Advance praise for

Innovative Approaches to Educational Leadership

"While there aren't quite as many books and treatises on leadership as there are, say, on cooking or on the history of the Cold War, educational leadership volumes sum to a large number compared to many other academic fields. How does another text on education leadership serve the field? [This book] seems destined to become a 'go-to-source' for those who are looking for a comprehensive and practical compilation of chapters that are carefully documented and provide clear examples of a variety of leadership approaches. This [book] puts a useful and surprising range of case studies in education leadership in current and emerging theoretical contexts."

—Dale Carpenter, Ph.D., Dean and Professor,
College of Education and Allied Professions, Western Carolina University

"The editors of *Innovative Approaches to Educational Leadership* have done a masterful job in coordinating a comprehensive set of chapters that provide innovative approaches needed for twenty-first-century educational leadership. These chapters provide us with the direction needed for our educational institutions to reach their full capacity and properly serve our key stakeholders—our students. I strongly encourage everyone who cares deeply about our educational institutions to add this book to your personal library. I thank the editors and contributors for showing us the way!"

—Chance W. Lewis, Ph.D., Carol Grotnes Belk Distinguished Professor
of Urban Education; Director, The Urban Education Collaborative,
University of North Carolina at Charlotte

"This book arrives at a time when there are BIG question marks about the future of education in the United States. Key among them is: do we have the right leaders in place to navigate highly questionable terrain? In *Innovative Approaches to Educational Leadership*, the editors have curated high-impact examples that can serve as guidance for other leaders in the nation to follow."

—Jerlando F. L. Jackson, Ph.D., Vilas Distinguished Professor of Higher Education;
Director & Chief Research Scientist, Wisconsin's Equity and Inclusion Laboratory,
University of Wisconsin-Madison

Innovative Approaches to Educational Leadership

Higher Ed

Questions about the Purpose(s) of Colleges & Universities

Norman K. Denzin and Shirley R. Steinberg
General Editors

Vol. 27

The Higher Ed series is part of the Peter Lang Education list.
Every volume is peer reviewed and meets
the highest quality standards for content and production.

PETER LANG
New York • Bern • Frankfurt • Berlin
Brussels • Vienna • Oxford • Warsaw

Innovative Approaches to Educational Leadership

Selected Cases

Edited by Carrie Rogers,
Kofi Lomotey, and Adriel Hilton

PETER LANG
New York • Bern • Frankfurt • Berlin
Brussels • Vienna • Oxford • Warsaw

Library of Congress Cataloging-in-Publication Data

Names: Rogers, Carrie, editor.
Title: Innovative approaches to educational leadership: selected cases /
edited by Carrie Rogers, Kofi Lomotey, and Adriel Hilton.
Description: New York: Peter Lang, 2017.
Series: Higher ed: questions about the purpose(s)
of colleges & universities; vol. 27 | ISSN 1523-9551
Includes bibliographical references.
Identifiers: LCCN 2017009348 | ISBN 978-1-4331-3311-4 (paperback: alk. paper)
ISBN 978-1-4331-3312-1 (hardcover: alk. paper) | ISBN 978-1-4331-4279-6 (ebook pdf)
ISBN 978-1-4331-4280-2 (epub) | ISBN 978-1-4331-4281-9 (mobi)
Subjects: LCSH: Educational leadership—Case studies.
Classification: LCC LB2806 .R63 2017 | DDC 371.2—dc23
LC record available at https://lccn.loc.gov/2017009348
DOI 10.3726/b11130

Bibliographic information published by **Die Deutsche Nationalbibliothek**.
Die Deutsche Nationalbibliothek lists this publication in the "Deutsche
Nationalbibliografie"; detailed bibliographic data are available
on the Internet at http://dnb.d-nb.de/.

The paper in this book meets the guidelines for permanence and durability
of the Committee on Production Guidelines for Book Longevity
of the Council of Library Resources.

29 Broadway, 18th floor, New York, NY 10006
www.peterlang.com

Printed in the United States of America

Contents

Section Two: Cases in P–12 School Leadership

Section Three: Cases in Higher Education Leadership

Foreword

GARY M. CROW

There is ample evidence in the literature that leadership matters for organizational improvement, culture building, and student achievement. However, not all leadership matters in a positive, innovative, and value-based way. Most of us have experiences of leaders who are culturally irrelevant, morally devoid, student insensitive, and aimed at maintaining the status quo. The editors and authors of *Innovative Approaches to Educational Leadership: Selected Cases*, have compiled rich descriptions and examples of a variety of innovative leadership approaches, which provide the opportunity for educational leadership researchers and scholar-practitioners to broaden our understanding of how leadership should matter.

The chapter authors broaden our perspectives on innovative leadership in a variety of ways. First, they provide rich literature reviews of diverse leadership perspectives, including authentic leadership, relational leadership, practical leadership, process educational leadership, culturally relevant leadership, servant leadership, and leaders who are researchers. This use of diverse leadership perspectives benefits us by identifying areas typically ignored in traditional leadership studies. Two examples seem relevant here. Horton, Willis and Brown's discussion of process educational leadership remind us that process and performance go hand in hand and that continuous improvement is a necessary part of leadership. This provides a much needed balance to the traditional outcome-based leadership practices and policies. Furthermore, two chapters, by Vaughan and Bogotch on imaginative action research and Crow and Ensley using improvement science frameworks, highlight exciting new avenues in which researcher and leader intersect. These chapters benefit us in understanding not only the importance of inquiry for leadership but also how two typically distinct roles can intersect in valuable ways.

Second, the authors broaden our leadership perspectives in regard to who leaders are. Instead of the traditional reliance on formal roles, the chapter authors open up leadership practice and thereby leadership capacity. Teachers, principals, students, higher education administrators, faculty and staff, and preservice teachers are among the types of individuals addressed in the chapters. A traditionally overlooked group, higher education mid-level administrators, is examined by Garcia, Nehls, and Florence in their chapter on shared governance. Although teacher leadership literature is not new, several chapter authors, including Sato and Rogers on teachers' practical leadership, Bricker and Tracy on teacher interactions, Vaughan and Bogotch on teacher leaders' use of action research, Crow and Ensley on teachers using improvement science, and Rogers and Scales on perceptions of teacher leadership among preservice and inservice teachers as well as teacher educators, provide valuable insights on this type of leadership approach. Broadening who enacts leadership helps to identify leadership practices, e.g., the "deliberative acts" (Bricker and Tracy) of teachers in their interactions that influence others. This broader notion of who leaders are also helps us understand how leadership capacity can be used and expanded within educational organizations.

Third, as several of the above examples demonstrate, context matters for innovative leadership. Part II focuses on K-12 school settings in various types of demographic contexts, while Part III emphasizes leadership in higher education settings. In addition to broadening our understanding of educational leadership to P-16(20) so that we recognize education as a system, the chapters on these various settings help remind us that context matters, be it a historically black college with a long term president (Washington, Esters, and Gasman), a Hispanic-serving institution with diversity issues (Pichon), or an African American principal struggling with supporting rigorous academic expectations (Lowery and Lomotey).

Fourth, one of the outstanding features of this book is the use in most chapters of one or more cases or stories about innovative leadership—its enactment, development, and struggle. Stories or narratives are rich tools for broadening our understanding of leadership. Used frequently and extensively in educational leadership preparation programs prior to the 1980s, stories got a "bad rap" mostly because they were often used to proudly demonstrate the storyteller's prowess without reflection or a variety of perspectives. For a period of time, these tools were eliminated in preparation courses. A recent re-awakening of cases and the use of stories not to privilege specific solutions but to enrich conversations and learning across multiple perspective, has the potential to broaden our understanding of how leadership is enacted and developed. The chapter authors provide rich examples/ narratives that not only enrich the description of the specific, innovative leadership approach but also the struggles that actual leaders encounter as they enact these approaches. The use of narratives allows us to drill deep into the practices, motivations, drive, values, and identities of those practicing leadership and then to interrogate those stories to identify their gaps, insensitivities, culturally dominant views, etc. For example, Tillman and Horsford's case of culturally relevant leadership in a high-performing, low income elementary school in the U.S. Mountain West provides a narrative rich with possibilities for individual and collective critical investigation and reflection. The chapters conclude with sample discussion questions to aid this type of investigation and reflection.

I commend Rogers, Lomotey, and Hilton and the various chapter authors for developing a book that broadens our perspectives on the nature, roles, contexts, and stories of leadership in various educational organizations. They present a valuable resource for scholar-practitioners who daily encounter the dilemmas and opportunities for leadership and for researchers, professors, and students who now have the opportunity to broaden their perspectives on enacting leadership in ways that matter to the children, youth, and adults in our schools and communities.

Acknowledgments

The editors would like to acknowledge the tremendous leadership and insight of Dale Carpenter, former Dean of the College of Education and Allied Professions at Western Carolina University (WCU). Dean Carpenter brought together a group of WCU education faculty, including the editors, in 2014 and described his sense that several of us had been exploring, often individually, different, creative and innovative conceptions of leadership in schools and higher education institutions. He suggested that we get together and think about how we might share our efforts in a collaborative way. This volume grew directly out of those conversations facilitated by Dean Carpenter.

From Carrie …

I would like to specifically acknowledge my colleagues who have led me to investigate teacher leadership deeply: Mistilina Sato has challenged my thinking about the capacity of teachers since graduate school; Roya Scales had aided and abetted, through finding funding and co-writing, our research into preservice teachers and the developmental notion of teacher leadership. I also thank my husband, Mike, whose faith in my capacity has never wavered. I am also deeply indebted to my co-editors for their mentoring: Thank you Kofi and Adriel.

From Kofi …

I would like to acknowledge my colleagues in educational leadership at WCU: Ann Allen, Robert Crow, Brandi Hinnant-Crawford, Casey Hurley, Kathleen

Jorissen, Dean Spaulding, and Jess Weiler. They are a group of creative, energetic, prolific and thoughtful scholars who inspire me and challenge me to seek to become the best teacher, scholar and service provider that I can. I also acknowledge with everlasting appreciation my wife, Nahuja; my children, Shawnjua, Juba and Mbeja; my grandchildren Ayanna, Isaiah and Nia; my sister, Saundra and my niece, Portia. They each motivate me beyond description.

From Adriel …

My deepest appreciation goes to my co-editors, Dr. Carrie Rogers and Dr. Kofi Lomotey, for their superb guidance and wise counsel. Their leadership and support have enhanced me intellectually and morally.

This text is dedicated to those who are closest to me (my support structure): my parents, Alphonso and Sarah Hilton, Jr.; my sister, Shaqauelia Blanding; and my beautiful niece, Sarah Nicole Penn. Had it not been for your sacrifice, guidance, and unwavering love, I would not have been able to accomplish this goal.

Finally, I wish to thank persons who aided in my development (since the inception of this project) from the villages of Western Carolina University, Grambling State University and now Webster University. I am truly indebted to these institutions as well as the faculty, staff and students who unselfishly gave of their time when I needed advice.

Introduction

CARRIE ROGERS, KOFI LOMOTEY, AND ADRIEL HILTON

Typically, when we think of an educational leader, whether at the primary, secondary or higher education level, we think of a man or woman who has a formal leadership role and title (e.g., principal, assistant principal, dean, president, provost, vice president, chancellor, headmaster, et cetera). The person in such a role has been hired by an individual or a group of individuals (e.g., a board of trustees or a board of education) to fulfill specific leadership responsibilities. They play vital roles that have been fulfilled since educational institutions were first established in this country.

These leaders perform administrative, managerial and supervisory roles within educational institutions. They are responsible for hiring, evaluating, training and (when necessary) terminating educators and other staff and managing budgets. They (1) insure that curricula are developed, (2) interact with politicians to secure adequate financial and human resources and (3) address community concerns and needs. We—as students, teachers, professors, parents and community people—expect these designated leaders to lead these institutions. More and more, individuals within educational institutions who do not hold official leadership titles are choosing to fulfill some of these leadership roles. Moreover, often those in traditional leadership roles have devised creative and non-traditional ways to lead their institutions.

This volume is about individuals and groups of individuals who serve leadership roles within educational institutions, though they do not hold official leadership titles and it is also about leaders in traditional roles who think and act inventively in fulfilling their responsibilities. We have invited a wide array of authors to offer theoretical perspectives on innovative leadership and to provide unique case studies of instances where people have taken on leadership roles for which they have not been hired or where leaders have creatively redefined their leadership.

These innovative cases illustrate how educational institutions are changing; individuals, sometimes viewing a void, take it upon themselves to create or redefine leadership roles in an effort to help in moving their schools or universities forward. In some instances, it is a teacher serving a leadership role in an elementary school, or a group of professors taking on added responsibility in a college or university. In each case, the desire is to advance the institution and to make better the experiences of the students therein. These cases, we believe, are important because they are reflective of institutions becoming stronger as a result of increased efforts to lead them with larger and more diverse groups of individuals providing creative leadership.

This text is unique and valuable for a number of reasons. First, we have gathered a diverse and scholarly group of academics and practitioners to tell this story of innovative leadership. There are seasoned as well as early career academics, current and former school-level administrators, current and former university administrators and more. Second, the volume focuses on such leadership at all levels of education: elementary, secondary and higher education. Third, the authors each provide provocative discussion questions for use by graduate students as well as practitioners in educational institutions.

Gary Crow of Indiana University provides a thought-provoking Foreword at the beginning of this volume.

PART ONE

In the first section of this book several authors provide theoretical discussions of leadership across all levels of the educational continuum. John Sherlock, a professor of human resources, begins this section in Chapter 1 with a broad, stimulating, and challenging conversation on the role of relational leadership (Uhl-Bien & Ospina, 2012) for educational practice. He outlines the three core elements of relational leadership and explores the ways other educational leadership perspectives (e.g., distributed leadership, shared leadership, transformational leadership, and instructional leadership) are complimentary to relational leadership.

In Chapter 2, Mistilina Sato and Carrie Rogers, former teachers and current teacher educators, push the definitions of teacher leadership. They offer a brief history of teacher leadership and a theoretical discussion based in Aristotelian ideas of practical reasoning declaring that teachers not only perform many acts of leadership but also enact leadership through negotiating relationships, deliberating on tough choices and *being* the kind of leaders they want to see within their schools. They explore the idea that teacher leadership is a form of practical leadership, which they call stewardship: collective responsibility of all members toward actions that sustain and help schools progress in response to the ethical and moral issues they face (e.g., school violence, poverty, and inequity).

In Chapter 3, Melvin (Jai) Jackson, a scholar of higher education, offers a theoretical discussion of leadership in higher education with a focus on informal leadership that is not limited to an official title nor the boundaries of an organizational chart. In this chapter he explores the relationship between culture and leadership and features illustrations of informal leaders in higher education.

In Chapter 4, Alonzo Flowers and Rosa Banda continue the discussion of leadership in higher education through a discourse on developments in social justice and global leadership. They do this through a detailed illustration that offers perspectives from the theories of social justice leadership (Theoharis, 2009), culturally proficient leadership (Robins, Lindsey, R. B., Lindsey, D. B. & Terrell, 2006), and cross-cultural competencies (Adler & Bartholomew, 1992) from varying stakeholders.

In Chapter 5, Joann Horton, Daria Willis and Isiah Brown extend the conversation of leadership in higher education through a discussion of Process Education (PE) leadership, a performance-based philosophy that integrates multiple theories emphasizing continuous improvement of learning skills, knowledge and abilities and uses assessment principles to produce learner self-development (Burke, Lawrence, El-Sayed, & Apple, 2009). The authors provide an overview of the theory and use it as a framework to explore effective leadership attributes and competencies.

PART TWO

In Chapter 6, Patricia Bricker and Kelly Tracy explore what teacher leadership looks like. They view the impact of teacher interactions in academia (e.g., attending conferences and conducting research). After defining teaching leadership, the authors draw upon interviews, field notes and documents to develop their case.

In Chapter 7, Kendra Lowery and Kofi Lomotey, both academics who once served as school leaders, offer a fictitious case study of an African American principal. The authors provide vivid illustrations of principal interactions with students, teachers and parents. While this case study is fictitious, it is built upon best practice and practical experience and allows the reader to see what is possible in interactions among teachers, students and the principal.

Jessica Weiler and Kathleen Topolka-Jorissen look at professional learning communities (PLCs) and the all-important relationship between school leaders and the PLCs in Chapter 8. The authors provide step-by-step guidance for principals interested in developing effective PLCs. The four steps are (1) developing a strong, collaborative team, (2) increasing the team's leadership capacity, (3) defining and creating a vision, and (4) building an infrastructure. Michelle Vaughan and Ira Bogotch introduce the concept of imaginative action research in exploring the role of educational researchers in relation to reform and social change. In Chapter 9, they use cases of 14 teachers. They contend that action research project data are key to decision making.

In Chapter 10, Linda Tillman and Sonya Horsford provide a case of culturally relevant leadership in an elementary school. They consider the implications for theory, leadership preparation and practice. In the chapter they offer valuable guidance for school leaders who seek to provide culturally relevant leadership. Chapter 11 focuses on a case study in an early college. In this chapter, Robert Crow and Rebecca Ensley use three improvement science frameworks as tools to enhance teacher leadership in a systematic way.

PART THREE

In the third and final section we share cases reflecting leadership at colleges and universities. These cases include an investigation of the leadership styles of administrators, the leadership challenges to administrators and the search for a way to define and measure leadership for students. In Chapter 12, Amanda Washington, Levon Esters and Marybeth Gasman offer an in depth portrait of one historically Black college or university (HBCU) and its leader. The transformation of Paul Quinn College under the servant leadership of president Michael Sorrell is richly described by the authors with specific examples of servant leadership in action.

Next we turn to the case offered by Carrie Rogers and Roya Scales. In Chapter 13, they present their program and university's effort to capture and measure teacher leadership of preservice teachers. They offer perspectives from multiple stakeholders on how teacher leadership should be defined at the University level. They compare findings from a survey of teacher education faculty about leadership development among preservice teachers with findings from the candidates' reflections on their required teacher leadership activities completed during student teaching and recent graduates' (first year teachers') perceptions of themselves as leaders.

In Chapter 14, Hugo Garcia, Kim Nehls and Kimberly Florence offer an insightful study of midlevel administrators at tertiary institutions and their perceptions of shared leadership and governance. Using their own data, they offer a conceptual model illustrating that collaboration + engagement + inclusion + involvement leads to shared leadership.

In Chapter 15, Henrietta Williams Pichon offers a case of authentic leadership in the face of challenges loosely based on a diversity issue that emerged at a research university in the Southwest that has been identified as a Hispanic-serving Institution (HSI). Pichon uses Robert Terry's (1993) authentic action wheel as a lens to analyze and critique the case.

Arnetha Ball provides an insightful Afterword reflecting her own thinking on the book and the notion of innovative leadership.

Enjoy.

SECTION ONE

Conceptual Understandings of Leadership in Education

CHAPTER ONE

Relational Leadership AND ITS Implications FOR Educational Leadership AND Practice

JOHN J. SHERLOCK

The intent of this chapter is to discuss the theoretical and practical understandings of relational leadership and to consider their implications for educational leadership and practice. While there has been general agreement for some time that leadership has a "relational" component (Follett, 1927; Graen & Uhl-Bien, 1995; Hollander & Julian, 1969; Stogdill & Coons, 1957), most of the attention in research and practice until recently has been limited to interactions initiated by designated "leaders" to "followers" (Wood & Dibben, 2015). Additionally, while the relational dimension of leadership has been discussed within educational leadership (Allen, Grigsby, & Peters, 2015; Gronn, 2002; Spillane, Halverson, & Diamond, 2001), it has not been the focus. Relational leadership views "relationship" as the fundamental aspect of leadership (Alvesson & Sveningsson, 2012; Uhl-Bien, 2006). While in her original conceptualization of relational leadership, Uhl-Bien (2006) referred to it as "Relational Leadership *Theory*" (RLT), her later work on relational leadership (Uhl-Bien & Ospina, 2012) describes relational leadership less of a theory and more of an overarching framework and "umbrella term" for research that "studies leadership as generated in social processes and relationships among people" (p. 573).

What follows begins with a discussion of the core elements of relational leadership. Given space limitations, the review of relational leadership literature is not intended to be exhaustive; rather, it draws heavily on the nearly 600+-page text *Advancing Relational Leadership Research* edited by Uhl-Bien and Ospina (2012), which is a recommended resource. The fact that such a voluminous publication focusing exclusively on relational leadership concepts exists is a testament to the interest in this perspective on leadership. Following the description of relational leadership's core elements is a brief discussion of the complementarity of relational leadership with other established leadership perspectives in the educational leadership literature, including distributed leadership, shared leadership, transformational leadership, and instructional leadership.

The chapter's final section discusses how employing a relational leadership perspective might impact our thinking about educational leadership practice. Given that I am a professor of human resources (HR), the operational lens used for the discussion focuses on HR-related areas of recruitment & selection, professional development, and performance management.

It is worth noting at this early juncture in the chapter that the varying perspectives presented on relational leadership may cause some "tensions" with readers' current paradigms related to what constitutes leadership and conceptualizations of "leader." For example, perceiving leaders as independent *entities* possessing certain qualities who *produce* leadership outcomes via relational exchanges with followers (e.g., an "entity" perspective of relational leadership) derives from a different ontological and epistemological paradigm than one perceiving leadership as dynamically constructed within the process of relating (e.g., a "constructionist" perspective of relational leadership) (Reitz, 2015; Uhl-Bien, 2006). Uhl-Bien and Ospina (2012, p. xxiii) note that studies of relational leadership typically fall somewhere along a continuum of "entity" and "constructionist" perspectives, and they challenge scholars and practitioners to embrace what Uhl-Bien and Ospina term "paradigm interplay," whereby differences in paradigms are not ignored but where the focus is on giving full consideration to connections and distinctions among paradigms with the purpose of advancing understanding. What follows, then, is a discussion of core interrelated elements of relational leadership: 1) Leadership as co-constructed; 2) Leadership as emerging through relational processes; and 3) Leadership as embedded in context.

LEADERSHIP AS CO-CONSTRUCTED

In the early leadership literature, leadership essentially was conceptualized as being *constructed* within the hierarchical "leader," with a mix of traits and behaviors that enabled the leader to influence "followers" to achieve desired outcomes. Dachler and Hosking (1995) asserted that this perspective reduces the relational process to basically an individual act, reduced to one-way causal relations with feedback. This "entity" view of leadership (Uhl-Bien, 2006), with its leader-centric, almost heroic characterization of the appointed leader has dominated popular leadership literature and much of academic literature (Alvesson & Sveningsson, 2012; Fitzsimons, 2012; Sveningsson, Alvehus, & Alvesson, 2012). However, as leadership research began to focus more on the relational aspects of leadership, such as the well-known Leader-Member Exchange (LMX) theory (Graen & Uhl-Bien, 1995), different views about the construction of leadership, and particularly the role of the follower in the leadership equation, began to emerge. Specifically, more consideration was given to the dyadic relation-building process between leaders and followers (Uhl-Bien & Ospina, 2012). Thus, the emphasis on leadership construction shifted from leader's traits and behaviors to the *process* of leadership construction via mutual influence. However, as Alvesson and Sveningsson (2012) point out, the division between leader and follower was typically assumed to be one where the appointed leader was the key agent in the influence process, while the follower was more often a passive receiver. To this point, Shamir in his correspondence with Hoskings (Hoskings & Shamir, 2012), acknowledges mutual influence and the co-creation of leadership, but asserts that the term "leadership" should be limited to situations where there is disproportionate influence in a social arena. He argues that in order for the term leadership to be useful some individuals have had to exert more influence on the group than others.

Coming from more of a constructionist perspective of relational leadership, Drath (2001) asserts that leadership is not "constructed" via personal dominance as in the more traditional leader-centric, primarily one-way influence models. Additionally, he adds that leadership is also more than acts of interpersonal influence, as articulated in Leader-Member Exchange (LMX) theory (Graen & Uhl-Bien, 1995). He describes leadership being constructed via a process of relational dialogue in which organizational members engage and interact to "co-construct" knowledge systems together. From this constructionist perspective, leadership is viewed as a "collective capacity" generated in and from the interactions and relationships among people (Drath, 2001; Uhl-Bien & Ospina, 2012). Additionally, the constructionist perspective sees that co-construction as "intersubjective," meaning it represents a shared understanding of a subjective reality (Cunliffe & Eriksen, 2011). These co-constructions occur via interactions that occur in everyday conversations in the workplace. Dachler and Hosking (1995) place the focus on communication as the medium in which all social constructions of leadership are created and potentially changed. Uhl-Bien and Ospina (2012) go further by conceptualizing relational leadership as a dynamic phenomenon—with "co-constructions" of leadership occurring continuously (Uhl-Bien & Ospina, 2012).

In attempting to find connections between an entity and constructionist perspectives concerning the construction of leadership, relational leadership scholars acknowledge that both perspectives include elements associated with both individuals and collective processes, thus supporting a general view of the "co-construction" of leadership. However, as the discussion above indicates, scholars who study relational leadership often vary in the extent to which they "privilege" the individual or the collective in that co-construction process (Uhl-Bien & Ospina, 2012, p. 571).

LEADERSHIP AS EMERGING THROUGH RELATIONAL PROCESSES

As noted in the introduction, the core elements of relational leadership are interrelated. As discussed in the previous section, one of those core elements is that leadership is co-constructed. This section addresses the relational processes *from* which, or *within* which, or *through* which (depending on one's perspective) those leadership co-constructions emerge. Alvesson and Sveningsson (2012) stress the importance of the relational process in asserting that leadership "emerges and manifests itself through relations and in relationships and cannot exist outside of these relations" (p. 211). While there's general agreement that leadership is "relational," what that actually means in terms of the leadership process has varying views. Within an organizational context, there is agreement that relational leadership processes are those that enable groups of people to work together in meaningful ways (Drath, 2001). Put another way, these relational, social processes are what enables ideas to be articulated that are then ideally recognized by others as progressing tasks that are important to them (Barge & Fairhurst, 2008; Fairhurst, 2007).

Hollander's work (Hollander, 1992; Hollander & Julian, 1969) stands out in the literature for promoting that leadership should be studied as a relational process rather than a set of individual traits or behaviors. Leader-member exchange (LMX) theory (Graen & Uhl-Bien, 1995) stressed not only the importance of leadership as a process but the essential importance of the "leader-follower" relational process. The more positively perceived the leader-member exchanges (as perceived by the member), the greater likelihood the overall relationship quality was high and that the member (follower) would then perform at a high level to produce outcomes. Those favoring more of an "entity" perspective of relational leadership identify *leadership* as being found in the skills and abilities of individuals for developing effective leader-member/follower relationships (Uhl-Bien & Ospina, 2012). Fitzsimons (2012) asserts that this entity perspective, although referring to relational processes, does not actually examine the "process." This assertion is based on the fact that often the measurements of leader-member/follower relations are typically "snapshots" in time of relational perceptions.

Those favoring a "constructionist" perspective of relational leadership locate leadership in the relational processes, considering social constructions of leadership generated through communication, negotiation, sensemaking, and meaning-making (Uhl-bien & Ospina, 2012, p. 545). A constructionist perspective seeks to better understand the process by which relationships develop to produce effective leadership. However, because these relational processes are dynamic and embedded in context (discussed in the next section of this chapter), it is very difficult to research and very difficult to produce generalized findings. The complexity in studying these relational processes are noted by Ospina and Uhl-Bien (2012) who refer to them as "the invisible threads that connect actors engaged in leadership ... " (p. xx). Cunliffe and Eriksen (2011) refer to the processes as the "the interplay of voices within dialogic or conversational spaces" (p. 1437). Bradbury and Lichtenstein (2000) describe relational processes in organizations as "the space of interaction between its members" (p. 551). A relational perspective brings attention to the "generative capacity of the spaces in between where people share or where they meet difference. Drath, in his correspondence with Day on this topic (Day & Drath, 2012) asserts that these "spaces" should be viewed less as barriers and more as opportunities to produce new ideas that integrate old ideas. This elusive "between space" Reitz (2015) asserts, is "a place where we 'sense' the 'quality' of our 'connection' with others."

Dialogue and Relational Processes

Processes of leadership then, arguably, are always underway via moments of interaction (Wood & Dibben, 2015). These moments of interaction typically involve the use of language in some type of dialogue. As Reitz (2015) notes, the general term "dialogue" often appears in leadership literature but the definitional use of the term is not consistent. As she remarks, the willingness and ability to encounter another in dialogue is more complex that being "good at open conversation" (p. 29).

Reitz (2015) notes that "entity" views of relational leadership tend to view these moments of interaction and discourse in "instrumental" ways where the leader interacts *so that* certain organizational aims can be achieved. She equates this type of discourse to Buber's (1923) conceptualization of "technical dialogue," referring to the objective transmission of information. Cunliffe and Eriksen (2011) compares this instrumental form of discourse to Bakhtin's (1981) conceptualization of "monologism," where the interaction consists of "talking to" rather than "talking with." Cunliffe and Eriksen (2011) suggest that relational leaders (not limited to only those in an appointed leader role), see dialogue not as an expression of something pre-conceived but as emerging and open. Reitz (2015) describes relational leadership as fundamentally as one's orientation to dialogue, which she defines as "a sensed quality of mutual encounter in the present moment where there is an honoring of personhood and intent to confirm the other, learn and create" (p. 177).

Despite the complexity of relational processes, Barge and Fairhurst (2008) assert that it is possible to examine the way meaning making unfolds during dialogue, noticing what seems to slow down or freeze the meaning making process as well as what enlivens and enriches meaning making. As an example of this type of research, Reitz (2015) identified a number of obstacles to dialogue and the meaning making process, including, issues of power, authenticity, judgment, conflict, "busyness," "worthwhileness" (i.e., the need to be "productive"), insecurity, "stilling the mind," and creating spaces for dialogue. Cunliffe and Eriksen (2011) identified similar challenges to dialogue in their study of the relational leadership practices of Federal Security Directors (FSDs) for the Transportation Security Administration (TSA). For example, the FSDs in the study expressed concern about "creating spaces" for true dialogue and found "town hall" type meetings were useful as well as just impromptu 1–1 conversations with their security screeners. The study's authors use the term "relational integrity" to characterize leaders who are attuned and responsive to moments of difference in dialogue and feel a sense of responsibility for working through those differences. For example, one FSD in the study spoke about observing women coming through security with baby harnesses holding newborns and how the FSD felt the need to act ("relate") in different ways [from standard screening protocols] in those instances; such instances were described as where concerns are "not just for following procedures but also for the moral task of treating people as human beings and understanding their differing needs" (p. 1439).

As demonstrated in the example above, the "relating" aspect of relational leadership involves not just the words spoken but the dispositions of the parties involved. Hosking, Shamir, Ospina, and Uhl-Bien (2012), label one relational leadership practice as "Being in the now rather than the know," which they assert is what enables true listening and heartfelt-felt participation in dialoguing (p. 531). Reitz (2015) identified from her research other practices that can facilitate dialogue, including having an orientation towards curiosity (about what new might come from the dialogue), modeling fragility (vulnerability), and striking a balance between advocacy and inquiry.

While true dialogue is difficult to achieve, it is essential to the relational process of leadership construction. Additionally, there are attitudes and practices that have been shown to improve the likelihood of true dialogue occurring. Reitz (2015) makes the point that dialogue, when it does occur, should not be expected to always be comfortable or harmonious. The relational processes of leadership construction require honoring—and working with—and through differences. It is through that authentic, heart-felt, and courageous interaction that new meaning can emerge (Reitz, 2015; Uhl-Bien & Ospina, 2012).

LEADERSHIP AS EMBEDDED IN CONTEXT

The previous two sections of this chapter have described relational leadership being co-constructed by individuals and emerging through relational processes. There's agreement that those relational processes are linked to context. Barge and

Fairhurst (2008), in describing relational leadership, articulate it as "a lived and experienced social activity in which persons in conversation, action, meaning, and *context* [emphasis added] are dynamically interrelated" (p. 228).

Age, gender, race, ethnicity, expertise, authority, formal structures, organizational culture are just some of the contextual variables that influence the relational work being done (Alvesson & Sveningsson, 2012; Denis, Langley, & Sergi, 2012). However, as with the discussion of other relational leadership elements, perspectives vary on the specific role and importance of these contextual variables in the leadership process. Those favoring an entity perspective of relational leadership view context as more of a set of variables that are antecedents to the leadership relationship. Viewed this way, contextual variables act as a moderator between the relationship and leadership outcomes (Uhl-bien & Ospina, 2012). As is exemplified in leader-member exchange theory (Uhl-Bien, 2006), the primary context where leadership occurs is the interpersonal one occurring between leaders and followers. From a leader-centric (entity) view, the leader should be sensitive to those contextual variables that may impact the quality of the leader-follower exchanges, and ultimately, followers' motivation and performance. Stereotypical examples might be a young appointed leader seeking out the expertise of a seasoned employee to demonstrate respect for their experience, or an appointed leader emphasizing the organization's commitment to diversity when talking about the organization's culture with a new Hispanic employee. Within this view of relational leadership, the appointed leader is the primary causal agent for the leadership outcome that is produced from the relational processes. "Leadership" is viewed as the property of individuals and their behaviors (Denis et al., 2012), and contextual considerations are important because of their relevance to how the "leader" approaches those relational processes.

From more of a constructionist perspective, Ospina and Foldy (2010) view context as a "constitutive dimension of the relational dynamics that call forth leadership" (p. 303). Uhl-Bien and Ospina (2012) assert that it is impossible to separate the construction of leadership from its context. Context is not considered as background or antecedent to leadership but as foreground, whereby leadership construction is embedded in and emerges from context (Uhl-Bien & Ospina, 2012). Alvesson and Sveningsson (2012) agree with this view, suggesting that the context goes beyond forming the outside scene for the influencing process, but it actually guides and frames what comes from the social interactions between individuals.

An implication of a constructionist perspective of relational leadership is that the meaning of terms like leadership, leader, follower, shared goals, etc. is not fixed. As Drath (2001) asserts, the meaning of such terms is continuously being framed and reframed from context to context. This view aligns with the research of Vine, Holmes, Marra, Pfeifer, and Jackson (2008) who describe leadership as a dynamic phenomenon that has to be continually enacted in relation to the changing context within organizations. Fitzsimons (2012) notes that relational dynamics occur in the context of on-going organizational social processes—i.e., "the actual day-to-day social interactions that constitute the experience of organizational members" (p. 162). Research by Carsten, Uhl-Bien, West, Patera, and McGregor (2010) demonstrated that organizations may consciously or unconsciously develop organizations contexts/cultures of "passivity" (valuing blind obedience and deference) or "proactivity" (emphasizing partnership or and/or co-leadership). Carsten and Uhl-Bien (2012) found in their study of the behavior of "followers" (i.e., those not in formally appointed leader positions) that in a context where the appointed leader is not open to follower contributions, the relational dialogue process was negatively impacted. Only where followers with strong "co-production" beliefs about leadership (i.e., a view that leadership did not reside with the appointed leader but was co-constructed) would engage in the relational dialogue process (p. 217). To the issue of passive or proactive cultures, Denis et al. (2012) assert that greater attention must be given to the issue of power within organizational contexts. They add that egalitarian and power-symmetric contexts that enable relational leadership to be robustly co-constructed do not just happen in a vacuum in organizations. They add that it requires considerable work, typically starting with the vertical hierarchy in place. Organizations embracing a constructionist perspective on relational leadership foster the view that leadership may occur in formal managerial contexts or in contexts that do not involve formal authority (Uhl-Bien & Ospina, 2012). This assertion is based on the view of leadership as a "contextual process where the ideas articulated in talk or action are recognized by others as progressing tasks that are important to them" (Barge & Fairhurst, 2008, p. 227). Barge and Fairhurst (2008) also highlight the fundamental role that context plays in leadership in addressing the question "What counts as leadership?" Their answer is "it depends," because it [leadership] is "highly contextualized and dynamic" where leadership actors negotiate its meaning (p. 232).

COMPLEMENTARITY WITH OTHER PROMINENT LEADERSHIP THEORIES IN EDUCATION

There is no shortage of leadership literature in the field of education. This chapter's discussion of relational leadership is not intended to supplant any of the prominent leadership theories already in practice within education settings; the emphasis that relational leadership places on leadership being co-constructed via relational processes is complementary with aspects of four popular educational leadership theories – distributed leadership, shared leadership, transformational leadership, and instructional leadership. That complementarity is briefly discussed below. It should be noted that the intention is not to provide in-depth discussion of the theories themselves; readers wishing to learn more about one of the theories discussed are encouraged to seek out the references cited and the many other resources available in the educational leadership literature.

Distributed and Shared Leadership

Distributed leadership and shared leadership perspectives have both received considerable attention in the field of education (Bolden, 2011; Duin & Baer, 2010; Gronn, 2008; Harris, Leithwood, Day, Sammons, & Hopkins, 2007; Latham & Wilhelm, 2014; Pienaar & Raymond, 2013; Spillane et al., 2001, 2004; Spillane, Harris, Jones & Mertz, 2015). Both theories align with relational leadership in that they can be considered part of the "post-heroic" representation of leadership that has encouraged a shift in focus from the attributes and behaviors of individual leader to more of a collective social process (Bolden, 2011). For example, Gronn (2002) asserts that distributed leadership offers a new unit of analysis that is on the collective and not the individual. He adds an individually focused analytical unit is restrictive because it fails to recognize interrelationships involved in the leadership process. Spillane et al. (2004) highlight two critical aspects of a distributed perspective on leadership; the first involves a "leader-plus" aspect acknowledging that the work of leadership involves not just those individuals in designated "leader" roles but is "distributed" across multiple individuals. The second aspect is the "practice" of leading and managing that they frame as a product of interactions of school leaders and followers. Spillane and colleagues suggest that of the two aspects, the more salient aspect is not the fact that leadership is distributed but *how* it is distributed. This point is complementary to relational leadership's emphasis on the relational process.

In regard to shared leadership, Pearce and Conger (2003) note that the purpose of their book on shared leadership was to advance inquiry into leadership processes outside the typical top-down paradigm of leadership. Their definition of shared leadership is as a:

> … dynamic interactive influence process among individuals in groups for which the objective is to lead one another to the achievement of group or organizational goals or both. This influence process often involves peer, or lateral, influence and at other times involves upward or downward hierarchical influence. (Pearce & Conger, 2003, p. 1)

While this definition of shared leadership arguably places greater emphasis on "influence" and "goal attainment" than relational leadership explicitly does, it is nevertheless complementary to relational leadership's emphasis on the dynamic nature of the leadership process. The shared leadership perspective, like distributed leadership, conceptualizes "leadership" as a collective social process of multiple social actors (Bolden, 2011; Pearce & Conger, 2003; Uhl-Bien, 2006).

Transformational and Instructional Leadership

Transformational leadership theory and instructional leadership theory have also been discussed extensively in the education literature (Aas & Brandmo, 2016; Balwant, 2016; Kahai, Jestire, & Rui, 2013; Zacher & Johnson, 2015). They are grouped together here because they both place an emphasis on the appointed "leader's" role (although in different ways). In that respect, they align most closely with "entity" perspectives of relational leadership. Wood and Dibben (2015) make the point that most of the research on transformational leadership styles, while acknowledging that leader-follower relations are important, affirm the leader's centrality. Among the key elements of transformational leadership theory (Bass, 1990, 1997) is what is termed *individualized consideration*, which focuses on the "leader's treatment of followers as unique individuals and providing specialized attention to followers" needs and lending support when necessary so that the followers can realize their full potential. Another key element is *intellectual stimulation* that involves leader actions that challenge "followers" to conceptualize, comprehend, and analyze problems in new ways. These two elements of transformational leadership align with the interactional social processes discussed in relational leadership.

In instructional leadership theory, the appointed "leader" also plays the central role in the leader-member interactions. However, Lee, Hallinger, and Walker (2012) identified in their research of instructional leadership practices across five schools that, while still "leader-driven," the principals often utilized a more distributed approach of instructional leadership, involving multiple staff members. The study also noted that effective instructional leadership practice included sustained interactions among staff. Supovitz and Poglinco (2001) note that one of the key elements of instructional leadership is the cultivation of a community of instructional practice via collaboration and network building. These points all support the essential role of relational processes to leadership; this comment from a participant in Taylor-Backor and Gordon's (2015) qualitative study of principals and instructional leadership really reinforces this: "Supervision [Instructional] should be a process of engaging teachers in dialogue about their teaching in a non-critical, not-judgmental way" (p. 110).

IMPLICATIONS FOR EDUCATIONAL LEADERSHIP PRACTICE

The discussion of relational leadership now turns to consideration of possible ways a relational perspective might impact particular human resource-related areas of educational leadership practice. As noted earlier in the chapter, the "entity" conceptualization of relational leadership has dominated the literature, and, until recently, has also dominated educational leadership practice (Kedian, Giles, Morrison, & Fletcher, 2016). Thus, particular attention will be given in the discussion that follows to the "constructionist" perspective of relational leadership. Given the emphasis of this perspective away from a leader-centric view of leadership and toward leadership as co-constructed via relational processes embedded in context, it is suggested that human resource-related areas such as recruitment & selection, professional development, workplace culture, and performance management should be approached differently than current models. Below is a brief discussion of how each of those areas might be impacted.

Recruitment and Selection in Education

The process for recruiting for a position typically involves creating a job description that describes the knowledge, skills, abilities, and other characteristics (KSAOs) required of the individual in the position (Henneman, Judge, & Kammeyer-Mueller, 2015). Henneman et al. (2015) stress the importance of conducting a "job analysis" process of studying jobs in order to gather, analyze, synthesize and report information about job requirements. While some job analysis approaches seek to identify and describe the specific tasks of the job, other approaches are more competency-based, describing "job requirements in the form of general KSAOs required across a range of jobs" (Henneman et al., 2015, p. 153). They add that a competency approach to job analysis focuses on how jobs relate to organizational strategy. It is suggested that job analyses, and subsequent job descriptions, for a variety of positions in educational settings would look quite different when approached from a relational leadership perspective. For example, common job description terminology like "team player," "collaborative," "leader," etc. take on deeper meaning from a relational leadership perspective that would need to be explicated. Research on relational leadership by Ospina et al. (2012) identified three leadership practices that help a group move their own collective effort forward: (1) "reframing discourse" to create new ways of seeing things; (2) "bridging difference" to create the conditions to facilitate joint work while maintaining, appreciating, and drawing on different perspectives; and (3) "unleashing human energies" via communication of the belief that people typically already come with a deep knowledge of the problem, which is derived from their own lived experience. These practices require particular mindsets and skillsets which are not addressed in most educational job postings (for hierarchical "leader" positions and others).

The selection process for job candidates typically involves some type of interview process where the candidate is asked questions that help the selection committee evaluate whether the candidate is qualified and would be a good fit within the organization's culture (Henneman et al., 2015). Barge and Fairhurst (2008), in discussing relational leadership, suggest that relational leaders are open to the "emergence of leadership" and demonstrate this by approaching their workplace conversations as new possibilities for meaning making and action. Candidates being interviewed for positions should be asked for examples from their experience of those types of workplace conversations as well as examples of the relational leadership practices mentioned above.

Professional Development in Education

A relational leadership perspective has significant implications for how educational institutions approach professional development. Leadership development activities have tended to follow an "entity" conceptualization of leadership where appointed leaders are given education to develop "interactional skills and competencies" to enable them to influence followers. However, considering leadership as a collective capacity and something socially constructed suggests a different approach to leadership development (Fletcher, 2012). Approaching professional development from a relational leadership perspective suggests that professional development should involve the "collective" to the maximum extent possible. Because context is a core element of relational leadership, leadership development should ideally educate individuals in the context of the collective processes through which leadership work is performed (Hosking, 2006; Uhl-Bien & Ospina, 2012).

In addition to the group/team education, those in appointed "leader" positions can benefit from individual professional development focused on relational leadership concepts. Barge (2012) advocates a need to help appointed "leaders" anticipate how they might act and be present within an unfolding relational interaction. He adds that it will be important to assist "leaders" in developing linguistic capacity to anticipate, to be present, and to reflect on their conversational experience. Here he is advocating for education in discursive practices that can help appointed "leaders" more effectively enable leadership constructions (Uhl-Bien & Ospina, 2012). Thus, development program content would need to give much more attention to the relational and dialogic nature of leadership discussed in this chapter. While there are not many examples of this type of leadership development programming, Kedian et al. (2016) highlight the positive results of their International Leadership Institute, a four-day alternative approach to learning involving 70 educational leaders from six countries. A distinguishing element of the program is the sustained immersion in "dialogue" activities. Reitz (2015) notes that the types of skills and attitudes needed for true dialogue (i.e., mindfulness, modeling curiosity and vulnerability, etc.) are typically not part of common managerial "boot camp" training.

Professional development in this area will need to differentiate programming designed to enhance the "work of the leaders" and programming designed to enhance the "work of leadership." The work of the *leaders* refers to those individual actions/practices carried out in context; the work of *leadership* refers to the development of collective practices that result in a collective capacity to produce shared agreements about concrete outcomes that will be viewed as collective achievement (Drath, 2001; Uhl-Bien & Ospina, 2012).

Performance Management in Education

Performance management includes setting individual performance goals for the year based on organizational strategy and goals, and typically includes ongoing individual performance feedback sessions with, potentially, a formal performance evaluation/appraisal once a year (Jackson, Schuler, & Werner, 2012). It is understood that many professionals in educational settings are subject to state-mandated performance evaluation criteria, but to the extent that modifications or additions can be made, incorporation of relational leadership practices is recommended. Drath (2012) operationalizes relational leadership as the organization's capacity to produce direction, alignment, and commitment. While many educational administration goals focus almost exclusively on goal attainment, a relational leadership perspective would place a performance management focus on *how* the goal was achieved.

One of the key areas for performance management attention are the relational practices that have been mentioned throughout this chapter. As discussed earlier, individuals in hierarchical leadership positions have probably been conditioned to engaging in discourse (via 1–1 meetings or staff meetings) with a primary goal of influencing others. The relational leader, however, is sensitive to the need for true dialogue that includes a balance of advocacy and inquiry and sees it has a matter of "relational integrity" to maintain this orientation to dialogue (Mossholder, Richardson, & Settoon, 2011). While some professionals in an educational setting may embrace this orientation with little encouragement, the human resource literature shows that having expectations and accountabilities formally documented is what is most effective in motivating some individuals (Jackson et al., 2012).

LIMITATIONS AND CONCLUSION

The intent of this chapter was not to advocate relational leadership as a "superior theory of leadership" vis-à-vis others. Rather, it is my hope that the chapter's content served to stimulate thinking about how a relational leadership perspective might enhance the ways those in educational practice identify and pursue the possibilities for leadership enactments in everyday activities. I purposely limited the discussion of the "entity" and "constructionist" perspectives of relational leadership to *descriptions* more than their *rationales* simply because the entity and constructionist rationales are ultimately connected to the long-standing, emotion-laden, contested nature of knowledge creation in the social sciences—which was not the chapter's focus. An in-depth discussion of the epistemological and ontological differences behind the entity and constructionist perspectives of relational leadership can be found in Uhl-Bien and Ospina (2012) and in cited sources in this chapter. I agree with Uhl-Bien and Ospina (2012) that embracing the concept of "paradigm interplay," as was encouraged in this chapter's introduction, is particularly helpful for considering the possibilities for what a relational leadership perspective could do for our understanding of leadership—in theory and in practice. That interplay is not about compromising one's world view, but rather, juxtaposing and linking ideas across paradigmatic perspectives (Uhl-Bien & Ospina, 2012, p. 538).

As Drath asserts in his correspondence with Day (Day & Drath, 2012), the variance in views about relational leadership may not be of great consequence at a pragmatic level:

> Seems like we can disagree ... while agreeing that leadership does not spring newborn from the mind of the leader, that it is not a protean force of the leader's personality, that followers are not passive receivers of the leader's thoughts, that it is, one way or another, the product of people working, thinking, talking, and acting together. This is the important bit of constructionism: Leadership in the sense we mean it (that is, as a non-coercive process) is not a naturally occurring biological fact, but a human-made, social artifact. (p. 241)

In order to be able to better operationalize relational leadership in education settings and elsewhere, there is a need for additional research and understanding of the social dynamics of the co-construction process of leadership (Reitz, 2015; Uhl-Bien, 2006; Uhl-Bien & Ospina, 2012). Additionally, while some "constructionist" perspectives on relational leadership focus almost exclusively on the co-construction process and not specific goal attainment, it is understood that applying a relational leadership perspective in educational settings will need to make this connection. Ospina and Sorenson's (2006) relational view of leadership supports this connection, describing relational leadership as "shared agreements" helping to create "results with collective value" (p. 188).

As Uhl-Bien and Ospina (2012) have noted, relational leadership is presented as a "framework" for studying and thinking about leadership. As such, this chapter was more conceptual than prescriptive. Given the current high level of scholarly interest in relational approaches to leadership, I am optimistic that more research attention will be given to the specific ways in which a relational leadership framework could be operationalized in the day-to-day practices of organizations. In the interim, I hope this chapter's brief discussion about recruitment, professional development, and performance management demonstrate that relational leadership concepts can and should be put into practice. Given the hierarchical structure that is common in most educational settings, enacting a number of the relational leadership practices discussed in this chapter will require the initiative of those in appointed "leader" positions. However, as has been emphasized throughout the chapter, relational leadership opportunities present themselves to everyone in the organization in their everyday interactions. As Cunliffe and Eriksen (2011) say so well: "Organizations are not understood as structures and systems but communities of people and conversations" (p. 1431).

REFERENCES

Aas, M., & Brandmo, C. (2016). Revisiting instructional and transformational leadership: The contemporary Norwegian context of school leadership. *Journal of Educational Administration, 54*(1), 92–110. doi: 10.1108/JEA-08-2014-0105

Allen, N., Grigsby, B., & Peters, M. L. (2015). Does leadership matter? Examining the relationship among transformational leadership, school climate, and student achievement. *International Journal of Educational Leadership Preparation, 10*(2), 1–22.

Alvesson, M., & Sveningsson, S. (2012). Un- and re-packing leadership: Context, relations, constructions, and politics. In M. Uhl-Bien, S. M. Ospina, M. Uhl-Bien, & S. M. Ospina (Eds.), *Advancing relational leadership research: A dialogue among perspectives* (pp. 203–225). Charlotte, NC: IAP Information Age Publishing.

Bakhtin, M. M. (1981). *The dialogic imagination: Four essays.* Austin, TX and London: University of Texas Press.

Balwant, P. T. (2016). Transformational instructor-leadership in higher education teaching: A meta-analytic review and research agenda. *Journal of Leadership Studies, 9*(4), 20. doi: 10.1002/jls.21423

Barge, J. K. (2012). Systemic constructionist leadership and working from within the present moment. In M. Uhl-Bien, S. M. Ospina, M. Uhl-Bien, & S. M. Ospina (Eds.), *Advancing relational leadership research: A dialogue among perspectives* (pp. 107–142). Charlotte, NC: IAP Information Age Publishing.

Barge, J. K., & Fairhurst, G. T. (2008). Living leadership: A systemic constructionist approach. *Leadership, 4*(3), 227–251. doi: 10.1177/1742715008092360

Bass, B. M. (1990). From transactional to transformational leadership: Learning to share the vision. *Organizational Dynamics, 18*(3), 19–31. doi: 10.1016/0090-2616(90)90061-S

Bass, B. M. (1997). Does the transactional–transformational leadership paradigm transcend organizational and national boundaries? *American Psychologist, 52*(2), 130–139. doi: 10.1037/0003-066X.52.2.130

Bolden, R. (2011). Distributed leadership in organizations: A review of theory and research. *International Journal of Management Reviews, 13*, 251–269.

Bradbury, H., & Lichtenstein, B. (2000). Relationality in organizational research: Exploring the space between. *Organization Science, 11*(5), 551–564.

Buber, M. (1923). *Ich und Du* [I and Thou], Leipzig: Insel Verlag.

Carsten, M. K., & Uhl-Bien, M. (2012). Follower beliefs in the co-production of leadership: Examining upward communication and the moderating role of context. *Zeitschrift Fur Psychologie, 220*(4), 210–220.

Carsten, M. K., Uhl-Bien, M., West, B. J., Patera, J. L., & McGregor, R. (2010). Exploring social constructions of followership: A qualitative study. *The Leadership Quarterly, 21*, 543–562. doi: 10.1016/j.leaqua.2010.03.015

Cunliffe, A. L., & Eriksen, M. (2011). Relational leadership. *Human Relations, 64*(11), 1425–1449, 25p. doi: 10.1177/0018726711418388

Dachler, H. P., & Hosking, D. (1995). The primacy of relations in socially constructing organizational realities. In D. Hosking, H. P. Dachler, K. J. Gergen, D. Hosking, H. P. Dachler, & K. J. Gergen (Eds.), *Management and organization: Relational alternatives to individualism* (pp. 1–28). Brookfield, VT: Avebury/Ashgate Publishing.

Day, D. V., & Drath, W. (2012). Dialogue: A dialogue on theorizing relational leadership. In M. Uhl-Bien, S. M. Ospina, M. Uhl-Bien, & S. M. Ospina (Eds.), *Advancing relational leadership research: A dialogue among perspectives* (pp. 227–251). Charlotte, NC: IAP Information Age Publishing.

Denis, J., Langley, A., & Sergi, V. (2012). Leadership in the plural. *The Academy of Management Annals, 6*(1), 211–283. doi: 10.1080/19416520.2012.667612

Drath, W. H. (2001). *The deep blue sea: Rethinking the source of leadership*. San Francisco, CA: Jossey-Bass.

Duin, A. H., & Baer, L. L. (2010). Shared leadership for a green, global, and Google world: The authors propose that shared leadership will foster institutional success in the green, global, and virtual future world of higher education. *Planning for Higher Education, 39*(1), 30–38.

Fairhurst, G. T. (2007). *Discursive leadership: In conversation with leadership psychology*. Thousand Oaks, CA: Sage Publications.

Fitzsimons, D. J. (2012). The contribution of psychodynamic theory to relational leadership. In M. Uhl-Bien, S. M. Ospina, M. Uhl-Bien, & S. M. Ospina (Eds.), *Advancing relational leadership research: A dialogue among perspectives* (pp. 143–174). Charlotte, NC: IAP Information Age Publishing.

Fletcher, J. K. (2012). The relational practice of leadership. In M. Uhl-Bien, S. M. Ospina, M. Uhl-Bien, & S. M. Ospina (Eds.), *Advancing relational leadership research: A dialogue among perspectives* (pp. 83–106). Charlotte, NC: IAP Information Age Publishing.

Follett, M. P. (1927). *Dynamic administration* (reprint 1942). New York, NY: Harper & Brothers Publishers.

Graen, G., & Uhl-Bien, M. (1995). Relationship-based approach to leadership: Development of leader-member exchange (LMX) theory of leadership over 25 years: Applying a multi-level multi-domain perspective. *The Leadership Quarterly, 6*(2), 219–247. doi: 10.1016/1048-9843(95)90036-5

Gronn, P. (2002). Distributed leadership as a unit of analysis. *The Leadership Quarterly, 13*, 423–451. doi: 10.1016/S1048-9843(02)00120-0

Gronn, P. (2008). The future of distributed leadership. *Journal of Educational Administration, 46*(2), 141–158. doi: 10.1108/09578230810863235

Harris, A., Leithwood, K., Day, C., Sammons, P., & Hopkins, D. (2007). Distributed leadership and organizational change: Reviewing the evidence. *Journal of Educational Change, 8*(4), 337–347.

Henneman, H. G., Judge, T., & Kammeyer-Mueller, J. (2015). *Staffing organizations* (8th ed.). New York, NY: McGraw-Hill Education.

Hollander, E. P. (1992). Leadership, followership, self, and others. *The Leadership Quarterly, 3*, 43–54. doi: 10.1016/1048-9843(92)90005-Z

Hollander, E. P., & Julian, J. W. (1969). Contemporary trends in the analysis of leadership processes. *Psychological Bulletin, 71*(5), 387–397.

Hosking, D., & Shamir, B. (2012). Dialogue: A dialogue on entitative and relational discourses.

In M. Uhl-Bien, S. M. Ospina, M. Uhl-Bien, & S. M. Ospina (Eds.), *Advancing relational leadership research: A dialogue among perspectives* (pp. 463–476). Charlotte, NC: IAP Information Age Publishing.

Hosking, D. (2006). Not leaders, not followers: A post-modern discourse of leadership processes. In B. Shamir, R. Pillai, M. Bligh, & M. Uhl-Bien (Eds.), *Follower-centered perspectives on leadership: A tribute to the memory of James R. Meindl* (pp. 1–36). Greenwich, CT: Information Age Publishing.

Hosking, D. M., Shamir, B., Ospina, S. M., & Uhl-Bien, M. (2012). Exploring the prospects for dialogue across perspectives. In M. Uhl-Bien, S. M. Ospina, M. Uhl-Bien, & S. M. Ospina (Eds.), *Advancing relational leadership research: A dialogue among perspectives* (pp. 501–535). Charlotte, NC: IAP Information Age Publishing.

Jackson, S., Schuler, R., & Werner, S. (2012). *Managing Human Resources* (11th ed.). Mason, OH: South-Western College Publishing.

Kahai, S., Jestire, R., & Rui, H. (2013). Effects of transformational and transactional leadership on cognitive effort and outcomes during collaborative learning within a virtual world. *British Journal of Educational Technology, 44*(6), 969–985.

Kedian, J., Giles, D., Morrison, M., & Fletcher, M. (2016). Leadership development as a dialogic process: The rationale and concept of an international leadership institute. *International Journal of Leadership in Education, 19*(2), 182–202, doi: 10.1080/13603124.2014.997800

Latham, M. E., & Wilhelm, T. (2014). Supporting principals to create shared leadership. *Leadership, 43*(3), 22–38.

Lee, M., Hallinger, P., & Walker, A. (2012). A distributed perspective on instructional leadership in International Baccalaureate (IB) schools. *Educational Administration Quarterly, 48*(4), 664–698.

Mossholder, K. W., Richardson, H. A., & Settoon, R. P. (2011). Human resource systems and helping in organizations: A relational perspective. *Academy of Management Review, 36*(1), 33–52. doi: 10.5465/AMR.2011.55662500

Ospina, S., & Foldy, E. (2010). Building bridges from the margins: The work of leadership in social change organizations. *The Leadership Quarterly, 21*, 292–307. doi: 10.1016/j.leaqua.2010.01.008

Ospina, S., & Sorenson, G. (2006). A constructionist lense on leadership: Charting new territory. In G. Goethals & G. Sorenson (Eds.), *Quest for a general theory of leadership* (pp. 188–204). Cheltenham: Edward Elgar Publishers.

Ospina, S. & Uhl-Bien, M. (2012). Mapping the terrain. In M. Uhl-Bien & S. M. Ospina (Eds.), *Advancing relational leadership research: A dialogue among perspectives* (pp. xix–xivii). Charlotte, NC: IAP Information Age Publishing.

Ospina, S. M., Foldy, E. G., El Hadidy, W., Dodge, J., Hofmann-Pinilla, A., & Su, C. (2012). Social change leadership as relational leadership. In M. Uhl-Bien, S. M. Ospina, M. Uhl-Bien, & S. M. Ospina (Eds.), *Advancing relational leadership research: A dialogue among perspectives* (pp. 255–302). Charlotte, NC: IAP Information Age Publishing.

Pearce, C. L., & Conger, J. A. (2003). Shared leadership: Reframing the hows and whys of leadership. *Shared Leadership: Reframing the Hows & Whys of Leadership, 1*. doi: 10.4135/9781452229539

Pienaar, C. F., & Raymond, E. B. (2013). Reflections on a shared leadership approach to curriculum development in higher education. *South African Journal of Higher Education, 27*(5), 1290.

Reitz, M. (2015). *Dialogue in organizations: Developing relational leadership*. New York: Macmillan Publishing.

Spillane, J. P., Halverson, R., & Diamond, J. B. (2001). Investigating school leadership practice: A distributed perspective. *Educational Researcher, 30*, 23–28. doi: 10.3102/0013189X030003023

Spillane, J. P., Halverson, R., & Diamond, J. B. (2004). Towards a theory of leadership practice: A distributed perspective. *Journal of Curriculum Studies, 36*, 3–34. doi: 10.1080/0022027032000106726

Spillane, J. P., Harris, A., Jones, M., & Mertz, K. (2015). Opportunities and challenges for taking a distributed perspective: Novice school principals' emerging sense of their new position. *British Educational Research Journal, 41*(6), 1068–1085.

Stogdill, R. M., & Coons, A. E. (1957). *Leader behavior: Its description and measurement.* Oxford: Ohio State University, Bureau of Busin.

Supovitz, J. A., & Poglinco, S. M. (2001). *Instructional leadership in a standards-based reform.* Washington, DC: ERIC Clearinghouse.

Sveningsson, S., Alvehus, J., & Alvesson, M. (2012). *Managerial leadership: Identities, processes, and interactions.* United Kingdom: Oxford University Press. doi: 10.1093/acprof:oso/9780199639724.003.0004

Taylor-Backor, K., & Gordon, S. P. (2015). Preparing principals as instructional leaders: Perceptions of university faculty, expert principals, and expert teacher leaders. *NASSP Bulletin, 99*(2), 105–126.

Uhl-Bien, M. (2006). Relational Leadership Theory: Exploring the social processes of leadership and organizing. *The Leadership Quarterly, 17*, 654–676. doi: 10.1016/j.leaqua.2006.10.007

Uhl-Bien, M., & Ospina, S. M. (2012). Paradigm interplay in relational leadership: A way forward. In M. Uhl-Bien, S. M. Ospina, M. Uhl-Bien, & S. M. Ospina (Eds.), *Advancing relational leadership research: A dialogue among perspectives* (pp. 537–580). Charlotte, NC: IAP Information Age Publishing.

Vine, B., Holmes, J., Marra, M., Pfeifer, D., & Jackson, B. (2008). Exploring co-leadership talk through interactional sociolinguistics. *Leadership, 4*(3), 339–360. doi: 10.1177/1742715008092389

Wood, M., & Dibben, M. (2015). Leadership as relational process. *Process Studies, 44*(1), 24.

Zacher, H., & Johnson, E. (2015). Leadership and creativity in higher education. *Studies in Higher Education, 40*(7), 1210–1225.

CHAPTER TWO

Practical Leadership

How Teachers Enact Leadership to Re-culture Their Schools

MISTILINA SATO AND CARRIE ROGERS

We present this chapter on the theory of practical leadership as a way to see teacher leadership as not only present in teachers' everyday actions but also as a way for teachers to see themselves as stewards of the teaching profession in their daily work within schools. Practical leadership, grounded in the ideas of Aristotelian practical reasoning, is bounded contextually and oriented toward action. This theory of leadership recognizes the everyday work of teachers as a place of leadership enactment. What we are learning and can continue to learn through the lens of practical leadership is that broadening the way teachers are viewed as leaders not only benefits teachers themselves, but can also work toward the re-culturing and improvement of schools. Below, we take up the history of teacher leadership and through illustrations of practical leadership, we push on common notions of what constitutes teacher leadership within US schools to get closer to leadership as stewardship.

TEACHER LEADERSHIP IN US SCHOOL SYSTEMS

Teacher leadership is not a new concept. Teachers were often referred to as classroom leaders in the mid–nineteenth century (Cuban, 1988) and the leaders of schools once bore the title of *principal teachers* (The National Commission on Teaching and America's Future, 1996, p. 110). As schooling moved to an industrial model in the early twentieth century, the work of teachers became equated with labor (Callahan, 1964; Mitchell & Kerchner, 1983; Troen & Boles, 1992); classroom teaching was cast in terms of following the policies and procedures established by the school administrators and viewing teachers as *ex officio* leaders became less common.

The notion of teacher leadership has re-emerged in recent decades. Silva, Gimbert, and Nolan (2000) identify three waves of how teacher leadership has been conceptualized by educational reformers, administrators, and policymakers over several decades of efforts to engage teachers as leaders. In the first wave, after the release of the Carnegie Task Force's (1986) report, *A Nation Prepared: Teachers for the 21st Century*, schools and districts provided a variety of work redesign structures to place teachers in leadership roles, including mentor programs that called on master teachers to work with other teachers; career ladders designed to allow teachers to "advance" within a traditionally flat career without moving out of teaching and into administration were created; and lead teachers were given decision making authority on site-based management teams. In summary, teacher leaders were viewed as serving in formal roles, often in a managerial capacity, which would enable the school to operate more efficiently (Smylie, 1997).

The second wave of teacher leadership conceptualization drew more directly on the instructional expertise of teachers, with hopes of leveraging greater impact on the curriculum and instruction in the school. Teachers took on greater responsibilities as curriculum leaders, staff developers, and mentors of new teachers. York-Barr and Duke (2004) reviewed 41 empirical studies on teacher leadership characterized within this wave of teacher leadership efforts. In their review, teacher leaders had significant teaching experience, were known to be excellent educators, and were respected by their peers. These authors argue that to be successful in leadership toward teaching and learning, teachers must have trusting and constructive relationships and build influence through both formal and informal avenues with peers and administrators. In the model of teacher leadership the authors put forward in this form of teacher leadership, the ultimate outcome of teacher leadership is anchored by seeing results in student learning outcomes.

The third wave of teacher leadership emphasizes teachers' roles in "re-culturing" schools as efforts toward school-wide instructional improvement have taken hold. The third wave emphasizes that teacher leadership is a process rather than a moment of locating leadership within a position or an instructional development role. Within this wave of teacher leadership, schools have turned to collective and team-based leadership approaches. For example, the concept of distributed leadership emerged from distributed cognition and socio-cultural learning theories in the early years of the 2000s (Spillane, Halverson, & Diamond, 2001). Within these conceptual frames, leadership not only comprises people and their roles and responsibilities, it also comprises the artifacts, the contexts, and the relationships among each of these parts of the socio-cultural system (Spillane, 2006). For example, Spillane argues that there is an interdependence among the identified leaders, the followers, and the situations in which interactions are taking place that creates a leadership practice. Leaders not only interact with and influence followers but are also influenced by them. Thus, leadership practice is an interdependent set of situated interactions among leaders and followers.

We see three limitations in the literature on teacher leadership with regard to this third wave of re-culturing schools. First, while distributed leadership has become popular within schools (as well as other organizations), the distributed nature of leadership within this framework gets portrayed differently depending on how it is taken up. Theoretically, the tasks on which leadership activity is centered are described as being "stretched" or distributed across the organization. In practice, however, the distribution of leadership is often understood as sharing the work of leadership across multiple people or a team within the organization to accomplish organizational goals. In the former view, teacher leadership would be tightly bound to the tasks in which teachers engage and the situated nature of teachers' work in schools and classrooms would be considered a dynamic part of the activity system. In the latter view, an identified leadership team distributes the work of establishing conditions, building consensus, and bringing about an organizational vision. The leadership work then gets translated to training and implementation rather than the situated tasks of instruction and school improvement being created, defined, and shaped by people across the organization. This approach harkens to older models of inserting teachers into new roles in order to accomplish instructional improvement work with greater efficiency.

Second, we find that in the empirical literature, tools or protocols by which we "measure" or describe teacher leadership tend to be limited to labeling teacher leadership activities within specific role-based forms of leadership or to naming discrete functions of leadership (Sato, Hyler, & Monte-Sano, 2014). Teacher leadership that is culturally and socially embedded in the daily activities of the school are much more difficult to capture given their non-specified nature and few studies have addressed this issue (Lieberman & Friedrich, 2010).

Finally, we propose that teacher leadership can be understood and described as a means toward re-culturing schools only if we shift our conceptualization of leadership away from roles and expertise, and even away from serving on distributed leadership teams, and toward recognizing the choices and actions—or enactment—in the everyday work of teaching. In our conceptualization of teacher leadership that follows, we recognize that the everyday work of teachers—conversations with school administration, collegial interactions, public displays of instructional practice—as having influence on their principal, their colleagues, and their parent community. These informal acts of influence are part of the fluid, culture-shaping practices of teachers. We also recognize that teachers make intentional and deliberated choices in their daily work that have lasting impacts on their relationships with colleagues, their school programs, and the organization as a whole (Collay, 2011; Lieberman & Friedrich, 2010). Rather than beginning with the person—or the leader—as the starting point for conceptualizing leadership, we will begin with an orientation toward everyday intentional action that continuously shapes and reshapes the culture of a school.

PRACTICAL REASONING

We will use practical reasoning as a conceptual frame for describing teacher leadership that is oriented toward action, morally driven with purpose, and deliberative within local contexts. In book six of the *Nicomachean Ethics,* Aristotle (trans. 1962) argues that there are two forms of reasoning: *techné* and *phronesis*. These forms of reasoning are distinct, drawing upon different intellectual processes and aimed at different outcomes. *Techné,* commonly Anglicized as "technique," is a kind of knowledge that allows one to make or produce a product or durable outcome (*poiesis*). In making, associated with craft or trade, the ends of *techné* reside beyond the activity. *Phronesis* is a kind of knowledge that is associated with practice, or for Aristotle, with *praxis*. The activity of *praxis* has no detached outcome from the person or from the activity; means and ends exist together in action. Thus, the actions one chooses are a representation of not only how one chooses to act, they are also an instantiation of how one wants the ends of actions—or outcomes—to be. Put simply in example, I want equity for students in schools, therefore the actions I choose will be equitable.

In contemporary discussions of these ancient ideas, we often make distinctions between technical reasoning and practical reasoning to create conceptual distinctions for understanding how actions are reasoned. *Reasoning* is needed for action—for making decision about how to act in particular circumstances. In Aristotle's terms, we can draw on a variety of knowledges for making decisions. *Episteme* is an abstracted and theoretical understanding of the world. Epistemic knowledge describes how things are in timeless and universal ways. Technical reasoning promises the potential to stabilize actions and the possibility to render predictable outcomes. One becomes skillful in a technique and reproduces actions that result in similar outcomes again and again. Practical reasoning requires acting within particular circumstances. The concept of *practical* here has more meaning than just "getting the job done" in a colloquial sense of practical. To engage in practical reasoning, one must choose a prudent course of action in uncertain circumstances. These can be the most difficult decisions to make and they can have long-lasting impact within particular situations.

Stephen Toulmin (2001) argued for a return to practical reasoning from the current climate of technical rationality (decision making driven by protocols and policy) across human activities such as politics, community development, organizational management, and living one's life. We argue, as others have (e.g., Atkin, Coffey, Moorthy, Author, & Thibeault, 2005; Coulter, 2002; Fenstermacher &

Richardson, 1993; Kessels & Korthagen, 2001; Orton, 1997; Sanders & McCutcheon, 1986; Sato, 2005), that teachers address everyday problems and uncertain situations not solely by understanding situations with theoretical knowledge or by learning a set of techniques that will help them get to similar outcomes again and again. They must read the situation at hand and take action based on what they think would best address that situation with both the desired outcome (ends) and the strategies (means) in mind. To describe teaching as a phronetic activity, or as one requiring practical reasoning, draws attention to the complex and uncertain work, to the everyday acts of teaching as a site for inquiry, to the moral dimensions of teachers' actions, and to approaches to teachers' development that are grounded in personhood and becoming.

PRACTICAL LEADERSHIP

Framing teacher leadership as practical leadership (Sato, 2005; Sato et al., 2014) recognizes that leaders act with purpose and fit their actions to the local context. Shifting away from a role-based frame of teachers as leaders, to a practical leadership frame views teacher leadership as the actions that teachers take within a context or situation. Different from distributed leadership, practical leadership values the purposes that drive those actions and places emphasis on the process of deliberation drawn from experience, identity, values, and local knowledge. This form of leadership is best seen and understood through the teacher's everyday choices and actions; that is, choosing to act in ways that are simultaneously who the teacher wants to be in action and the desired outcomes the teacher wants to see in the contextual situation in which the leadership is enacted. Given this overview, we can see that three primary dimensions are part of practical leadership.

First, within a framework of practical leadership, understanding the context and culture in which one works is very important. Having knowledge of the history of the working situation among teachers and approaches to developing relationships with people allows for leadership that is responsive not only to a particular situation, but to the people who are bound up in that situation.

Practical leadership is also purposeful. Here, purpose is most linked to the idea of intention. The question is not only what drives one toward leadership, but also why is one driven toward leadership in particular moments or situations. These questions can be answered with a traditional leadership idea such as a "vision" for leadership. But purposes do not always have to look outward to the future. One's purpose for leadership can look deep into one's desires in order to respond to something current that needs attention and action. One's guiding purpose for leadership serves as a compass that provides direction for the influence one exerts on others. When leadership draws from purpose, actions and the outcomes are merged. In Aristotelian notions of moral virtue, leadership is not only present in the means by which the teacher exerts influence—acting courageously, caring for others, using just practices—but is simultaneously the ends toward which the teacher is seeking to influence others.

Third, choosing action draws on processes for deliberation, a core feature of leadership that is practical and situated. Deliberation is a process of weighing alternatives and reaching decisions about actions that are both strategic and also reasoned through for what is right for the situation. For a decision to be right does not necessarily mean that it is true or accurate or factual. A decision is right if it is reasonable in light of virtues such as being a just decision, a fair decision, or a fitting decision. Making choices about how, when, and why to act also requires exercising judgment. Judgment is influenced by both normative pressures that suggest what should be done as well as inner desires that reflect purpose. Nussbaum (1990) captures the essence of practical decision making as the "sheer complexity and agonizing difficulty of choosing well" (p. 55).

LEADERSHIP ENACTMENT

Enacting leadership is different from performing acts of leadership that we associate with role-bound expectations of leadership. Acts of leadership are performed in moments when we have a leadership role and must carry out certain responsibilities. Leadership is the purpose behind why the action was performed. For example, a teacher serves on a curriculum committee in a leadership role and she must engage in curriculum writing activities as part of serving in that leadership role. Or, a teacher serves as a mentor teacher and he must engage in difficult coaching conversations with a struggling teacher as part of his responsibilities in the role of mentor. These are actions that are taken as part of one's diligence and responsibility to particular assigned roles commonly associated with teacher leadership.

Leadership enactment may not be located in a single event or connected to a particular role. Enactment of leadership is bound up in the practical actions of teachers and leadership is the result of the action, not the cause. In the following section, we explore leadership enactment through examples from teachers' lives collected through interviews as a means of both illustrating what enactment looks like (as opposed to seeing acts of leadership) and to further illustrate the practical nature of this enactment.

Illustrations of Leadership Enactment

Leadership enactment is harder to pinpoint than leadership acts because it is not necessarily planned in advance and is in response to a local situation. In interviews with teachers in which we solicited stories about how teachers felt like they had made a difference in their schools, we heard many stories (Sato, 2002). The following three stories from the teachers will help illustrate the leadership enactment of teachers and demonstrate how the enactment unfolds over time, with intention and purpose, and relies on deliberation with specific contextual knowledge of the situation—the practical aspects of leadership.

Melissa was a kindergarten teacher in an urban elementary school. She saw two situations at her school that she thought to be problematic—the primary grades did not have access to outdoor education opportunities as the upper elementary school grades did, and the school science fair was a traditional competition in which, she suspected, the parents may have been more involved than the students. Melissa had years of experience as an environmental educator. She knew the high quality of experiences available to young children in outdoor education within easy access to the school. She was dismayed that the school did not take advantage of such opportunities. Given her experience, qualifications, and motivations, Melissa sought to change the school policy about outdoor education for the primary grade levels. Through knowledgeable and consistent argument at parent–teacher meetings, Melissa convinced the parents and the principal that a redistribution of funds for outdoor education across the grade levels was warranted.

Melissa also had hurtful experiences in childhood competitions. She felt that communal learning experiences could be more productive than competitive learning experiences. Drawing on her personal and professional experiences, Melissa championed, designed, and implemented a school-wide science night to replace the traditional science fair competition in her school. She took on these two issues with passion and desire for change, knowing that she would have to convince other teachers, the administration, and the parent community on both issues. By giving persistent attention to all constituencies and by offering potential solutions with strong rationale for change, Melissa managed to change both situations into policies that she thought were more equitable and provided better learning experiences for children. Even though Melissa felt strongly that teachers should be compensated for additional responsibilities they take on at the school, she advocated for these changes in the science programs without additional compensation because she so strongly believed that these programs were the right choices on behalf of her students.

Carole was a second grade teacher in a suburban elementary school. She was faced with the decision of whether to move to the first grade to help remedy a dysfunctional grade level team situation, or to stay at the second grade level, thereby risking the loss of a highly qualified teacher in the first grade who was frustrated with the dysfunctional team. Carole chose to make the grade level change in an effort to keep her colleague from leaving the school and to act as a catalyst for change on the first grade team. In agreeing to make this move, Carole sacrificed her own professional and personal comfort and took on the challenge of managing new professional relationships. The situation was sensitive, requiring knowledge of the history of the working situation among the teachers and a diplomatic approach to developing working relationships among the newly constituted team. Carole's decision was driven by her desire to ensure that the school did not lose a teacher whom she thought to be highly qualified and by her sense of obligation to the teacher for having traded grade level places with her previously. In making her decision, Carole demonstrated her willingness to make a personal and professional sacrifice for the greater good of the school. Carole anticipated that she would be able to negotiate the new grade level context and felt confident that she could help facilitate a productive working relationship among the members of the grade level.

Kerri was a special education teacher who worked in the classroom with the regular sixth grade science teacher. She guided a steady change in the science curriculum, which she saw as needing an overhaul from a traditional textbook-based curriculum to a hands-on, investigative approach to teaching science. This transition would not only align with Kerri's own beliefs about effective science instruction, but would also help the school align better with new science standards. Kerri believed that an authoritarian approach with her partner teachers would not bring about the transition she wanted to advocate. Rather, given the team situation in which she taught, her reading of the needs of the teachers with whom she worked, and her own personality, she chose to nudge the curriculum change along gently in a non-aggressive manner.

To begin the change process, she made suggestions directly to the science teacher with whom she worked and provided curriculum materials where she could. Then she worked on the science frameworks and curriculum committee to write curriculum and pilot new materials at her grade level, thus bringing her co-teacher into the new curriculum adoption process. Finally, she promoted professional development experiences for her grade level partners. She did not make proclamations and she did not preach her message, even though she believed strongly in a particular kind of instruction she wanted to see in classrooms. Kerri unobtrusively steered the science curriculum toward a more hands-on approach over the course of three years. She made careful choices about how to approach her work, drawing not only on her expert knowledge, but also her knowledge of the situation and people with whom she worked.

Melissa's actions demonstrated her purposes and drive for providing meaningful science education experiences for young children and she used the democratic processes of the school governance system to promote more equality in access to outdoor education experiences and sharing science knowledge. Carole enacted practical leadership when she deliberated how to prevent a highly regarded teacher from leaving the school community. Her actions went beyond fulfilling an internal sense of obligation she felt to one teacher. She put the grade level team and the overall quality of instruction in the school above her own sense of comfort. Kerri had a professional drive for engaging special education students more fully in engaging science curriculum. She knew the teachers on her team and she enacted leadership in how she chose a contextually sensitive approach to manage a significant curricular change. All three of the teachers were guided by the purpose of making the school and the classroom better places for students to learn and leveraged their local knowledge in their deliberations about what action to take. In order to reach their desired outcomes, they had to live those outcomes in their process of enactment. Their actions show us who they are as teachers and as leaders.

Interestingly, these teachers did not identify these illustrations as stories of leadership. One teacher reflected on her experience after we recast a story she told as a story of leadership:

> I never thought of it as leadership, but that's what I've done. I think that, in a way, I've almost internalized it, and it's just a way of being, of teaching, of thinking, of sharing in an unobtrusive way, of thinking things out so that you can work with a colleague to the betterment of the students and of the school and make things function more easily. I think I've always been that way, to a degree, but I never really thought of it in a leadership sense.

Through these illustrations of leadership enactment we can see that teachers are astute decision makers, negotiating interactions with many different groups of people and individuals on a daily basis and their professional work takes place both inside and outside of the classroom. As we listened to the stories the teachers told about dilemmas that they faced in their everyday work and how they coped with them in deliberative and purposeful ways, we understood that these teachers were *living a kind of leadership* that was not connected to particular roles or labels they had acquired. They were not only performing many acts of leadership that keep programs running, curriculum updated, and committees talking, they were also *enacting leadership* through negotiating relationships and deliberating on tough choices and *being* the kind of leadership they wanted to see within their schools.

PRACTICAL LEADERSHIP AND RE-CULTURING SCHOOLS

Conceptualizing and understanding teacher leadership is a task that many researchers have embarked upon. This chapter makes a small effort to contribute to that conceptualization by describing the idea of practical leadership and illustrating leadership enactment that may go unrecognized because it does not fit within traditional leadership conceptions that rely on definitions within bureaucratic and often hierarchical organizational structures (Forster, 1997). Forster contrasts a structural view of leadership (for example, membership on a committee) with what might be considered a more cultural view of leadership (for example, continual collaboration). The difficult aspect about shaping one's own culture is that our cultural norms and practices are often not visible to us when we live within them—like a fish not understanding that they live within an environment made of water (Barth, 2006). Therefore, understanding the construct and compositional dynamics of school culture is an important aspect for teacher leadership to be a culture-shaping process (Collay, 2011; Holland, Eckert, & Allen, 2014; Sato, Bartiromo, & Elko, 2016).

Our practical leadership framework helps us move closer to a cultural view of leadership. In the practical leadership framework, contextual knowledge and attention to the local and particular relationships within the school are needed for enactment to be embedded within existing relationships and histories. The role that the cultural dimensions play within a school, though, could be further developed in practical leadership through more explicit attention to understanding the school culture and its dynamics. A deeper cultural understanding of the school would address how the school culture supports relationships among members of the school community, communication and decision making practices, and a general feeling of efficacy among teachers for being successful with students and in their agency for participating in school level decision making (Holland et al., 2014; Sato et al., 2016).

Schools need strong, professional cultures to foster teacher learning and teacher leadership (Deal & Peterson, 1999). A school's culture can support or sabotage the quality and effectiveness of professional learning and leading for teachers as well as for students (Fullan, 2001). School principals are often charged with the responsibility for creating and nurturing a healthy or positive school culture. Culture, however, when viewed as a dynamic and relational process rather than something that is created and becomes fixed in time, is everyone's responsibility to shape. We argue here that the practical leadership in which teachers engage can be a culture shaping process. With more explicit attention to helping teachers understand the cultural dynamics of the school, teachers' practical leadership can be more intentionally focused on shaping and reshaping school culture.

PRACTICAL LEADERSHIP AND STEWARDING THE PROFESSION OF TEACHING

Given the illustrations depicting leadership enactment, it is also important to ask why a teacher might choose to take on the additional work that Melissa took on, the risks that Carole took on, and the long-term change process that Kerri took on. To answer this, so far the discussion about practical leadership has steered us toward the notion of having purpose—an internal drive for something that is morally good and worth fighting for. We want to also propose that this professional stance might also be characterized through the concept of stewardship. In this discussion, we consider how teachers who choose to enact practical leadership are driven by purposes that are not only internally strong, but are also purposes that reach outside of their personal goals and link to a broader organizational or societal purpose.

The role and status of the steward harkens to a time of kings leaving their lands in the capable hands of a trusted steward—someone with the talents to care for the kingdom's economic well-being and the wisdom to lead the people in the absence of the ruler. From this history, standard definitions of stewardship emphasize the responsible management and care of something entrusted to one in the absence of the owner. In Judeo-Christian life, stewardship is defined as one's responsibility for systematically sharing time, talent, and possessions in the service of God and for the benefit of mankind. Environmental advocates have adopted the notion of stewardship of the Earth as a means of conveying the long-term commitment we, as humans, have to manage the resources of the earth and care for the environment. The message conveyed by these groups does not only portray a responsibility to preserve resources, but is strongly imbued with the obligation to nurture, sustain, and improve, if we can, the earth's environment that belongs to none of us so that we, as well as future generations, benefit from our forethought today.

Thomas Sergiovanni used stewardship as a conception of leadership in his 1992 book *Moral Leadership*, a work that focused on the leadership of schools by principals. Sergiovanni explains:

> Stewardship represents primarily an act of trust, whereby people and institutions entrust a leader with certain obligations and duties to fulfill and perform on their behalf. For example, the public entrusts the schools to the school board. The school board entrusts the school to its principal. Parents entrust their children to teachers. Stewardship also involves the leader's personal responsibility to manage her or his life and affairs with proper regard for the rights of other people and for the common welfare. Finally, stewardship involves placing oneself in service to ideas and ideals and to others who are committed to their fulfillment. (p. 139)

In his discussion of stewardship, Sergiovanni focuses on the idea of servant leadership (Greenleaf, 1977, cited in Sergiovanni, 1992, p. 273)—leadership enacted in the service of the people one is leading. The examples he draws upon invoke a sense of selflessness of the leader as he or she engages in work that is less bureaucratic and closer to the needs of the people. We are less drawn to the altruistic conception of stewardship that Sergiovanni conveys as we want to uphold a strong sense of agency for teacher leadership as well as advocate for teachers' working conditions to not be portrayed as voluntary and non-remunerated. We are, however, drawn to how Sergiovanni focuses his attention to questions that drive a deeper understanding of purpose such as "What are we about? Why? Are the students being served? Is the school as a learning community being served? What are our obligations to this community? With these questions in mind, how can we best get the job done?" (p. 277). These questions bring sharper focus to the collective responsibility of all members of the organization to attend to how decisions to take action shape the work, relationships, organization, and community.

Peter Block writes about stewardship as a form of leadership in the world of business in his 1996 book *Stewardship: Choosing service over self-interest*. This work focuses on shifting the conception of the leadership within businesses from one that emphasizes control and compliance of the workforce to one that enables choice over how to serve the customer and establishes accountability as a professional norm rather than a set of controls. He writes:

> Stewardship begins with the willingness to be accountable for some larger body than ourselves—an organization, a community. Stewardship springs from a set of beliefs about reforming organizations that affirms our choice for service over the pursuit of self-interest. When we choose service over self-interest we say we are willing to be deeply accountable without choosing to control the world around us. It requires a level of trust that we are not used to holding (p. 6). … Stewardship questions the belief that accountability and control go hand in hand. We can be accountable and give control to those who are closer to the work, operating from the belief that in this way the work is better served. (p. 18)

For Block, stewardship is about redistributing power, purpose, and wealth within the organization. Three ideals govern the shift of the leadership to stewardship: (1) working in partnership so that the productivity of the company is built on joint work; (2) developing the empowerment of each employee so that accountability arises from doing meaningful work; and (3) similar to Sergiovanni's conceptualization, stewardship is built on a foundation of service to the company, the customer, and the community.

Introducing stewardship as a concept to help understand why leadership enactment is taken up by teachers recognizes moral and service-oriented purposes of leadership for teachers (Margolis & Deuel, 2009). Purposes provide both a reason for acting and a direction, vision, or potential outcome for the action. The teachers' purposes for their actions are far-reaching goals on the educational horizon (Gadamer, 1994). These purposes may never be fully realized but, through their ongoing work, the teachers hope to move closer to their goals.

The concept of stewardship also provides a concept to describe a professional stance toward leadership enactment that is rooted in the belief that teachers' contributions and actions can make a difference for the larger community—the students, the school, and the profession. In the illustrations provided, we saw that teachers did not only look out for themselves and the students in their classrooms, they saw themselves as part of a larger educational endeavor. They could contribute to the betterment of the school and uphold the covenants of being a teacher.

Not only were the teachers acting as stewards of the students they served, they were also stewards of the school and stewards of the profession of teaching.

CLOSING THOUGHTS

This chapter is not an argument against role-based forms of teacher leadership. Certainly specific roles and functions contribute to the work in classrooms and schools and provide access to differentiated work within the flat structure of the teaching profession in the US. The argument for more attention to *practical leadership* is a call to pay attention to the untapped potential of teacher leadership within our schools. We propose that a different language for describing leadership can help us actually see what teachers are doing and potentially encourage more enactment in a time when teachers are feeling restricted in how much agency they have.

We recognize that practical leadership captures the embedded nature of leadership enactment while also needing some further descriptive work to help teachers develop and hone their own sense of practical leadership. We propose here that further conceptualizing practical leadership with intentional focus on re-culturing schools and toward professional stewardship can help teachers both recognize and further develop their practical leadership and alleviate some of the resistance from teachers who so adamantly deny their own leadership because of the historical and hierarchical images that the word leader conjures. Teachers who take a practical leadership stance toward their everyday work may not have a designated position of leadership. They can, however, have a sense that their ideas are important, that they have expertise that can be shared with others, and that they have a responsibility to participate in shaping the work and culture of the school.

REFERENCES

Aristotle. (1962). The Nicomachean ethics (M. Ostwald, Trans.). Indianapolis, IN: Bobbs-Merrill.

Atkin, J. M., Coffey, J. E., Moorthy, S., Author, M., & Thibeault, M. (2005). Designing everyday assessment in the science classroom. New York, NY: Teachers College Press.

Barth, R. S. (2006). Culture in Question. In *The Jossey-Bass reader on educational leadership* (2nd ed.) San Francisco, CA: Jossey-Bass Publishers.

Block, P. (1996). *Stewardship: Choosing service over self-interest.* San Francisco, CA: Berrett-Koehler.

Callahan, R. E. (1964). *The cult of efficiency*. Chicago: University of Chicago Press.

Carnegie Task Force on Teaching as a Profession. (1986). *A nation prepared: Teachers for the 21st Century*. Washington, DC: Carnegie Forum on Education and the Economy.

Collay, M. (2011). *Everyday teacher leadership: Taking action where you are.* San Francisco, CA: Jossey-Bass.

Coulter, D. (2002). What counts as action in educational action research? *Educational Action Research, 10*(2), 189–206.
Cuban, L. (1988). *The managerial imperative and the practice of leadership in schools.* Albany, NY: State University of New York Press.
Deal, T. E., & Peterson, K. D. (1999). Shaping school culture: The school leader's role. San Francisco: CA. Jossey-Bass.
Fenstermacher, G., & Richardson, V. (1993). The elicitation and reconstruction of practical arguments in teaching. *Journal of Curriculum Studies, 25*(2), 101–114.
Forster, E. M. (1997). Teacher leadership: Professional right and responsibility. *Action in Teacher Education, 19*(3), 82–94.
Fullan, M. (2001). *Leading in a Culture of Change.* Hoboken, NJ: John Wiley and Sons.
Gadamer, H.-G. (1994). *Truth and method.* (J. Weinsheimer & D. G. Marshall, Trans.). New York, NY: Continuum (Original work published, 1960).
Holland, J., Eckert, J., & Allen, M. (2014). From preservice to teacher leadership: Meeting the future in educator preparation. *Action in Teacher Education, 36*(5/6), 433–445.
Kessels, J., & Korthagen, F. A. J. (2001). The relation between theory and practice: Back to the classics. In F. A. J. Korthagen, with J. Kessels, B. Koster, B. Lagerwerf, & T. Wubbels (Eds.), *Linking practice and theory: The pedagogy of realistic teacher education* (pp. 20–31). Mahwah, NJ: Lawrence Erlbaum.
Lieberman, A., & Friedrich, L. D. (2010). *How teachers become leaders: Learning from practice and research.* New York, NY: Teachers College Press.
Margolis, J., & Deuel, A. (2009). Teacher leaders in action: Motivation, morality, and money. *Leadership and Policy in Schools, 8*(3), 264–286. doi: 10.1080/15700760802416115
Mitchell, D., & Kerchner, C. (1983). Labor relations and teacher policy. In G. Sykes & L. Shulman (Eds.), *Handbook of teaching and policy* (pp. 215–219). New York, NY: Macmillan.
The National Commission on Teaching and America's Future. (1996). *What matters most: Teachers for America's future.* New York, NY: Author.
Nussbaum, M. C. (1990). The discernment of perception: An Aristotelian conception of private and public rationality. In M. C. Nussbaum (Ed.), *Love's knowledge: Essays on philosophy and literature* (pp. 54–105). New York, NY: Oxford University Press.
Orton, R. (1997). Toward and Aristotelian model of teacher reasoning. *Journal of Curriculum Studies, 29*(5), 569–583.
Sanders, D. P., & McCutcheon, G. (1986). The development of practical theories of teaching. *Journal of Curriculum Studies and Supervision, 2*(1), 50–67.
Sato, M. (2002). *Practical Leadership.* Unpublished doctoral dissertation. Stanford, CA: Stanford University.
Sato, M. (2005). Practical leadership: Conceptualizing the everyday leadership work of teachers. *The New Educator, 1*(1), 55–71.
Sato, M., Bartiromo, M., & Elko, S. (2016, March). Investigating your school's science teaching and learning culture. *Phi Delta Kappan, 97*(6), 42–47.
Sato, M., Hyler, M. E., & Monte-Sano, C. B. (2014, Fall). Learning to lead with purpose: National Board Certification and teacher leadership development. *International Journal of Teacher Leadership, 5*(1), 1–23.
Sergiovanni, T. J. (1992). Moral leadership: Getting to the heart of school improvement. San Francisco, CA: Jossey-Bass Publishers.

Silva, D. Y., Gimbert, B., & Nolan, J. (2000). Sliding the doors: Locking and unlocking possibilities for teacher leadership. *Teachers College Record*, *102*(4), 779–804.

Smylie, M. A. (1997). Research on teacher leadership: Assessing the state of the art. In B. J. Biddle, T. L. Good, & I. F. Goodson (Eds.), *International Handbook of Teachers and Teaching*, *1*, 521–592. Dordrecht, The Netherlands: Kluwer.

Spillane, J. (2006). *Distributed Leadership*. San Francisco, CA: Jossey-Bass.

Spillane, J. P., Halverson, R., & Diamond, J. (2001). Investigating school leadership practice: A distributed perspective, *Educational Researcher*, *30*(3), 23–28. doi: 10.3102/0013189x030003023

Toulmin, S. (2001). *Return to reason*. Cambridge, MA: Harvard University Press.

Troen, V., & Boles, K. (1992, April). *Leadership from the classroom: Women teachers as a key to school reform*. Paper presented at the Annual Meeting of the American Education Research Association, San Francisco.

York-Barr, J., & Duke, K. (2004). What do we know about teacher leadership? Findings from two decades of scholarship. *Review of Educational Research*, *74*(3), 255–316.

CHAPTER THREE

Leadership in Times of Social Change

ALONZO M. FLOWERS III AND ROSA M. BANDA

Personal and systemic change processes are constructed with recognition of the moral imperative of our work.

—Franco, Gutierrez Ott, & Robles (2013, p. 110)

INTRODUCTION

Critical ideologies associated with leadership development are fundamental as we examine the educational pipeline, specifically as it pertains to the moral imperative inherent in higher education. In addition to an understanding of individual thoughts and feelings related to change, knowledge of the complexity of groups, organizations, and systems as well as a commitment to navigating change in diverse and intersecting contexts remain at the forefront of leadership style in times of profound social change. Research and policy literature on current issues in global education is used to examine topics that include, but is not limited to, cross-border education, colorism, feminism, student and scholar mobility patterns, and the impact of emerging technologies (Bell, Jones, & Johnson, 2002; Hafner, 2005; Jean-Marie, 2008; Karpinski, 2006). This chapter is designed to broaden and deepen the reader's understanding of contemporary developments in social justice and global leadership and to develop analytical skills for understanding the social, political, and economic processes shaping education. More specifically, this chapter will examine effective leadership theories that are applicable and necessary for leaders to be effective social change advocates in the 21st century.

:standing leadership development in a global world is an invaluable tool for administrators who want to provide opportunities for students to become socially and globally aware leaders on their respective campuses. The development of critical social justice leadership is considered to have a profound beneficial impact on students within the higher education environment and the larger society (Lindsey, Robins, & Terrell, 2009; Northouse, 2013). Today we live in a world that is rapidly changing due to technology, and the higher education arena is no exception as an increasing number of postsecondary courses are implementing technological innovations. Advances in technology, in other words, has globalized the society in which we currently live. As a result, the need for leadership frameworks to be inclusive of broader world perspectives and more importantly, understanding of these world perspectives is warranted. In view of the changing educational landscape, several educational researchers have questioned the social justice process for leaders (Gurin, Nagda, & Lopez, 2004). The literature covered by this chapter will provided an overview of the concept of social justice and leadership in higher education and integrate contemporary perspectives of social justice in a time of change (Purdie-Vaughns, Steele, Davies, Ditlmann, & Crosby, 2008).

CONTEMPORARY SOCIAL JUSTICE LEADERSHIP MODEL

The literature on social justice and leadership exists in a complex space that focuses on the development of society and the role of creating social structures that seeks to benefit the greatest number of participants. McInerney (2004) highlighted three forms of injustices that might impede the development of a socially justice context: socioeconomic disadvantage, racism, and cultural oppression. For students in higher education, their identities as a leader are significantly influenced by the role the student had within their campus community (Komives, Longerbeam, Owen, Mainella, & Osteen, 2006). In addition, Patton, Shahjahan, and Osei-Kofi (2010) assert that social justice in higher education "requires a multi-faceted, holistic, and contextual approach to understanding the concept of social justice in a broader sense" (p. 269). Social justice, in other words, remains a complex and multifaceted call to action that remains situational in nature. As such, there is no single theory that can be utilized as a barometer for how to best develop leaders (Lindsey, Graham, Westphal, & Jew, 2008).

CONCEPTUAL LEADERSHIP THEORIES THAT ENCOMPASS GLOBAL PERSPECTIVES

The development of social justice leaders must rely on a conceptual understanding of theories that promote action-oriented leadership. What follows is an explication, albeit brief, of three leadership theories that emphasize *social justice leadership* (Theoharis, 2007, *culturally proficient leadership* (Robins, Lindsey, Lindsey, & Terrell, 2006), and *cross-cultural competencies* (Adler & Bartholomew, 1992) as building blocks to aid in the conceptual understanding of leadership that should be at the forefront of social change (Frattura & Capper, 2007). To be clear, this is not to suggest that these are the only leadership theories that can cultivate social justice leaders. Rather the aforementioned leadership theories should begin to build a repertoire of knowledge and skill set to be utilized in the development of 21st century leaders in the globalized world.

Social justice leadership. Extant research continues to examine leadership for social justice from various lenses (see Gewirtz, 2006; North, 2006; Singh, 2011; Theoharis, 2009). Singh (2011) posits that "Social justice has kinships and associations with notions of human and socio-economic rights, social inclusion, equity, and access to resources and capabilities for human well-being" (p. 482). Rather than a definition of social justice that focuses on race, sexual orientation, religion, to name a few, Singh (2011) argues that social justice should encapsulate a perspective that focuses on how social structures embedded in higher education shape the inequitable distribution of resources at a global level. Gewirtz (1998) similarly asserts that exclusionary and marginalized processes must be dismantled.

Social Justice Leadership

As such, the role of knowledge acquisition permeates the quest for parity in social justice. Such sentiments align with Theoharis's (2007) social justice leadership. Theoharis outlines essential characteristics associated with being a social justice leader that include:

1. Places significant value on diversity, deeply learns about and understands that diversity, and extends cultural respect;
2. Ends segregated and pull-out programs that prohibit both emotional and academic success for marginalized children;
3. Strengthens core teaching and curriculum and insures that diverse students have access to that core;
4. Embeds professional development in collaborative structures and a context that tries to make sense of race, class, gender, and disability;
5. Knows that school cannot be great until the students with the greatest struggles are given the same rich opportunities both academically and socially as their more privileged peers;
6. Demands that every child will be successful but collaboratively addresses the problems of how to achieve that success;

7. Seeks out other activist administrators who can and will sustain her or him;
8. Sees all data through lens of equity;
9. Knows that building community and differentiation are tools to ensure that all students achieve success together;
10. Becomes intertwined with the life, community, and soul of the school. (p. 252)

As noted in Theoharis's (2007) characteristics associated with social justice leaders, a lens of equity filters the manner in which data and opportunity are analyzed. In addition to a significant value on diversity, Theoharis (2007) also recognizes the role of administrators to be activist-oriented so as to not only invoke change via practice and curriculum but to invest in community building that works to achieve parity in the success of all students. Such characteristics, though it does not specifically mention race, gender, sexual orientation, to name a few marginalized populations, begin to reframe and account for how policies in place might work counterproductive to a socially just mission. We argue that this is a strength of Theoharis's (2007) model in that the characteristics outlined do not remain bifurcated in nature.

Culturally Proficient Leadership. According to Robins et al. (2006), cultural proficiency is the "set of values and behaviors in an individual, or the set of policies and practices in an organization, that create the appropriate mindset and approach to effectively responding to the issues caused by diversity" (p. 11). What is of particular interest is the creation of an "appropriate mindset and approach" to respond to diversity issues. This suggests that an integral aspect of culturally proficient leadership is often situated in a mindset—one that must be cultivated via a critical consciousness lens (Banda, Flowers, Robinson, & Allen, 2016)—that allows for individuals to develop into leaders of action rather than simply theorists.

The cultivation of a critical consciousness lens must begin in college classrooms (Banda et al., 2016) via critical dialogues that problematize and deconstruct quality and access in education (Singleton & Linton, 2006). Critical consciousness lens, according to Freire (1970), requires individuals to critically self-examine the systematic structures of inequality and more importantly, recognize their role in their respective positionality as a change agent within those unjust systems. A critical consciousness lens delves deeper in the self-reflection of social injustices so much so that the conscious is readily aware of an individual's agency and how such agency can serve as a catalyst for social change (Banda et al., 2016). For instance, a critical consciousness of culture often initiates a greater understanding and appreciation for those outside of our own cultures. As such, culturally proficient people capitalize on teachable moments that welcome diversity in safe environments (Robins et al., 2006).

Nuri-Robins, Lindsey, Terrell, and Lindsey (2007) propose five characteristics associated with being a culturally proficient leader. These characteristics include one's ability to:

1. *Assess culture.* An assessment of culture suggests that one must be not only cognizant of one's own culture but recognize the effect it has on peers. In a community of learners who assess culture, one seeks to interact as a means to experience dissonance and further expand one's initial assessment of culture.
2. *Value diversity.* To value diversity means that one must welcome diverse learners in the class and more importantly, recognize and welcome the challenges that inherently result from a diverse group of individuals. The latter suggests that learners in your class will work to build a community premised on comprehension and appreciation of diversity.
3. *Manage the dynamics of difference.* Much like nuances in similarities encountered, one must recognize that within diverse learners conflict and challenges encountered remain a normative process. As such, such conflicts and challenges provide opportunities for learners to effectively manage conflict associated with personalities and found within diverse cultures. What appears to be clashes in personalities may in fact be conflicts in culture.
4. *Adapt to diversity.* A true adaptation to diversity suggests that continuous learning must be a key component of how one chooses to negotiate differences. The aforementioned seeks to utilize principles of cultural proficiency to structure courses.
5. *Institutionalize cultural knowledge.* Characteristics of cultural proficiency must be embedded in the policies and practices found in the culture of any organization. Teachable moments are not only reserved for students but instructors, managers, and communities can all benefit from a shared cultural understanding.

Nuri-Robins' et al. (2007) model of culturally proficient leadership provides a critical framework pertinent to leadership in times of social change. One's ability to assess culture, value diversity, manage dynamics of differences, and adapt to diversity culminates in an institutionalized cultural knowledge found in the policies of an organization. As a leader in times of social change, one's ability to encompass culturally proficient characteristics remains a necessary set of skills for leadership found at any capacity.

Cross-Cultural Competencies. A leadership framework associated with cross-cultural competencies in an era of globalization is warranted to train future leaders and to further unpack social change that transcends a national level (Northouse,

2013). To achieve such a feat, Adler and Bartholomew (1992) contend that leaders must develop the following five cross-cultural competencies:

1. Leaders must possess a worldwide understanding of business, politics, and culture associated with environments;
2. Leaders must grasp trends, tastes, perspectives, and technologies associated with world cultures;
3. Leaders must be able to effectively collaborate with people from diverse, global cultures;
4. Leaders must be able to adapt to multiple forms of communication and to interact with the community of world cultures;
5. Leaders must forego notions of dominance and act on notions of equity as a means to establish genuine relatability to members of other world cultures.

Adler and Bartholomew (1992) understand the environmental context of the world. For instance, their cross-cultural competencies emphasize the relationship between politics, business, and culture as interdependent components that shape world cultures. To grapple with diverse trends, tastes, perspectives, and technologies, these competencies highlight the importance of collaboration as key components of cross-cultural competencies. Relinquishing normative frames of cultural superiority enables leaders to seek social change from a lens of equitable parity at multiple levels. A similar assertion by Ting-Toomey (1999) posits that "transcultural visions" are critical for global leaders.

While the previously noted social justice leadership (Theoharis, 2009) and culturally proficient leadership (Robins et al., 2006) models of leaders focus on social justice from a Westernized normative lens that gives credence to marginalized populations, the cross-cultural competencies (Adler & Bartholomew, 1992) framework is the culmination of the progression of how leadership development should astutely build on and cultivate socially just leaders for social change in the era of globalization. This is not to say that these leadership frameworks do not hold individual merit; rather, what we argue is that one cannot simply become a global leader without knowledge of how to promote social justice on a national level. Proactive leaders, in other words, must be well-versed and consistently action-oriented while extending their leadership capabilities to be inclusive of global societies. Leadership in silos stifles development of leadership warranted to build on various conceptualizations of socially just leadership theories. Even with aforementioned theories or any other leadership theories one chooses to ascribe to, it is important to utilize a critical consciousness to deconstruct theories as a necessity to understand what characteristics best serve an increasing global perspective.

CASE STUDY: SPRINGTOWN STATE UNIVERSITY (SSU)

As administrators and leaders on college campuses, acknowledging the critical discussion around issues of diversity and inclusion must incorporate both national and global social changes. The aim of this case analysis is to provide readers with an example of how social justice and leadership theories can be utilized to prompt effective decision making towards university policy. To accomplish this, social justice leadership theory (Theoharis, 2007), culturally proficient leadership theory (Robins et al., 2006), and cross cultural competencies (Northouse, 2013) will frame the processes in which the administrators understand and conceptualize the issues presented. Below we share the case and an analysis from varying stakeholders' perspectives. The appendix includes a suggestion for a course assignment with this case study.

SPRINGTOWN STATE UNIVERSITY (SSU)

Springtown State University (SSU) is a rural regional public institution founded in 1940 that is in the process of becoming a comprehensive research institution. Springtown State University is located 45 miles from Main City, one of the state's largest metropolitan areas. With a current student enrollment of 15,000 and a projected enrollment of 20,000 students in the next five years, SSU is seeking to diversify its' student population. Springtown State University President Lena Stone aims to implement her *2021 Social Justice* plan over the next five years. According to President Stone, "Creating a Social Justice platform for SSU is one of the most important actions we can take to ensure that diversity, inclusion, and globalization become integral to the way our institution functions, both internally and externally." She further noted that, "the *2021 Social Justice* plan involves several steps, one that includes revising SSU's mission statement so that the institution addresses diversity and global initiatives in a meaningful and relevant way." As a result, President Stone and the Board of Trustees revised the college's mission statement to read:

> The mission of Springtown State University is to seek exceptionally promising students of all backgrounds from across the nation and around the world and to educate them, through academic discipline and social experience, to develop their intellectual, moral, civic, and creative capacities to the fullest. The aim of this education is the cultivation of citizens with a rich awareness of our heritage to lead and serve in every sphere of human activity.

While the President's *2021 Social Justice* plan seeks to diversify the student population at SSU, there has been limited discussion about the organizational implications of the President's vision. Furthermore, the President's *2021 Social Justice* plan fails to address the disproportionate number of racially and culturally diverse faculty currently employed at SSU. Campus demographics indicate that out of the 1,800 faculty and staff currently employed at SSU less than 5% represent a diverse population. While the President's *2021 Social Justice* plan has enjoyed broad support among the campus community, several key stakeholders have expressed concern about the impact of significant student and faculty demographic shifts on the SSU campus. As a result, the President has convened a special committee to examine the impact of a significant demographic shift on the SSU campus.

CASE ANALYSIS: ANALYZING PROFESSIONAL PERSPECTIVES

The role of student affairs leaders continues to focus on the holistic development of students (Dung & Gordon, 2011). As such, among the responsibilities of student affairs professionals is to cultivate the social, moral, and ethical aspects of students. The aforementioned remain central and necessary to instill the competencies and tenets often aligned with social justice frameworks. Building social justice and global awareness remains a vital responsibility and need during these social times which is why the role of student affairs professionals is becoming increasingly important on college campuses.

Within this case study, the mission of the *2021 social justice plan* and shift in demographics is certain to change the structural and compositional diversity at SSU. This shift requires leaders to understand how social justice leadership theories can impact the direction of decision-making processes across the institution. For instance, the Director of Multicultural Affairs might integrate cross cultural competencies as a way to provide collaboration in the establishment of programs that seek to impact and build community among a multitude of diverse student populations. Leaders must be able to adopt multiple forms of communication to interact with communities of world cultures. This collaboration must happen between various leaders on campus. To achieve true diversity and more importantly, inclusion the Director of Multicultural Affairs cannot be the sole, leading voice when it comes to diversity matters on campus. True inclusion on college campuses is not a result of the lone effort of one leader or office but rather the result of consistent and collective effort of all leaders and offices.

As such, the demographic shift at SSU highlights an ongoing change on most college campuses today. Shifting demographics and increased access to higher education has reshaped the compositional diversity found within student body at postsecondary institutions. Theoretically, leaders must first be cognizant of how the shifting demographics at SSU will shape their values and affect the development of policies and programs as it pertains to diversity (Robins et al., 2006). Such policies and programs, in other words, essentially create the mindset associated with diversity at SSU. Foundational to the diversity at SSU is a social justice framework that also must focus and develop its' commitment to global awareness as it relates to a critical examination and comprehension of the impact that the unequal allocation of resources has on the global community (Singh, 2011).

In order for SSU to create an institutional culture that aligns with the vision of *2021 social justice* plan there must be leaders who utilize the five characteristics of a culturally proficient leader (Nuri-Robins et al., 2007). According to the five characteristics, a culturally proficient leader must be able to: (1) Assess the culture; (2) Value diversity; (3) Manage the dynamic of differences; (4) Adapt to diversity; and (5) Institutionalize cultural knowledge. Given the shift in demographics, SSU must begin to assess the changing culture and diversity now found on campus. In addition to policies and programs that favor diversity, SSU leaders must be cognizant of how to incorporate and to welcome diverse ways of knowing into the college experience. An important inherent component of valuing diversity are leaders' abilities to manage the dynamic of differences within the collegiate environment. Differences must be understood as unique rather than divisive in nature. Managing the dynamics of differences will not be an easy feat for SSU leaders. As such, leaders must be willing to adapt to diversity with an institutional commitment to continuous learning to help mediate the differences and nuances associated with diverse environments. This continuous learning and valuing of diversity should become the fabric of policies and programs that essentially institutionalize cultural knowledge at SSU.

To institutional cultural knowledge as it pertains to a commitment to diversity and global awareness, we offer the following recommendations.

1. Conduct SWOT Analysis: To assess a change in culture, SSU can employ a SWOT analysis so as to systematically examine the current strengths, weaknesses, opportunities, and threats as it pertains to the changing diversity on campus. Analysis of the findings can help SSU assess the current state of diversity amidst the demographic changes and goals of the *2021 social justice* plan.
2. Train Leaders in Social Justice Frameworks: Leaders of the 21st century must be exposed to social justice frameworks in these times of social change. Frameworks included in this chapter can be a good starting point for SSU when it comes to leadership training development and institutes. Understanding the social context transcends national issues and must encompass a global awareness that reflects a critical consciousness lens.
3. Provide an Open Forum for Critical Dialogue: The leaders at SSU must proactively create an open forum for critical dialogue to collect qualitative data in order to frame the perspectives of key stakeholders (e.g., students,

faculty, staff, professional communities) on campus. This allows for a snapshot of a collective understanding of diversity as well as an examination of how cultural and diverse knowledge is being or not being institutionalized at SSU.

In alignment with the revised mission statement of SSU that seeks "exceptionally promising students of all backgrounds from across the nation and around the world … to develop their intellectual, moral, civic, and creative capacities to the fullest", the *2021 Social Justice* plan seeks to ensure that diversity, inclusion, and globalization become an integral aspect of how cultural knowledge is institutionalized at SSU. The demographic shift and the global awareness at SSU will empower students to attend a university that addresses diversity and global initiatives from an institutionalized lens rather than one of mere compositional diversity. In this time of vast social change, revitalized mission statements and university social justice plans must move forward an agenda that empowers leaders to become the image of what social justice leadership should embody in the 21st century.

IMPLICATIONS FOR ADVOCACY FOR 21ST CENTURY LEADERSHIP

The social landscape of this country and world has changed dramatically since the onset of technology that has resulted in globalization. With an understanding that a globalized world has localized even the furthest places, it is critical that the development of leaders epitomize a social justice component. As such, we argue that leaders can no longer just be formally appointed but rather that leaders must embrace advocacy as an inherent aspect of their leadership. The Kellogg Foundation similarly asserts that every individual has the potential to be a leader—one who acts as a "social change agent" (Astin & Astin, 2000). Komives and Wagner (2009) posits that to be a social change agent one must be willing to learn trial by fire, to listen to people especially those affected by an injustice, and to admit when they are wrong and in need of more information. Further aligned with the Kellogg Foundation is the belief "that effective leadership is an essential ingredient of positive social change. No society can continue to evolve without it, no family or neighborhood holds together in its absence, and no institution prospers where it is unavailable" (Astin & Astin, 2000, p. iv). Much like social change, conceptualizations of leadership must also be altered and extended from their previous constructions to be more inclusive of a globalized perspective.

CONCLUSION

The next generation of leaders must be cognizant of social justice, cultural proficiency, and cross-culturally aware of the spaces in which they lead. Institutions of higher education play a critical role in the development of leaders who will serve as advocates for the common good (Astin & Astin, 2000). More importantly, leadership in times of social change necessitates leaders to be politically, socially, and culturally astute. The aforementioned lead to a deeper understanding of the interconnectedness of our global society. Leadership in times of social change calls for global leaders who are more than symbolic in stature; rather, 21st century leaders must be global advocates who encapsulate their role as a social change agent.

APPENDIX

Challenge

You were assigned to this committee by your supervisor; the goal is to examine the impact of a significant demographic shift on campus. You will be operating from *one of the following professional perspectives*. From the professional perspective, you will provide the committee with a section of a white paper that outlines your organizational feedback on the President's *2021 Social Justice* plan.

- **Director of Multicultural Affairs**—The Director is responsible for providing leadership, mentorship and support for students of color and for underrepresented populations on campus.
- **Director of Globalization and International Student Services**—The Director is responsible for the international student population through administration of immigration documents and regulations; advising of student organizations; individual counseling on cultural, financial, and limited academic issues.
- **Assistant Director of Admissions**—The Assistant Director manages a specific territory, develops collegial relationships with high school personnel, identifies and recruits applicants, manages, evaluates, and implements outreach and recruitment programs.
- **Assistant Director—Residence Life**—The Assistant Director is responsible for training and supervision for the Resident Assistant Staff in planning, organizing, advertising, implementing and evaluating the success of campus-wide programming. Oversees the Resident Assistant program, including the planning and implementation for interactive and comprehensive training sessions and on-going development.

- **Director of Student Advisement and Success**—The Director is responsible for developing/coordinating the introduction of student Personal Success Plans and work with the Assistant Dean for Career Services to help guide students.

Case Guidelines: Demonstrate your ability to integrate your knowledge gained in the completion of your courses and relevant literature in your field of study.

1. Describe the overall significance of the issue presented in the case study (institutional diversity in American higher education), noting its historical significance as well as its impact on the future of higher education institutions.
2. Select one of the professional perspectives above. Based on this perspective, articulate three social justice implications of the President's *2021 Social Justice plan, more specifically the impact of a significant demographic shift on campus.* Please note that your perspective should be grounded in credible, high-quality, and relevant/current literature from your coursework.
3. Choose competencies and/or characteristics from one of the aforementioned social justice models that you deem necessary for SSU to successfully implement the President's 2021 *Social Justice* plan. Provide a rationale grounded in a synthesis of case study information and theoretical understanding as evidence to support competencies/characteristics chosen.
4. Outline recommendations you would provide to the committee regarding your unit's involvement in the President's *2021 Social Justice Plan.* Your recommendations should focus on your selected professional unit involvement in implementing the vision.
5. Provide a short conclusion that connects with both Springtown State University's mission statement and the President's *2021 Social Justice Plan.*

REFERENCES

Adler, N. J., & Bartholomew, S. (1992). Managing globally competent people. *Academy of Management Executive, 6*, 52–65.

Astin, A. W., & Astin, H. S. (2000). *Leadership reconsidered: Engaging higher education in social change.* Battle Creek, MI: W. K. Kellogg Foundation.

Banda, R. M., Flowers, A. M., Robinson, P., & Allen, A. (2016). Developing global citizenship through activism in higher and adult education. In C. Newman, A. Hilton, B. Hinnant-Crawford, & S. Platt (Eds.), *Multicultural education in the 21st century: Innovative research and practices.* Charlotte, NC: Information Age Publishing.

Bell, G. C., Jones, E. B., & Johnson, J. F. (2002). School reform: Equal expectations on an uneven playing field. *Journal of School Leadership, 12*, 317–336.

Dung, G., & Gordon, S. A. (2011). The development of student affairs. In J. H. Schuh, S. R. Jones, S. R. Harper, & Associates (Eds.), *Student Services: A Handbook for the Profession* (pp. 61–79). San Francisco, CA: Jossey-Bass.

Franco, C. S., Gutierrez Ott, M., & Robles, d. P. (2013). Lessons learned: Cultural assets inform actions. In M. Grogan (Ed.), *The Jossey-Bass reader on educational leadership* (3rd ed., pp. 93–110). San Francisco, CA: John Wiley.

Frattura, E., & Capper, C. A. (2007). Leadership for social justice in practice: Integrated comprehensive services (ICS) for all learners. Thousand Oaks, CA: Corwin Press.

Freire, P. (1970). *Pedagogy of the oppressed.* New York, NY: The Continuum International Publishing Group.

Gewirtz, S. (1998). Conceptualizing social justice in education: Mapping the territory. *Journal of Education Policy, 13*, 469–484.

Gewirtz, S. (2006). Towards a contextualized analysis of social justice in education. *Educational Philosophy and Theory, 38*(1), 69–81.

Gurin, P., Nagda, B. R. A., & Lopez, G. E. (2004). The benefits of diversity in education for democratic citizenship. *Journal of Social Issues, 60*(1), 17–34.

Hafner, M. M. (2005). Teaching strategies for developing leaders for social justice. In C. Marshall & M. Oliva (Eds.), *Leadership for social justice: Making revolutions in education* (pp. 167–193). Boston, MA: Pearson.

Jean-Marie, G. (2008). Leadership for social justice: An agenda for 21st century schools. *The Educational Forum, 72*, 340–54.

Karpinski, C. F. (2006). Social justice and educational administration: Mutually exclusive? *Journal of Educational Administration, 44*(3), 278–292.

Komives, S. R., Longerbeam, S. D., Owen, J. E., Mainella, F. C., & Osteen, L. (2006). A leadership identity development model: Applications from a grounded theory. *Journal of College Student Development, 47*(4), 401–418.

Komives, S. R., & Wagner, W. (Eds.). (2009). *Leadership for a better world: Understanding the social change model of leadership development* (2nd ed). San Francisco, CA: Jossey-Bass.

Lindsey, R. B., Graham, S. M., Westphal, R. C., & Jew, C. L. (2008). *Culturally proficient inquiry: A lens for identifying and examining educational gaps.* Thousand Oaks, CA: Corwin Press.

Lindsey, R. B., Robins, K. N., & Terrell, R. D. (2009). *Cultural proficiency: A manual for school leaders* (3rd ed.). Thousand Oaks, CA: Corwin Press.

McInerney, P. (2004). Making hope practical. Flaxton, Queensland: Post Pressed.

North, C. (2006). More than words? Delving into the substantive meaning(s) of "social justice" in education. *Review of Educational Research, 76*(4), 507–535. Retrieved from http://www.jstor.org/stable/10.2307/4124413

Northouse, P. G. (2013). *Leadership: Theory and practice* (6th ed.). Thousand Oaks, CA: Sage.

Nuri-Robins, K., Lindsey, D., Terrell, R., & Lindsey, R. (2007) *Cultural proficiency: Tools for secondary school administrators*, NASSP Principal Leadership, V8. Retrieved from http://www.nassp.org/Portals/0/ Content/56015.pdf

Patton, L., Shahjahan, R., & Osei-Kofi, N. (2010). Introduction to the emergent approaches to diversity and social justice in higher education. Special issue. *Equity & Excellence in Education, 43*(3), 265–278.

Purdie-Vaughns, V., Steele, C. M., Davies, P. G., Ditlmann, R., & Crosby, J. R. (2008). Social identity contingencies: How diversity cues signal threat or safety for African Americans in mainstream institutions. *Journal of Personality and Social Psychology, 94*(4), 615–630.

Robins, K. N., Lindsey, R. B., Lindsey, D. B., & Terrell, R. D. (2006). *Culturally proficient instruction: A guide for people who teach* (2nd ed.). Thousand Oaks, CA: Corwin Press.

Singh, M. (2011). The place of social justice in higher education and social change discourses. *Compare: A Journal of Comparative and International Education, 41*(4), 481–494.

Singleton, G. E., & Linton, C. (2006). *Courageous conversations about race: A field guide for achieving equity in schools.* Thousand Oaks, CA: Corwin Press.

Theoharis, G. (2007). Social justice educational leaders and resistance: Toward a theory of social justice leadership. *Educational Administration Quarterly, 43*(2), 221–258.

Ting-Toomey, S. (1999). *Communicating across cultures.* New York, NY: The Guilford Press.

CHAPTER FOUR

Direction Through Authentic Leadership in Higher Education

MELVIN (JAI) JACKSON

LEADERSHIP IN HIGHER EDUCATION

Leadership is recognized by many as the most important characteristic for bringing about inspired change and progress in higher education. Leadership is one of many traits that helps to stimulate growth, jumpstart transformation, and provide advocacy for the underrepresented and underserved populations in colleges and universities. Leaders are often times characterized in various ways depending on the university and its environment. However, a leader is not relegated to an official title nor the boundaries of an organizational chart. A leader is defined by their actions, vision, and their ability to inspire others regardless of one's title or operational charge. Informal (or authentic) leaders in the United States higher education system provide unendorsed governance and contribute to the proliferation and success throughout colleges and universities. Within the culture of higher education, leaders are presented as figures that embody what it means to be a contributing member of that organization. An informal (or authentic) leader in higher education exists to advocate, to guide, and to build up those who recognize their leadership as not necessarily endorsed by traditional titles but, substantially valued for their contributions and positive influence.

Exploring informal leadership in higher education involves examining guidance and direction through various theoretical lenses. Higher education leadership can most commonly be envisioned through individual frames of support, governance, or advocacy. Though individuals in higher education all contribute to the general leadership and achievement of the college/university, individual leadership is not inherent. The recognition of one's leadership should not simply be associated to a role but has to be acknowledged and accepted by the group of individuals to be led. In higher education leaders are not born to assume command over an office or an organization. They are molded and shaped through experiences and opportunities. Higher education professionals acknowledge that there is no undergraduate major for college/university administration, so it is a commonly held understanding that to successfully lead within the field one must take the necessary steps to develop the toolkit for success. Leaders are bestowed with a title and granted the confidence and respect of a group of individuals. Nevertheless, authentic leaders and their leadership can often be revealed or assumed as a method of providing guidance, service, and vision to colleges/universities based on the power they are granted through their position, longevity, or influence within the greater institution (formally and informally). The purpose of this chapter is to explore an underserved concept of leadership that exposes the presence and influence of authentic (informal) leaders in higher education through an exploration of relevant research that exists within the American higher education system.

WHAT IS LEADERSHIP IN HIGHER EDUCATION?

Leadership in higher education is rooted in several theoretical frames (Kezar, Carducci & Contreras-McGavin, 2006). Kezar et al. (2006) state three paradigms have influenced leadership and provided function and form to the concept. Social constructivism, postmodernism, and positivism represent the three leadership paradigms (Kezar et al., 2006). In social construction, there exist different realities that represent the perception of individuals within the group. Collegiality is the foundation, as much emphasis is placed on arriving at a consensus when making decisions. Significance is also placed on achieving input from all involved in the decision making process. A core function of social constructivism is to inspire and empower individuals (Bolman & Deal, 2013). A postmodernism paradigm of leadership considers reality to be subjective and emphasis is placed on experiences that shape perspectives (Kezar et al., 2006). Foucault and Derrida made the assumption that knowledge is power and a postmodernist view of leadership empowers marginalized voices (Cooper & Burrell, 1988). The positivist paradigm of leadership places considerable prominence on improving efficiency and effectiveness of leading (Kezar et al., 2006). The positivist idea extols a single shared vision that can be seen as truth (Kezar et al., 2006).

In working with several community organizations I have observed a social constructivist model of leadership being implemented. The organizations were led by individual boards of directors ranging in age, level of education, and societal status. Though there were many differences in the experience levels of each of the board members, the groups placed much value in a system of shared governance. The decisions of a few did not dictate the decisions and the direction the organizations would progress towards. While the organizations looked to the leadership of the chair, it was promoted and accepted that the social constructivist model was preferred. Though the chair of the groups helped to frame a vision for the organizations, (s)he promoted shared decision-making and group consensus.

In modern theories of leadership, an individual is assigned the distinction of leader and they make the decisions and are considered the lead (Esmaceeli & Afshani, 2014). In the postmodern era, leadership is not a concept that promotes an individual to make decisions and lead. Every decision made is relative and fits on track with a divine purpose of natural fit (Esmacelli & Afshani, 2014). This natural fit dictates that decisions, opportunities, occurrences will fall into place as they should be and that the advent of a leader will not have any effect on the end product (Cooper & Burrell, 1988; Tierney, 1988). While serving as a member on an academic search committee I faced postmodernist leadership first-hand. The committee was led by the chair that was designated to confer over the group. Our committee chair believed that leading the group would inadvertently prevent the ideal candidate from being selected if it was assumed that all decisions and ideas had to be vetted through a centralized leader. While granted the responsibilities associated with leadership, he believed that leadership should be shared amongst all individuals in order to allow for things to naturally occur and fall into place.

A positivist view can be observed happening at many United States higher education institutions. Institutions are forced to do more with less and the need for dynamic leadership in this area is causing a shift from traditional figurehead leadership towards a more active and innovative university leader. The new leader is bringing to reality a vision of a university that operates with lean resources while still generating top graduates. In working in a state that severely devalued higher education and education altogether, I witness the collapse of a once tall operating structure into a lean organizational chart that forced the maximization of benefit from the minimization of resources. The university leadership was drastically shifted in order to bring forth this realization and make the reality of a 21st century institution of higher learning a lasting certainty.

THE ACTIONS OF LEADERSHIP IN HIGHER EDUCATION

In 1989, Bensimon identified six theories of leadership in higher education. The six theories were subdivided into categories that explore the characteristics one may possess in order to contribute to their success in a leadership role. The theories include power and influence, which focus on the origin, amount, and use of power to lead a group of individuals. Birnbaum and Edelson (1989) references one typology that has identified five kinds of power used in organizations. The powers identified and often used in higher education leadership include coercive, the power to punish those not influenced; reward, the ability to provide incentives for loyalty or hard work; legitimate, power agreed upon by both parties; referent, readiness to be influenced by another based on previous relationships; and expert power, when individuals accept subordinate status because they believe the other person has higher competency or knowledge (Birnbaum, 1988). Behavioral theories study leadership through patterns associated with a task or responsibility and explore what leadership actually does to lead (Bensimon, 1989). Contingency theories investigate situations that may occur in leadership. They examine what could happen and develop methods to combat negative outcomes that may arise (Bass, 1991; Bass, Stogdill, & Stogdill, 1990). Cultural and symbolic theories explore the culture and symbols that represent the organization. Leaders must be capable of understanding the culture and symbols and accurately interpret them to others in order to properly get all parties on the same accord. Finally, cognitive theories allow individuals to make meaning of the environment around them, be it leadership practices, policies, or procedures.

Leadership extends beyond individuals and their characteristics. Bolman and Deal (2013) identified four frames of organizational development and each can have considerable influence from leadership. The frames consist of structural, human resource, political, and symbolic frameworks. Leaders must utilize more than one lens to conceptualize and properly lead an organization (Bolman & Deal, 2013). In her focus on overall governance Bensimon (1989) posited that leadership differs based on the structure and the type of institution. Leadership at a small private liberal arts college is dissimilar to that of a large public institution. Leadership in higher education must contend with a twofold system that focuses on academics and administration individually (Bensimon, 1989). To address the question posed, leadership may differ in higher education based on the mission and vision of an institution and the direction and vision for those at the helm.

DEFINED LEADERSHIP AND THE DYNAMICS OF POWER

Institutional leaders in higher education hold the responsibility of promoting an environment of success towards the progress of achieving institutional mission, visions, and values (Bruno, 2008; Meek, Goedegebuure, Santiago, & Carvalho, 2010). For defined leaders to achieve this success, there is a degree of sense making that needs to take place in order to successfully gather all stakeholders into one accord. Sense making arrives at an intersection of being rational and trying to achieve perfect knowledge before making the final decision (Birnbaum, 1988). While the head of the institution generally holds the responsibility of making the final decision, it can be important to remember that the college/university also stands accountable. The governing boards of institutions bestow agency power on the head of the institution and allow that individual to make decisions on behalf of the college/university. Administrators are merely agents acting on behalf of the university. Similar to that of the business field, higher education institutions have developed hierarchical structures that promote ranks of supervision and administration.

THE CULTURE OF LEADERSHIP IN HIGHER EDUCATION

Leadership extends beyond individuals and their characteristics. Leaders must utilize more than one lens to conceptualize and properly lead an organization (Bolman & Deal, 2013). Bensimon (1989) asked if leadership is different in the higher education landscape and while leadership studies focus on theories and frameworks that can guide leadership practices, leadership in higher education must contend with a two-fold system that focuses on academics and administration respectfully (Bensimon, 1989). Furthermore, leadership may be different in higher education based on the mission and vision of an institution and its leadership.

Deal and Kennedy (1983) stated, "Organizational culture profoundly influences managerial culture." Culture in higher education has been a focal area that has spawned many theories on the inner workings and manifestation of the philosophy. Culture is made up of influential employees guided by leadership, the impact on commitment, performance, and productivity, and values (Tierney, 1988). Deal and Kennedy (1983) suggested there are six dovetailing elements that serve as the basis for organizational culture. History is a collective narrative that establishes the foundation for culture. Traditions rooted in history provide a framework and an anchor to underlying values. Cultural identity is further established within a system of values and beliefs. The values of an organization govern what the organization stands for and the beliefs that are emphasized that most important. The symbolism of rituals and ceremonies further provide the glue for cultures. Daily practices and procedures help to strengthen the culture of an organization. Narration of stories illustrates organization values and idolizes members who promote the values and beliefs of the organization. Within cultures, heroes are presented as figures that embody what it means to be a contributing member of that organization. Finally, many cultures maintain an informal network of role players who serve as agents to maintain the culture of the organization (Deal & Kennedy, 1983).

In order for culture to be maintained and promoted, it takes a network of formal and informal roles to perpetuate values, beliefs, rituals, and narratives of the organizational culture. This network includes: guardians, gossipers, storytellers, spies, and individuals who have considerable influence (Deal & Kennedy, 1983). These roles are played out differently and organizational culture ebbs and flows based on the type of institution. Small institutions tend to have strong institutional cultures in comparison to large schools based on the close community imbedded within them (Lutz, 1982). Colleges and universities that are tightly coupled, meaning elemental changes have a direct and predictable outcome on other elements, have a stronger culture because of interdependency (Lutz, 1982). Additionally, the history of an organization has an effect on the institutional and organizational culture. In April 2007, Virginia Polytechnic Institute and State University (Virginia Tech) experienced an active shooter on campus that resulted in the deaths of 32 people and injury of several others (Library, 2016). The unfortunate events that took place during that day in April have served to strengthen the community and in turn, the culture of the institution through the joining of individuals throughout the University community. Though recent, the incident rekindled the togetherness engrained in the institutional culture. Newer institutions tend to lack a historical framework in which an individual culture may be established (Lutz, 1982). According to Tierney (1988), "Institutions certainly are influenced by powerful, external forces such as demographic, economic, and political conditions, yet they are also shaped by strong forces that emanate from within." Culture exists as the internal force that binds organizations together and creates a community.

THE IMPACT OF CULTURE ON LEADERSHIP

The culture of an institution is what binds together the mission, the people, the traditions, and the rituals (Lutz, 1982). If culture provides the glue, leadership must provide the direction in higher education. The intersection of culture and leadership may be composed of administrators whose leadership is guided by the traditions engrained in their home institutions. Leadership largely influences organizational culture and leadership can be affected by the organizational culture present at colleges and universities (Bass & Avolio, 1993). As mentioned earlier, the culture of an institution is developed through history, traditions, and rituals. Culture has the ability to shape various institutional functions including leadership and governance (Kezar & Eckel, 2002). While colleges and universities have centuries of operation, leadership is temporary and the tenure of any college administrator is not guaranteed through the life of the institution. Leadership acknowledges organizational culture through informed and intentional practices (Bass & Avolio, 1993).

Culture has and will always be an existing influence that leadership will have to address and consider when assuming governance of colleges and universities.

The cultures at institutions across the country have existed throughout leadership terms whether recognized or underground. Leaders accept cultures, formal and informal, because of the benefit it has bringing together key stakeholders and propelling universities forward in times of celebration and sorrow. Leadership must collaborate with culture in order to promote the mission, vision, and values of an institution (Kezar & Eckel, 2002). The intersection of culture and leadership in higher education exists in the students, faculty, staff, symbols, rituals, and traditions of the universities. Leadership governs the institution that is a symbol for the students, faculty, and staff (stakeholders). Culture is engrained within the stakeholders, and leadership must work to influence those who carry the culture in order to impact culture. Culture and leadership are two dominant forces in higher education that can directly influence one another and higher education administrators are the agents that maintain or change the way the two factors affect each other and the greater institution.

WHAT IS AUTHENTIC (INFORMAL) LEADERSHIP?

Authentic (Informal) leaders are individuals who are recognized as leaders within their organization though, this recognition is traditionally not documented or realized in official organizational charts (Foster, 1989; Howell & Avolio, 1993; Pielstick, 2000). Without position power, formal authorization of one's power based on a position held (Bal, Campbell, Steed, & Meddings, 2008), informal leaders are bestowed with the concept of leadership through their actions, values, and beliefs. Pielstick (2000) contends that informal leaders are authentic leaders (p. 13). The concept of authenticity in leadership focuses primarily on leaders without the power dynamics of a formal leadership declaration but on those who often lead from behind the scenes. In her analysis of informal leadership during the Civil Rights era Herda-Rapp (1998) discerned that more often, informal leaders are individuals who possess the ability to influence others and develop a loyal following without the need to impose formalized leadership titles or hierarchies to seek authority. Authentic (informal) leaders possess several qualities that elevate them to the position and recognition of leadership. For many of these characteristics, they can be observed in official leaders but their existence is merely a byproduct of the formalization of their leadership within the hierarchies of college and university organizational structures. The difference in the representation of these qualities can be recognized as being prescribed or presented qualities. Informal leaders present the many merits of leadership naturally and without coaxing from higher-ups and position expectations. Formal leaders are prescribed with a plethora of role responsibilities and traits that they must possess in order to be successful in their position. Often times, these desirable traits are presented by formal leaders on a "fake it, till you make it" basis until they can become mastered and naturally engrained in the leader, if at all.

Authentic leaders possess characteristics that define their leadership as being authentic and legitimate (Pescosolido, 2001; Smart, 2005). Pielstick (2000) identified vision, communication, relationships, community, character, and hypotheses that define informal (authentic) leadership. Vision for colleges and universities is essential in bringing about inspired change and progressing one's institution. A leader must hold the capability of creating and realizing a shared vision for an organization (Bennis, 1993). Authentic leaders in higher education promote a shared vision with their colleagues through engaging individuals and groups into recognizing their higher purpose for the greater success of the organization (Bennis, 1993; Bryman, 2007; Pielstick, 2000). In the promulgation of this shared vision, authentic leaders help to transform individuals into groups and influence a positive shift towards the success of the institution (Duignan & Macpherson, 1993). These leaders do not force or inflict their own vision for the institution on those who follow their guidance and look to them for leadership. Authentic leaders simply initiate the ideas that lead to the creation of a shared vision through an analysis and acknowledgement of the shared needs, common purpose, and shared values amongst those influenced by their leadership (Doloff, 1999; Han, 1993; Pielstick, 2000). Wheatley (1992) points out that shared beliefs, vision, and values work together to shape and guide the core of an organizational culture, which we will explore further in the chapter.

Communication in higher education is often a top-down process with lines of dissemination that flow through formalized leaders and their penchant for information sharing. Formal leaders determine both how and when information is communicated and they also establish the rules of communication in college/university environments. In practice, formal leaders should broadcast information widely and in easy to understand mediums, but some formal leaders operate on a "one size fits all" communication standard and this often leads to misinformation and misinterpretation (Birnbaum, 1992; Birnbaum & Edelson, 1989; Molina, 2001). Authentic leaders allow communication to serve as the medium for developing purpose and developing the shared vision for their colleagues (Pescosolido, 2001; Zemke & Zemke, 2008). These leaders recognize that communication should be utilized to inspire, motivate, and unify all stakeholders (DeZure, Shaw, & Rojewski, 2014; Posner & Kouzes, 1988). Pielstick (2000) states, "Communication is a dialog, a two-way sharing that facilitates the process of elevating the moral purpose of the shared vision, building relationships, and shaping the culture of the organization" (p. 3). Furthermore, authentic leaders extend communication down this two-way street by listening as much as they speak, if not more. Listening offers colleagues the opportunity to exhibit influence and the willingness to be influenced showcases openness for communications and opinions by the informal leader (Birnbaum, 1992; Cronin, 1993). Authentic leaders intentionally use their communicative influence to inspire others, encourage open dialogue, and recognize success (Johnston, n.d.; Stincelli & Bathurst, 2014; Wheelan & Johnston, 1996). They lead by example because they understand they are commonly well regarded by their peers and know their influence is substantial (Smart, 2005; Wheelan & Johnston, 1996).

Relationships in higher education carry considerable influence. The interconnectedness of professionals can send a wave of support or detriment in one's direction. Relationships play an integral role for authentic leaders in higher education. The formation of genuine relationships with constituents may foster an exchange of support and encouragement for both parties and this strengthens a bond rooted in influence, communication, and trust (Foster, 1989; Howell & Avolio, 1993; Whitaker, 1995). While formal leaders operate on a supervisor-subordinate operating structure, authentic leaders promote a peer-to-peer level of equality that favors no individual over another (Meek et al., 2010; Northouse, 2004). This method of leadership creates a social exchange in which both the authentic leader and the peer are innately more concerned with maintaining a positive and beneficial relationship with the other, respectful of opinions and advice (Bass et al., 1990; Birnbaum & Edelson, 1989). The characteristics that make this relationship possible and extremely likely amongst informal leaders over formal leaders' rests with the openness and treatment of their constituents. Authentic leaders are more inclined towards being approachable, friendly, and informal (Duignan & Macpherson, 1993). This allows for engagement of all individuals on a person by person basis and not through the arduous and top heavy hierarchies of organizational structures. The act of building relationships with constituents' aids in the creation of communities within the institution.

Community within higher education establishments is integral to promoting a unified and cohesive message outward to external stakeholders and inward towards organizational members. As community members, authentic leaders foster community through the construction and promotion of an organizational culture that encourages shared values, endorses open dialogue, and builds genuine/lasting relationships (Han, 1993; Howell & Aavolio, 1993). Sashkin and Rosenbach (1993) conclude, "Culture may be the only important thing leaders do" (p. 99). In addition to supporting community, authentic leaders are consciously representing and promoting their values towards all members of the community, especially marginalized and underrepresented individuals (Johnston, n.d.). These leaders believe in altruism and often pass their success onto others, they are fair with praise, recognition, and acts of kindness, they believe in treating all with fairness and grandeur, and they promote social justice (Meek et al., 2010; Zemke & Zemke, 2008). Bennis and Nanus (1985) state, "Leaders build trust through their actions, knowing what is right and necessary and being tirelessly persistent" (p. 45). Within a organization you have a binary of teachers and students. Authentic leaders are those individuals who teach without the pedagogue title. The leadership they exhibit represents the necessity for teachers (or leaders) to instruct and support students (constituents) into becoming leaders of their own right (Molina, 2001; Whitaker, 1995). Opportunities for individual growth and progress are considered an intrinsic reward for authentic leaders, as they find personal satisfaction in observing individual and organizational success from their peers and constituents (Bass et al., 1990).

Leadership is not inherent. An individual is not born with all the qualities and characteristics that define an authentic leader. One must follow before they can lead, they must learn before they can teach, and finally, an authentic leader must learn and develop the necessary leadership traits before they can model true leadership for others. In his study of informal leadership, Pielstick (2000) determined that authentic leaders possess specific traits that differentiate them from their peers who assume their role through formalized structures. The first trait, self-confidence, is important because in the changing landscape of higher education, authentic leaders must be confident in their actions and emotionally sound (Howell & Avolio, 1993; Johnston, n.d.). As the colleges and universities transform due to budget cuts, increased competition, and the revolving political climate, constituents will look to authentic leaders to be grounded in confidence and determined to continue to set positive examples (Hall, 1986; Pielstick, 2000). Motivation is the next trait that authentic leaders may embody. Authentic leaders work to motivate those around them regardless of work environment and they help others to focus on a set of primary goals that all can agree are essential and important (Cronin, 1993; Doloff, 1999). This motivation is more so intrinsically focused and does not harbor intentions regarding extrinsic forces such as money and status (Bal et al., 2008). The ability to motivate others is commonly used to empower constituents to succeed towards both the goals of the institution and their individual organizational goals (Wheelan & Johnston, 1996). Intellect is also attributed to authentic leaders. These leaders demonstrate an ability to comprehend and empathize with their constituents. Additionally, they approach and address difficult challenges and situations with new, unique, and innovative methods of problem solving that incorporates a vast degree of emotional intelligence (Smart, 2005; Stincelli & Bathurst, 2014). Along with their emotional intelligence, authentic leaders are also organizationally adept at understanding and navigating the intricacies of the network of policies, procedures, and politics of the higher education landscape (Smart, 2005). This is often approached by authentic leaders with caution and from a neutral standpoint because of a desire to not impress one's personal opinions or experiences on others, in fear of jeopardizing potential relationships and organizational success (Birnbaum & Edelson, 1989; Cronin, 1993). Finally, authentic leaders are humble and think not of themselves and their personal gain but focus greatly on how they can help others to succeed and achieve their personal goals (Bryman, 2007; Zemke & Zemke, 2008). While not all traits are existent in all authentic leaders, many individuals occupy a combination of these qualities.

Authentic leadership embodies characteristics that appeal to constituents and peers because of its genuine capacity to lead with compassion, vision, guidance, community, and a higher commitment (Zemke & Zemke, 2008). These leaders provide meaning for those who look to them and they help to make sense of the environment around (Doloff, 1999; Wheelan & Johnston, 1996). The inclusivity promoted by authentic leaders is welcomed as individuals within higher education want to operate with a sense of belonging and a sense of purpose. With formal leadership, there is a slight exclusivity apportionment allocated to those within an "inner circle" and this creates an informal hierarchy amongst constituents that breeds inadequacy and the perception of inequity (Hall, 1986; Johnston, n.d.). Authentic leaders pride themselves on collaborative efforts and emphasize the importance of diminishing the inner circle mentality in favor of an open invitation to all. Piestick (2000) states, "Informal leaders treat everyone with dignity and respect" (p. 11). Authentic leaders are represented throughout the traditional organizational charts of higher education institutions. These individuals are not relegated to managerial or administrative positions and are even represented in student leaders throughout colleges and universities.

WHO ARE THE AUTHENTIC LEADERS?

In higher education, leadership is promoted amongst students, staff, and faculty. It is essential for the success of the institution and considered a core objective for colleges and universities throughout the world. Many universities present formalized leadership academies for students to engage with faculty and staff as a means for building and harnessing their true leadership potential. There are also opportunities for the very staff members who promote and teach leadership to gain and develop their skills in institutes and programs that promote leadership based on years of experience, operational structures, and institutional types.

A prolific and oftentimes overlooked group of authentic leaders are the students attending our institutions. Student leaders are, in fact, leaders but they are more often shuffled to the side when recognizing their impact on the community and university culture and decision making. Because of the word "student" in front of their designation, they are commonly disregarded for their knowledge, leadership, and influence (Pescosolido, 2001; Tierney, 1988). Student leaders are authentic leaders because their motivation is intrinsic and they operate with the greater good of the university community in mind. For instance, when the students of Duke University determined that the institution's support staff (housekeepers, dining workers, etc.) were not being paid a living wage, they organized and led a campaign against the unfair wages for these employees (Bowen, 2016). Their informal and altruistic leadership led to the university standardizing a nearly 15% pay increase for employees (Bowen, 2016). Student leaders are authentic leaders because they carry no formalized power towards decision making in traditional universities, yet they can advocate for the marginalized, model unselfish behavior and are looked to for their leadership capabilities.

One of the greatest treasures a higher education institution maintains is its history and the history of many colleges and universities is not isolated to webpages and bound volumes. The peoples' history of a university provides a richer observation into the past, complete with little known details and facts specific to individuals and offices. This history is captured and recorded in the hearts and minds of individuals and its that institutional memory that establishes some individuals as leaders within organizations. Institutional memory is a common phrase when referencing faculty/staff members in higher education who have served for several years at the same college or university. These individuals being referenced are held in high regard for their longevity and also their resilience during the transitional growing pains of recessions, expansions, and contractions of higher education. These individuals are the face of authentic leadership in higher education. Not limited to one position or another, they represent a knowledge base of institutional memory that is valued for its completeness and information. While working at a medium-sized public institution I met an administrative assistant; we'll call her Mrs. May, who had been employed with the university for 35 years. In her time at the institution, Mrs. May served in several capacities ranging from Desk Secretary for housing to Executive Assistant for the Vice-Provost. Professionals and students regarded Mrs. May for her knowledge and wisdom for navigating the intricacies of the red tape associated with the political and bureaucratic system at the university and she was always requested for special committees and taskforces. Her leadership was not conferred by an organizational chart but by display of characteristics representative of authentic leadership. Mrs. May was reliable, and she was always willing to go the extra mile to help a student or staff member in need. She promoted a 'one accord' mindset in that she wanted to make sure that everyone was aware and on the same page when representing the office and the university. She held her relationships in high regard. Mrs. May did not undervalue any relationships with peers or students because she saw value in every person and wanted them to see value in her. She promoted community, she always wanted to organize opportunities for staff bonding and collegiality and she always celebrated birthdays. She was the advisor that everyone from the top administrative officer to the newest student always went to when needing advice on university matters. Mrs. May, along with others like her, are authentic leaders of higher education because their leadership is not based on formal organizational authority.

They are highly influential leaders who are regarded for their institutional memory, rapport, and inspiration. They are able to utilize their referent power, leadership by example, expert power, knowledge of the institutional landscape and its exceptionalities, and even reward power, ability to offer sincere praise and recognition, to form the foundation of their authentic leadership (Bal et al., 2008; Foster, 1989).

Leadership in higher education ebbs and flows with the change in leaders and the governance and culture of colleges and universities are representative of those who assume command of the institutions. Leadership is not inherent but developed and leadership in higher education exists as a function of skills and experiences that set the foundation for the success of an authentic leader. Authentic leaders accept cultures, formal and informal, because of the benefit it has bringing together key stakeholders and propelling universities forward in times of celebration and sorrow. The authentic leader is a keeper and influencer of institutional culture and the overall success of the office or institution will rely on the leadership of these unsung heroes. Leadership must collaborate with culture in order to promote the mission, vision, and values of an institution (Kezar & Eckel, 2002). The intersection of culture and leadership in higher education exists in the students, faculty, staff, symbols, rituals, and traditions of a university. Leadership governs the institution while culture is engrained within the stakeholders, and authentic leadership must work to influence those who allow the culture to guide the direction of the university. Culture and leadership are two dominant forces in higher education that can directly influence one another and authentic higher education leaders are the agents that maintain the balance the two factors have on each other and the greater success of colleges and universities. An authentic leader is defined by their actions, vision, and their ability to inspire others and these leaders contribute to the proliferation and success of higher education. Authentic leaders exist to advocate, guide, and to build up those who follow and equally contribute to the overall success of colleges and universities everywhere. The existence and continued representation of authentic leaders in higher education represents a driving force in the overall success of colleges and universities throughout the world.

REFERENCES

Bal, V., Campbell, M., Steed, J., & Meddings, K. (2008). The role of power in effective leadership. *Center for Creative Leadership*. Retrieved from www. ccl.org.

Bass, B. M., & Avolio, B. J. (1993). Transformational leadership and organizational culture. *The International Journal of Public Administration, 17*(3–4), 541–554.

Bass, B., Stogdill, R., & Stogdill, R. (1990). *Bass & Stogdill's handbook of leadership*. New York, NY: Free Press.

Bass, B. M. (1991). From transactional to transformational leadership: Learning to share the vision. *Organizational Dynamics*, *18*(3), 19–31.

Bennis, W. (1993). *An invented life: Reflections on leadership and change*. New York: Basic Books.

Bennis, W., & Nanus, B. (1985). Leaders: The strategies for taking charge. New York, NY: Harper. Row.

Bensimon, E. M. (1989). *Making Sense of Administrative Leadership: The "L" Word in Higher Education. ASHE-ERIC Higher Education Report 1, 1989*. ASHE-ERIC Higher Education Reports. The George Washington University, One Dupont Circle, Suite 630, Dept. RC, Washington, DC 20036-1183.

Birnbaum, R. (1988). *How Colleges Work: The Cybernetics of Academic Organization and Leadership* (1st ed.). San Francisco: Jossey-Bass.

Birnbaum, R. (1992). *How academic leadership works: Understanding success and failure in the college presidency*. San Francisco, CA: Jossey-Bass, 94104.

Birnbaum, R., & Edelson, P. J. (1989). How colleges work: The cybernetics of academic organization and leadership. *The Journal of Continuing Higher Education*, *37*(3), 27–29.

Bolman, L., & Deal, T. (2013). *Reframing organizations: Artistry, choice, and leadership* (5th ed.). San Francisco, CA: Jossey-Bass.

Bowen, J. (2016). *Duke students end week-long sit-in: WRAL.com. WRAL.com*. Retrieved April 24, 2016 from http://www.wral.com/duke-students-end-week-long-sit-in/15629558/

Bruno, L. (2008). *Leadership and performance beyond expectations*. E-Leader Bangkok.

Bryman, A. (2007). Effective leadership in higher education: A literature review. *Studies in Higher Education*, *32*(6), 693–710. http://dx.doi.org/10.1080/03075070701685114

Cooper, R., & Burrell, G. (1988). Modernism, postmodernism and organizational analysis: An introduction. *Organization Studies*, *9*(1), 91–112.

Cronin, J. F. (1993). Four misconceptions about authentic learning. *Educational Leadership*, *50*(7), 78–80.

Deal, T. E., & Kennedy, A. A. (1983). Culture: A new look through old lenses. *Journal of Applied Behavioral Science*, *19*(4), 498–505.

DeZure, D., Shaw, A., & Rojewski, J. (2014). Cultivating the next generation of academic leaders: Implications for administrators and faculty. *Change: The Magazine of Higher Learning*, *46*(1), 6–12. http://dx.doi.org/10.1080/00091383.2013.842102

Doloff, P. (1999). Beyond the organization chart. *Across the Board*, *36*(2), 43–47.

Duignan, P., & Macpherson, R. (1993). Educative leadership: A practical theory. *Educational Administration Quarterly*, *29*(1), 8–33. http://dx.doi.org/10.1177/0013161x93029001003

Esmaeeli, M., & Afshani, M. (2014). Postmodern leadership in organization. *Interdisciplinary Journal Of Contemporary Research In Business*, *6*(3), 266–272. Retrieved from http://euabr.com/ijcrbjul14/266-272jul14.pdf

Foster, W. (1989). Toward a critical practice of leadership. *Critical Perspectives on Educational Leadership*, *3*, 39–62.

Hall, C. (1986). The informal organization chart. *Supervisory Management*, *31*(1), 40–42.

Han, P. (1993). The informal organization you've got to live with. *Supervisory Management*, *28*(10), 25–28.

Herda-Rapp, A. (1998). The power of informal leadership: Women leaders in the civil rights movement. *Sociological Focus*, *31*(4), 341–355.

Howell, J. M., & Avolio, B. J. (1993). Transformational leadership, transactional leadership, locus of control, and support for innovation: Key predictors of consolidated-business-unit performance. *Journal of Applied Psychology*, *78*(6), 891.

Kezar, A. J., Carducci, R., & Contreras-McGavin, M. (2006). *Rethinking the "L" word in higher education: The revolution of research on leadership: ASHE higher education report.* San Francisco: John Wiley & Sons.

Kezar, A. J., & Eckel, P. D. (2002). The effect of institutional culture on change strategies in higher education: Universal principles or culturally responsive concepts? *The Journal of Higher Education, 73*(4), 435–460.

Library, C. (2016). *Virginia tech shootings fast facts—CNN.com. CNN.* Retrieved July 18, 2016 from http://edition.cnn.com/2013/10/31/us/virginia-tech-shootings-fast-facts/

Lutz, F. W. (1982). Tightening up loose coupling in organizations of higher education. *Administrative Science Quarterly, 27*(4), 653–669.

Meek, V. L., Goedegebuure, L., Santiago, R., & Carvalho, T. (Eds.). (2010). *The changing dynamics of higher education middle management* (Vol. 33). Berlin, Germany: Springer Science & Business Media.

Molina, J. (2001). The informal organizational chart in organizations: An approach from the social network analysis. *Connections, 24*(1), 78–91.

Northouse, P. (2004). *Leadership.* Thousand Oaks, CA: Sage.

Pescosolido, A. (2001). Informal leaders and the development of group efficacy. *Small Group Research, 32*(1), 74–93. http://dx.doi.org/10.1177/104649640103200104

Pielstick, C. D. (2000). Formal vs. informal leading: A comparative analysis. *Journal of Leadership & Organizational Studies, 7*(3), 99–114.

Posner, B., & Kouzes, J. (1988). Relating leadership and credibility. *Psychological Reports, 63*(2), 527–530. http://dx.doi.org/10.2466/pr0.1988.63.2.527

Sashkin, M., & Rosenbach, W. E. (1993). A new leadership paradigm. *Contemporary issues in leadership, 3*, 87–108.

Smart, M. (2005). *The role of informal leaders in organizations: The hidden organizational asset.* Moscow, Idaho: University of Idaho.

Stincelli, E., & Bathurst, T. (2014). A grounded theory exploration of informal leadership qualities as perceived by employees and managers in small organizations. *International Journal of Business Management and Economic Research, 5*(1), 1–8.

Tierney, W. (1988). Organizational culture in higher education: Defining the essentials. *The Journal of Higher Education, 59*(1), 2. http://dx.doi.org/10.2307/1981868

Wheatley, M. (1992). *Leadership and the New Science: Learning about Organization from an Orderly Universe* (1st ed.). San Francisco: Berrett-Koehler Publishers.

Wheelan, S., & Johnston, F. (1996). The role of informal member leaders in a system containing formal leaders. *Small Group Research, 27*(1), 33–55. http://dx.doi.org/10.1177/1046496496271002

Whitaker, T. (1995). Accomplishing change in schools: The importance of informal teacher leaders. *The Clearing House: A Journal of Educational Strategies, Issues and Ideas, 68*(6), 356–357. http://dx.doi.org/10.1080/00098655.1995.9957270

Zemke, D., & Zemke, S. (2008). Identifying roles and behaviors of informal leaders on student design teams. *American Society for Engineering Education, 13*(682), 1–12.

CHAPTER FIVE

Process Education Leadership

Shifting the Paradigm

JOANN HORTON, DARIA J. WILLIS, AND ISIAH BROWN

LEADERSHIP DYNAMICS

Good leadership at the top is not sufficient for the environment of the 21st century! We are living in a time when two crucial elements for social change are present—new values and economic necessity. Globalization, deregulation, democratization and technology are characteristics of the competitive arena of the Knowledge Age (Uhl-Bien, Russ, & McKelvey, 2007). The complexity of problems and issues demands that corporate and higher education institutions be managed differently. Institutions must deal with shrinking resources and demands for greater outcomes (Growe, 2011). If organizations are to meet these challenges, new leadership models must be examined (Uhl-Bien et al., 2007). Effective leadership can transform organizations by creating visions of potential opportunities, securing staff commitment to change and instilling new cultures. They can also adapt strategies to mobilize individuals and resources.

Our history shows that varied structures and requirements have placed us in a milieu that is more authoritarian than collaborative. The Industrial Age (early 20th century) was highly structured, with power directed from the top creating an environment that tended to be rigid. People and processes operated in a closed system. Institutions were highly organized, with a singleness of perspective that included management being Eurocentric and male-dominated. Leaders were trained to lead from the top of the organization, with limited input from others. They were given theoretical frameworks to understand how organizations function, budgeting and finance frameworks, and aspects of administrative process. Little, if any, emphasis was placed upon the human aspect of the organization, other than charts with defined roles, responsibilities and benefits (Hallett, 1987).

The emergence of the Information Age in the late 20th century brought global orientation and technological changes that required flexibility in how people led and how organizations were run (New Zealand Council for Educational Research, 2015). Other evident characteristics included human resources with information, knowledge, and creativity as the strategic resource; computerization; focus on innovation; new variegated work force—younger, better educated, and increasingly minority and female; and evolving career patterns. And, the need for new basic skills forced education to reinvent itself and build alliances with businesses (Naisbitt & Aburdene, 1990). Characterized by high tech/high touch, within a world economy, the information age emphasized effectiveness of communication and application of information.

We are now solidly in the 21st century and the Knowledge Age, a new economic age, in which organizations are facing a complex competitive landscape driven largely by globalization and the technological revolution. The Knowledge Age brought with it the acknowledgement of the importance of people in fostering essential change through acquisition, use and creation of knowledge to meet key needs (New Zealand Council for Educational Research, 2015). The focus is on transformation. Leaders must be able to adapt and empower others to change in order to meet the new demands of the workplace. In this economy, knowledge (its development and application) is a core commodity and new models of leadership are essential if organizations are to survive (Uhl-Bien et al., 2007).

Administrators and managers must now deal with new dynamics: an environment that requires greater interaction, structures that may lack stability of prior years and increasing interaction with diverse groups under multiple circumstances and globalization (Friedman, 2005). This fact requires a shift in perspective and orientation to leadership. Not only must leaders make tough decisions about their interactions, they must be more tolerant of competing viewpoints and the significance of new demographics, cultural differences, biases, and overt and convert discrimination.

Colleges and universities have to respond to higher expectations for effectiveness, shifting faculty roles, and developing criteria for performance excellence. Translated by experienced educators in 2007, The Malcolm Baldridge National Quality Program defines criteria that work across types of organizations within diverse communities. These include leadership; strategic planning; student, stakeholder and market focus; measurement, analysis and knowledge management; workforce focus; process management and results (Lindborg, 2007).

Leadership is deeply embedded in complexity where organizations with limited resources are both process- and product-oriented. Diverse perspectives and cultures are integral to the environment. Responsibility and example, rather than command and authority, are exercised to accomplish goals through mutual learning, purpose, communication of vision, and culture rather than merely by formal rules, roles, and procedures. Communication is open and multidirectional. Emphasis is on opportunities and learning from errors. Ambiguity, change, and uncertainty are the order of the day (Uhl-Bien et al., 2007).

Overview of Leadership in Higher Education

Currently university faculty and administrators are struggling to negotiate the balance of power as they face the dynamic challenges brought on by the 21st century changes taking place in higher education. The challenges and changes require a reconceptualization of leadership in the academy (Mutisya, Osler II, Bitting, & Rotich, 2014). As part of institutional assessment, institutions are required to demonstrate learner knowledge, skills, and dispositions. Most accrediting bodies expect this to include a high standard for faculty development (Lindborg, 2007). Based on that assumption, faculty are educated in modern methods of teaching in their discipline and kept current in professional standards of practice beyond their discipline.

Consolidation of decision-making power within traditional administrative offices has diminished faculty voice and constrained deployment of expertise in areas of campus culture, institutional mission, community outreach, changing student demographics, and response to fiscal pressures (Mutisya et al., 2014).

> Amongst the professorate, there is great wisdom about the problems of modern society—in creating social capital (through education), in generating intellectual capital (through scholarship), in promoting citizenship (through the professions and through political involvement), and in pursuing social justice (through' psychological and philosophical perspectives). (Mutisya et al., 2014, p. 48)

The call for leadership in higher education is constantly evolving. Uhl-Bien et al. (2007) use the concept of complex adaptive systems, proposing that leadership should not only be seen as a position, but as an emergent, interactive, dynamic interplay that fosters change. Leadership is defined as a process by which an individual has the ability to influence a group of people towards the consciousness of goals (Amanchuckwu, Staneley, & Ololube, 2015; Wolinski, 2010). Leaders within institutions and department often rotate. With active turnover, professional development and support are essential for progress. Black (2015) notes, academic leadership roles are subjected to anomalies where senior or established professionals in the faculty ranks are often called to lead. Preparing these leaders to meet tomorrow's challenges is critical to the success of educational institutions (Basham, 2010). Educational leaders who are called to serve their institutions are not always trained in leadership principles, but are considered to be individuals who are well respected by the faculty and the administration. They must be sensitive to modeling best practices to better serve students, faculty and staff (Davis, 2012). Twenty-first century leaders must espouse positive leadership qualities that allow for building and managing key stakeholder relationships. This will allow for a better understanding of how to effectively lead based on a specific set of needs (Davis, 2012). Having the right leadership style to meet institutional needs is a key element that warrants consideration.

Davis (2012) discussed two specific types of leadership styles as being effective within tertiary institutions. "Effective leadership at the university level often points away from acting as an authoritarian and utilizes more transformational styles that include collaboration and mentorship" (p. 2). Collaborative and transformational styles are models that are prevalent in higher education. Collaborative leaders use inclusive and supportive methods as they work with others to address agreed upon issues (Davis, 2012). A collaborative leadership style ensures that all people affected by a decision are part of the change process. Black (2015) argues that the traditional models where senior professors are called to lead are problematic due to the nature of skills and development required for effective leadership in the 21st century. Collaborative approaches must be strategic and institutions must invest in a leadership development process for those called to lead.

Transformational leadership has been the sole dominant style over the past 20 years (Black, 2015). "Transformational leaders tend to have the attributes to learn across their specialist discipline" (Basham, 2010, p. 4). These qualities and attributes have been proven to be effective when working with university professionals. Davis (2012) also notes college administrators act as transformational leaders, integrating a shared vision of change, reflecting on its value, and empowering voices in a collaborative community. Table 5.1 (Appendix A) provides an analysis of key transformational leadership characteristics based on research literature. According to Kaya, Kaplan, Mutisya, and Beyerlein (2015), these traits are central to a transformational leader profile and are tied to personal or interpersonal attributes.

Leadership Attributes, Skills, and Competencies

Leadership attributes are constantly being reshaped by the context from which the leader operates in the 21st century. The multitude of leadership styles offers varying perspectives of what dispositions yield success. Ultimately, the process of developing attributes is critical to the success of any educational leader. There is no one best leadership style or approach that will dictate success. Every situation is different and requires that leaders consult with internal and external experts when solving specific institutional problems. The leader's ability to collaborate across interdisciplinary contexts is vital to gaining credibility from those that follow their lead. The transformational characteristics outlined in Table 5.1 (Appendix A) provide a framework for measuring effective leadership.

Amanchuckwu et al. (2015) assert leadership qualities between managers and leaders are notably different. Key skills and traits of managers include: problem solving, consulting, rationalizing, persistence, tough mindedness, analytical, structured, deliberate, authoritative, and stabilizing. Alternatively, leaders are considered to be visionaries, passionate, creative, flexible, inspiring, innovative, courageous, imaginative, experimental, and change agents (Naylor, 1999). The Leadership Foundation for Higher Education identified key behaviors associated with effective leadership. The leader will espouse a clear strategic direction; consideration of others; supportive and collaborative environment for faculty and staff; integrity; transparency; open communication; credibility; positive and collegial work environment; performance feedback and resources for scholarship and research. They are proactive in advancing the institution's cause and making academic appointments to enhance its reputation (Bryman, 2007). What lies at the center of this argument is that leaders must find ways for faculty and staff to foster a collegial environment in which autonomy and mutual support are respected and encouraged within the college community (Bryman, 2007).

Higher Education Effective Leadership Qualities, Skills, Competencies

Quality leadership is demonstrated when effective results are recognized and realized (Black, 2015). Quality leadership embodies (a) risking personal image for team benefit; (b) listening to critical inputs; (c) making firm decisions; (d) promoting others; (e) facilitating team growth; (f) and reviewing performance to achieve key outcomes (Apple, 2009). Successful leaders must be adept at establishing partnerships in a non-hierarchal manner while maintaining accountability (Amey, 2006; Black, 2015). Leadership attributes that define effective leadership are categorized as group and individual competencies. For example, individual traits identified include managing and building relationships, commitment, integrity, demonstrated competence through work experience, and compassion. At the group level, understanding shared governance, collaboration, and professional disagreement with respect to others are essential (Astin & Astin, 2000; Black, 2015). While this is not a comprehensive list of all competencies required for effective leadership, it provides a framework for consideration of effective qualities, skills, and competencies.

Leadership is a process. Building and maintaining positive relationships with key stakeholders matters and progress can be stifled if this aspect is not managed well by leaders, whether they lead at the institutional or department level. As Gardner (2004) points out, it is a process of continually assessing the primary role of one's institution and crafting a consistent message and approach.

A GENERALIZED MODEL OF HIGHER EDUCATION LEADERSHIP

When the discussion arises around assimilation models for effective leadership in higher education, effective leaders need to model transactional and transformational leadership styles (Bass & Avolio, 1993; Black, 2015). Apple (2015) offers a process education transformational leadership model that embodies key attributes and provides a greater understanding of how the PE leader functions. Identification of the most realistic leadership qualities must account for the context, the leader, and their followers. Effective leadership qualities for higher education fall into four broad themes with at least ten specific attributes supporting each category (Black, 2015; Black, Groombridge, & Jones, 2011). A fifth category illustrates the importance of personal attributes of leaders (see Table 5.2, Appendix B). Consideration of the competencies and skills in this detailed framework provides useful insight and are broadly valid for higher educational leadership consideration.

Table 5.2 (Appendix B) provides an analysis of a generalized model of higher education leadership. Identified traits are central to a transformational and process educational leadership profile with a crosswalk of personal and interpersonal attributes. The PE leadership approach adds to the leadership research literature. It considers competencies and processes essential to facilitating transformative organizational change within dynamic, complex environments. It supports challenging leaders to focus on how to transform institutions into learning colleges that set high standards and measure results (O'Banion, 1997).

Process Education Leadership

The current dynamics in education are a clarion call for a change in leadership style. Effective leaders must (a) be action oriented; (b) believe in the intelligence, capability and awareness of the customer; and (c) sustain contact with constituencies (Peters & Waterman, 1982). Leadership is also the presence and spirit of the individual who leads and relationships created with those who are led. Leadership is an internal and an external process. Quality leadership (a) adapts to the needs and values of those led; (b) takes into account the skills and capabilities of those with whom the leader shares leadership; (c) and adjusts to organizational purpose and future needs (Scholtes, 1998).

At the same time, leaders must be responsive, passionate and relentless about the pursuit of quality as they facilitate change to transform institutional outcomes. The challenge is to combine the very best knowledge, insight, and wisdom to improve on a continuous basis. Leaders cannot force individuals to work harder or smarter; however they can create a shared vision and a culture where each employee realizes that he can change the organization by constructively contributing to goal accomplishment. When facilitating change, superb leadership effectively communicates a positive vision; consistently articulates change plans and progress; values and engages teams in plans, decision-making and problem solving (Apple, 2009). These leaders are transformational.

With the transformational leader, vision is the driving force—its creation and integration into the environment where ideas on how to achieve organizational goals are rewarded; open communication in mobilizing commitment; and institutionalizing the vision to allow staff the freedom to do things on their own. Leaders must be in the center of the web where the internal and the external environments come together, dealing with constant change—the past, the present, and the future at the same time.

Process Education (PE) leaders are transformational (Burke, Lawrence, El-Sayed, & Apple, 2009). Process education leadership is derived from a performance-based philosophy of education, which evolved over the past twenty-five years. PE integrates many different educational theories, processes, and tools in emphasizing the continuous development of learning skills. It uses assessment principles in order to produce learner self-development (Apple, Ellis & Hintze, 2016).

For purposes of this research, process education leadership is described as an inner journey of self-growth (behaviors, skills, attributes), which includes having a personal vision that provides context for how one leads. Analysis of quality leadership vis-à-vis process education leadership results in five key areas that form a profile of a PE leader: risk taking, emotional resilience, quality orientation, mentoring and self-growth (see Table 5.3, Appendix C). Table 5.3 illustrates theory into action in these key areas. PE leadership involves building relationship networks, organizational development, strategy mastery and continuous performance improvement. Effective process education leadership embodies active engagement of people using a variety of processes: mentoring, facilitating, delegating, assessing, visioning, planning, problem solving and teambuilding. With PE, growth of leadership skills is as essential as other skills required to accomplish tasks.

In PE, self-growth is based upon the premise that any person can seek to improve any performance, create their own challenges, serve as a leader and mentor, take control of their own destiny, and self-assess and self-mentor to facilitate their own growth (Apple, Morgan, & Hintze, 2013). Self-growth is a process that requires an enduring practice compelling numerous steadfast behaviors, actions, and activities (Jain, Apple, & Ellis, Jr., 2015). Self-growers are learners who seek to improve their own learning performance. Process education leaders are focused on transforming learning, individuals, institutions and outcomes (Burke et al., 2009).

Leadership Development for Faculty & Staff

Leadership development is not only to ensure the best use of current talent; it is also important to succession planning. One of the critical dynamics that institutions will face within the next few years is the retirement of many administrators, faculty and staff who have led and contributed to college and university advancement for decades. The talent pool needs to be strengthened if educators, students and communities are to meet the needs of the 21st century. Given that leadership is dispersed throughout organizations (Heifetz & Laurie, 1997), we must examine how to grow leaders at the faculty and staff levels, where individuals without the traditional titles are able to make major contributions.

Leadership development from within tertiary institutions continues to present challenges for higher education. The development of effective leaders is critical to their performance and success. Several studies have shown the positive effects of leadership development on faculty and staff (Braun et al., 2009; Koester & Martinez, 2016; University of California Berkeley, 2007). Substantial investments have been made in faculty and staff development programs for those who aspire to administrative leadership. Higher education leaders must continue to critically assess and evaluate whether or not faculty and staff training programs are developing the required knowledge, skills and abilities needed for institutional success (Koester & Martinez, 2016). Effective leadership development programs should foster engagement that enhances faculty and staff commitment and satisfaction with the institution (Horton & Apple, 2009).

A number of leadership development programs are available for faculty and staff within academic institutions nationally. Colleges and universities have programs specific to their needs and dedicated to developing future leaders. For example, some institutions have developed PE oriented profiles and measures to ensure appropriate development of faculty and staff leaders (Kettering University, 2008; Kirkwood Community College, 2011).

Higher education literature suggests that the transformation of educational institutions is tied to the role and effectiveness of leaders. Their action orientation and ability to identify and prioritize workplace issues are vital to moving the transformation agenda (Bennis & Townsend, 1995). Leaders facilitate educational outcomes, stakeholder engagement and growth of learning colleges.

Other researchers recommend improving incentives, integration of topics relevant to future leaders teaching content, use of multiple training methods, such as small group and one-on-one development experiences, scientific based evaluation of leadership development programs, and strategic cooperation within the higher education leadership community of practitioners to share empirical based knowledge and experiences across contexts to facilitate systematic development (Braun et al., 2009; University of California Berkeley, 2007).

Additional recommendations include: developing a holistic understanding and appreciation of the academic enterprise, developing and maintaining competent interpersonal relationships, being open to entrepreneurship, developing strong leadership teams, and knowing how to listen and how to deliver strategic planning (Koester & Martinez, 2016).

Higher education could benefit from a coherent, broadly applicable conceptual framework that can stimulate more effective collective leadership in the academy at local, national, and global levels (Mutisya et al., 2014). The Compass of Higher Education offers a comprehensive framework that can inform professional development for faculty and staff to strengthen institutions and develop those interested in becoming leaders. The Compass of Higher Education (Figure 5.1) provides a visual representation of integration of process education in an organization (25 Years of Process Education, 2016). It highlights five key development areas: self (self-assessment and reflective practice); learner (growth of learning skills and processes); institutional (continuous quality improvement); intellectual (construction of knowledge); and professional (use of best researched practices) (Beyerlein, Holmes, & Apple, 2007).

In 2008, North Carolina Central University (NCCU) piloted the Compass of Higher Education leadership model, with the goal of creating a culture of engagement between administration and faculty to solve leadership challenges (Mutisya et al., 2014). This model was affirmed as a conceptual framework to diffuse tensions surrounding shared governance. Pacific Crest provided training for university faculty and administrators to assess five points of the compass: (1) self, (2) learner, (3) institutional, (4) faculty and (5) intellectual development. It also facilitated the development of professional learning communities as a means to develop solutions to the challenges of interdisciplinary collaboration within the university.

Academic freedom and shared governance were used as the platform to engage and develop faculty and administrators (Mutisya et al., 2014). The integration of the compass of higher education explores individual and community actions that could synergize actions related to shared governance. Educative processes identified in the model connect compass points that support leadership performance skills for attaining high levels of organizational outcomes across academic and student support units. Administrator support was provided for faculty development within each point of the compass framework to address the challenges of shared governance. The nurturing of faculty and staff following principles embodied in the Compass of Higher Education could generate human capital for the overall reconstruction of the university as an entity that is a vibrant laboratory for shared governance, open communication and collaboration (Mutisya et al., 2014, p. 47).

As a result of this study, researchers suggest this new conceptual framework for academic leadership helped to ameliorate concerns within a toxic work environment (Mutisya et al., 2014). The perception of maintaining an evaluative culture often stymies roles for faculty academic leadership, compromises academic freedom, and leads to protracted innovation that typifies higher education today. Faculty perceptions about the level of collegiality, ability to influence academic policy and overall communication of key information were explored. The tri-squared statistical analysis model showed a significant difference in the pooled survey responses between similar and non-similar items, a result that is counter-intuitive to what should be found in a thriving university setting (Mutisya et al., 2014, p. 49). Data obtained from this survey will allow for the application of a tri-squared model. This approach will allow for the success of faculty and administrator actions within each of the "points" to be compared in a statistically rigorous manner (Mutisya et al., 2014). The core purpose of the Compass is to empower students, faculty and institutions in processing challenges by increasing capability through expansion of abilities, skills and support.

Best practices and the scholarship of process education are documented in the Faculty Guidebook (Beyerlein et al., 2007) based on Compass themes. This comprehensive resource is the foundation of professional development institutes for faculty and staff at a number of community colleges and universities. Institutes are not only designed to improve student learning outcomes, they are learning environments that address knowledge, skills and understandings essential to leadership within college-wide environments. For example, the PE Teaching Institute engages participants in becoming successful change agents to help their colleges increase educational outcomes. This process utilizes key components of PE, such as problem solving, cooperative learning, mentoring, peer coaching, and assessment (Apple, 1991). These skills are fundamental to effective, transformative leadership. Recommendations presented here will help to enhance and develop an avenue to achieving greater success with the individuals selected for further leadership development.

CONCLUSION

In conclusion, Process Education has been introduced with the intent of improving the leadership development of faculty and staff in higher education. Leadership development cannot be realized if faculty and staff are not developed accordingly and resources are not available. We explore the literature around transformative leadership and aspects of process education leadership. We posit, dynamics of the Knowledge Age require more than the traditional models of leadership to support organizational transformation. A generalized model of transformational leadership in higher education is presented, identifying essential competencies, skills and attributes for consideration. Research and the higher education context support the move toward a leadership model anchored in PE principles. A comprehensive approach to growth of talented leaders with the capabilities to facilitate individual and organizational change is essential. The Compass of Higher Education provides a viable framework for development of leadership competencies. It responds to our constantly changing environments and contexts that require growing skills and processes in order to ensure success.

Recommendations for Further Study

Based on the review of the literature and findings, the following recommendations are offered for higher education leaders involved with decision-making about developing faculty and staff for leadership roles.

1. Use of Compass of Higher Education as a comprehensive framework for process education leadership development for faculty and staff;
2. Mixed methodologies studies of non-traditional higher education leaders (faculty and staff) in diverse settings; and
3. Measures for competences defined in the generalized transformational leadership model.

APPENDIX A

Table 5.1. Transformational Leadership Characteristics.

Characteristics or Attributes	Source
Visionary	Davis, 2012; Apple, 2009; Black, Groombridge & Jones, 2011; Covey, 2004; Black, 2015; Bass & Avolio, 1994; Kaya et al., 2015; Apple, 2015; Friedman, 2005; Horton & Apple, 2009
Role model	Apple, 2009; Kaya et al., 2015; Apple, 2015; Covey, 2004
Self-grower	Burke et al., 2009; Apple, 2015
Lifelong learner	Basham, 2010; Apple, 2009; Black, Groombridge, & Jones, 2011; Black, 2015; Apple, 2015
Collaborator	Davis, 2012
Team builder	Apple, 2009; Bass & Avolio, 1994; Kuhnert, 1994; Bass, 1994; Kaya et al., 2015; Apple, 2015
Visible	Black et al., 2011; Black, 2015; Bass, 1994; Guilliani, 2002
Problem solver	Apple, 2009; Bass, 1994; Guilliani, 2002
Communicator	Apple, 2009; Bass & Avolio, 1994; Apple, 2015
Risk taker	Apple, 2015
Delegator	Apple, 2009; Kuhnert, 1994; Kaya et al., 2015; Apple, 2015
Advocate/politician	Kaya et al., 2015; Apple, 2015

(*Continued*)

Table 5.1. (*Continued*)

Characteristics or Attributes	Source
Planner/ organizational alignment	Kaya et al., 2015; Apple, 2015; Covey, 2004
Mentor	Kaya et al., 2015; Davis, 2012; Apple, 2015
Assessor (individual and team)	Kaya et al., 2015; Apple 2015; Kouzes, 2002; Greenleaf, 2004
Stewardship of resources (resourceful)	Apple, 2015; Kaya et al., 2015
Diplomat	Kaya et al., 2015
Change agent/ change oriented	Naylor, 1999; Horton & Apple, 2009
Quality Results oriented	Apple, 2015
Ethical	Apple, 2015
Accessible/ open-minded; servant leader	Apple, 2015; Greenleaf, 2002
Decisive	Apple, 2015

APPENDIX B

Table 5.2. Generalized Model of Higher Education Leadership.

Higher Education Transformational Leader	Process Education Transformational Leader
1-Vision & Goals: direction, motivation & means to realize future • Establishes shared vision and systems • Identifies results • Sets clear achievable goals • Ensures inclusive planning process • Seeks stakeholder views • Sets clear & high expectations • Embraces institutional aims & culture • Measures performance	Visionary: Thinks outside the box; sees future trends, gaps, opportunities and new paths Storyteller: Uses vibrant stories to excite stakeholders about positive future Planner: Defines strategic plans, goals, operational strategies and project plans aligned via strategic thinking

(*Continued*)

Higher Education Transformational Leader	Process Education Transformational Leader
• Advocates shared governance • Aligns plans, actions, results & assessments	Risk Taker: Deviates from the norm to make a difference in challenging situations Emotionally Resilient: Exhibits strong self-esteem and self-affirmation
2-Big Picture and Details: increasing efficiency & effectiveness • Understands organizational dynamics • Discerns solvable problems • Establishes budgets & resource development strategy • Examines financial systems and procedures • Identifies information, technology & resource needs • Cooperates with external partners • Anticipates unexpected outcomes • Seeks external specialist advice • Manages professional flexibility and academic rigor • Determines institutional data needs	Decisive: Uses evidence; seeks stakeholder input, incorporates feedback, deliberates and makes timely tough decisions Resourceful: Anticipates needs and matches internal and external resources for optimal allocation Planner: Guides implementation of strategic goals through alignment of operational strategies and project plans Politician: Clarifies current and future needs of stakeholders through dialogue and connections to vision Team Builder: Creates teams with passion and expertise to ensure success Emotionally Resilient: Exhibits strong self-esteem, self-image and self-affirmation
3-Hands-on Leadership: managing action and implementation • Utilizes "hands-on" management • Possesses highly developed skills • Assesses priorities constantly • Knows institutional assets • Is sensitive to cultural differences • Empowers faculty and staff • Engages personnel in data analysis, decisions and implementation • Delegates responsibility and information control • Understands what matters • Maintains multi-faceted communication • Ensures managers lead • Makes decisions in timely manner	Delegator: Articulates responsibilities, expectations and accountabilities; provides freedom and resources to produce success Results oriented: Establishes goals, measures, milestones and monitoring systems Quality-oriented: Improves existing performance standards through continuous assessment Affirmer: Uses inclusive language to acknowledge others' ideas, accomplishments and value

(*Continued*)

Table 5.2. (*Continued*)

Higher Education Transformational Leader	Process Education Transformational Leader
4-Improvement and Learning: grow capacity to perform better • Provides faculty and staff development • Seeks alternative solutions • Enables risk taking for learning • Strives for high standards • Expects institutional needs to evolve over time • Understands risk factors and contingencies • Judges systems, manages people and celebrates success • Guides improvements by understanding data • Recognizes capability • Allows for alternative methods to improve performance	Mentor: Establishes growth outcomes, builds trust, advocates, assesses, and challenges growth Assessor: Improves individual and team performance via assessment Self-grower: Has a guiding life vision, self-assesses and self-mentors towards vision Lifelong Learner: Creates opportunities to increase knowledge and performance Identifies and develops talent
5-Personal Attributes • Establishes clear direction • Is considerate • Fosters collaborative & supportive environment • Exhibits integrity • Is transparent • Promotes open communication	Personable: Values others; culturally appropriate; empathetic Role Model: Constantly models behaviors consistent with personal and professional values; passionate Ethical: Values-based; Exhibits integrity in decision-making Communicator: Shares organizational vision, challenges, and opportunities Accessible: Makes and takes advantage of opportunities to connect; proactive Open minded: Seeks diverse perspectives; challenges assumptions Responsible: Is dependable and accountable

APPENDIX C

Table 5.3. Profile of Process Education Leader (Key differences from quality or transformational leader).

PE Leadership Case Statement by Dr. Daniel Litynski

Characteristic	Description	Leadership Illustrations
Risk Taking	Understands importance and gets outside comfort zone personally and institutionally to establish a growth culture	As Dean, led the College of Engineering and Applied Sciences (CEAS) team in strategic planning articulating a new vision, mission, values, goals and objectives plus their implementation. Also led the CEAS and university team in the conceptualization, design, and construction of a new engineering campus on 270 farmland acres at a cost of over $100 million. Both plan and design were based on a culture of collaboration and flexibility. Had virtually the entire CEAS faculty attend Process Education (PE) faculty workshops and many implemented them in their instructional techniques. Supported other PE workshops, such as curriculum design. Subsequently, initiated strategic planning at the provost, division director, and vice president for research levels to move outside comfort zone and establish a growth culture. For example, as vice president for research, initiated multi-year strategic planning process that included Discovery Plans by all departments, units, and colleges. This included self-assessment by all of their level of research, scholarship, and creative activities stratified at the local, regional, national, or global levels.
Emotional Resilience	Embraces challenges and failures; learned that successful cultural change has temporary failures on the way	Most strategies worked across leadership roles; some did not. We celebrated our successes and analyzed our failures to build forward momentum and cultural transformation.

(Continued)

Table 5.3. (*Continued*)

Characteristic	Description	Leadership Illustrations
Quality Orientation	Embraces assessment (over evaluation) as essential set of practices, systems, and processes leading to stakeholder growth and development	At each leadership level, held organizing and communication meetings very early in the process of developing projects and performances. They covered very basic philosophy, expectations, and procedures. Meetings incorporated core values, such as respect, integrity, collaboration, teamwork, leadership, open communication and assessment. This approach supported growth and development of all team members.
Mentoring	Assists key leaders with articulation of growth goals and plans; mentors them to strengthen their performance in line with annual plans	In each position, used both formative and summative assessment and evaluation in accomplishing organizational goals and plans. The university and the federal government have mandatory periodic performance mentoring. These were supplemented with frequent spontaneous feedback in various forms.
Self-Growth	Publically models the fundamental practices of a self-grower, self-challenger, self-assessor; invests in growth and development; and publishes self-assessment report for office	Have worked to provide developmental opportunities for all staff and modeled behavior by personally participating in professional development. Also called for periodic growth feedback by division staff on informal and formal bases. The formal assessment included surveys by all faculty of the functioning of staff members. At annual retreats, we furnished self-assessments of our individual and group progress. Leadership also called for similar self-assessments by all staff, plus feedback on leader performance.

Biosketch: Dr. Dan Litynski is vice president of research and a professor of Electrical and Computer Engineering at Western Michigan University. The former dean of the College of Engineering and Applied Sciences, provost and vice president for academic affairs, and president (interim), he has over 25 years in research and teaching. Further, Litynski served three years with the National Science Foundation as a program director (physics) and as acting division director for undergraduate education.

APPENDIX D

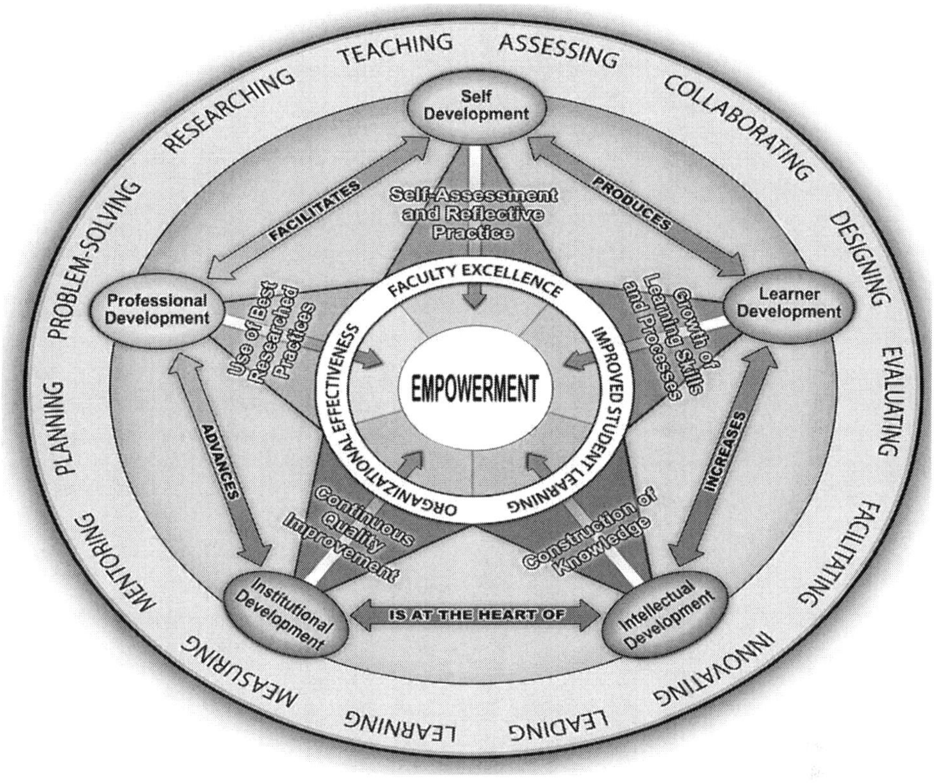

Fig 5.1. Compass of higher education.

REFERENCES

Amanchuckwu, R., Staneley, G., & Ololube, N. (2015). A review of leadership theories, principles and styles and their relevance to educational management. *Management, 5*(1), 6–14. Retrieved December 12, 2015 from https://www.researchgate.net/publication/283081945_A_Review_of_Leadership_Theories_Principles_and_Styles_and_Their_Relevance_to_Educational_Management

Amey, M. J. (2006). Leadership in higher education. *Change: The Magazine of Higher Learning, 38*, 55–58.

Apple, D. K. (1991). Notes for the 1991 teaching institute. Corvallis, OR: Pacific Crest.

Apple, D. K. (2015). *Profile of a transformational educational leader*. Unpublished manuscript. Hampton, NH: Pacific Crest.

Apple, D. K. (2009). *Profile of quality leadership. Leading change and transformation*. Unpublished leadership curriculum. Hampton, NH: Pacific Crest.

Apple, D. K., Morgan, J., & Hintze, D. (2013). *Learning to learn: Becoming a self-grower.* Hampton, NH: Pacific Crest.

Astin, A. W., & Astin, H. S. (2000). *Leadership reconsidered: Engaging higher education in social change.* Battle Creek, MI: W. K. Kellogg Foundation.

Baldrige National Quality Program. (2007). *Education criteria for performance excellence.* Gaithersburg, MD: National Institute of Standards and Technology (NIST).

Bass, B. M., & Avolio, B. J. (1993). Transformational leadership and organizational culture. *Public Administration Quarterly, 17,* 112–121.

Basham, L. (2010). Transformational and transactional leaders in higher education. *International Review of Business Research Papers, 6*(6), 141–152. Retrieved December 12, 2015 from http://www.irbrp.com/static/documents/December/2010/11.%20Lloyd%20Basham.pdf

Bennis, W. G., & Townsend, R. (1995). *Reinventing leadership: Strategies to empower the organization.* New York, NY: William Morrow.

Beyerlein, S. W., Holmes, C., & Apple, D. K. (Eds.). (2007). *Faculty guidebook: A comprehensive tool for improving faculty performance* (4th ed.). Lisle, IL: Pacific Crest.

Black, S. (2015). *Qualities of effective leadership in higher education.* Retrieved December 12, 2015 from http://file.scirp.org/pdf/OJL_2015061617461002.pdf

Black, S. A., Groombridge, J. J., & Jones, C. G. (2011). Leadership and conservation effectiveness: Finding a better way to lead. *Conservation Letters, 4,* 329–339. Retrieved December 12, 2015 from http://dx.doi.org/10.1111/j.1755-263X.2011.00184.x

Braun, S., Nazlic, T., Weisweiler, S., Pawlowska, P. C., & Frey, D. (2009). Effective leadership development in higher education: Individual and group level approaches. *Journal of Leadership Education, 8*(1), 195–206. Retrieved May 1, 2016 from http://leadershipeducators.org/Resources/Documents/jole/2009_summer/JOLE_8_1_Braun_Nazlic_Weisweiler.pdf

Bryman, A. (2007). Effective leadership in higher education: A literature review. *Studies in Higher Education, 32,* 693–710. Retrieved December 12, 2015 from http://dx.doi.org/10.1080/03075070701685114.

Burke, K., Lawrence, B., El-Sayed, M., & Apple, D. (2009). Process Education™—Past, present and future. *International Journal of Process Education, 1*(1), 35–42.

Davis, L. (2012). *Leadership in higher education.* Pepperdine University. Retrieved December 12, 2015 from http://shayesliedavis.com/wp-content/uploads/2012/10/Leadership-In-Higher-Ed.pdf

Friedman, T. (2005). The world is flat: A brief history of the twenty-first century. NY: Farrar, Straus and Giroux

Gardner, H. (2004). *Changing minds: The art and science of changing our own and other people's minds.* Boston: Harvard Business School Press.

Growe, R. (2011). Collaborative leadership in the era of new normal. *National Forum of Educational Administration and Supervision, 29*(4), 1–6.

Hallett, J. (1987). Worklife Visions: Redefining Work for the Information Economy. Alexandria. VA: American Society for Personnel Administration.

Heifetz, R. & Laurie, D. (1997). The work of leadership. Obtained on Jan 1, 2015 from http://admin.kasa.org/Professional_Development/documents/TheWorkofLeadership.pdf. Harvard Business Review.

Horton, J., & Apple, D. K. (2009). *Leading change and transformation: Unpublished leadership curriculum.* Hampton, NH: Pacific Crest.

Jain, C. R., Apple, D. K., & Ellis, W., Jr. (2015). What is self-growth? *International Journal of Process Education, 7*(1), 41–52.

Kaya, A., Kaplan, M., Mutisya, P. M., & Beyerlein, S. (2015). Internalizing principles of transformational global leadership in a graduate education course. *International Journal of Process Education, 7*(1), 29–40.

Kettering University. (2008). *Performance measures for leadership: Kettering university leader.* Flint, MI.

Kirkwood Community College. (2011). *Profile of a Kirkwood faculty leader.* Cedar Rapids, IA.

Koester, J., & Martinez, A. (2016). *Closing the gap: Leadership development and succession planning in public higher education.* American Association of State Colleges and Universities. Retrieved May 1, 2016 from https://www.tiaainstitute.org/public/pdf/aascu_closing_the_gap.pdf

Lindborg, H. (2007). Introduction to expectations and change movements in higher education. Retrieved May 2, 2016 from www.pcrest3.com/fgb/efgb4/1/1_1_1.htm

Mutisya, P. M., Osler II, J. E., Bitting, P. F., & Rotich, J. P. (2014). The need for a conceptual framework for leadership and shared governance between faculty and administrators (pp. 43–52). *International Journal of Process Education, 6*(1), 43–52.

Naisbitt, J., & Aburdene, P. (1990). *Megatrends 2000: Ten new directions for the 1990s.* New York, NY: William Morrow and Company.

Naylor, J. (1999). *Management.* Harlow: Prentice Hall.

New Zealand Council for Educational Research. (2015). "Shifting to 21st century thinking—The knowledge age". Retrieved from http://www.shiftingthinking.org/?page_id=58

O'Banion, T. (1997). *A learning college for the 21the century.* Westport, CT: Oryx Press for the American Council on Education and the American Association of Community Colleges, League for innovation n the Community College.

Pacific Crest. (2007). *The compass of higher education.* Hampton, NH: Pacific Crest. Retrieved December 12, 2015 from http://www.pcrest.com/LO/star_final/1.htm

Peters, T., & Waterman, R. (1982). *In search of excellence.* New York, NY: Harper & Row.

Scholtes, P. R. (1998). *The leader's handbook.* New York, NY: The McGraw Hill Companies.

Uhl-Bien, M., Russ, M., & McKelvey, B. (2007). Complexity leadership theory: Shifting leadership from the industrial age to the knowledge era. *The Leadership Quarterly, 18*, 298–318.

University of California Berkeley. (2007). Preparing faculty for academic management. *Creating Academic leaders at CAL: Leadership development program.* Retrieved May 1, 2016 from http://hrweb.berkeley.edu/sites/default/files/attachments/07academicmanagement.pdf

Wolinski, S. (2010). *Leadership theories.* Retrieved June 14, 2015 from http://managementhelp.org/blogs/leadership/2010/04/21/leadership-theories/

SECTION TWO

Cases in P–12 School Leadership

CHAPTER SIX

Elementary Teachers Leading From THE Classroom

Cases of Practical Leadership

PATRICIA BRICKER AND KELLY N. TRACY

Understanding teachers as leaders is not a new concept, but conceptualizing what teacher leadership actually looks like takes on a myriad of forms. In York-Barr and Duke's (2004) extensive review of the literature on teacher leadership, they describe its roots and evolution. Beginning in formal designated roles intended to further the purposes of administration (e.g., increasing efficiency), teacher leadership has evolved to include instructional leaders in curriculum and mentoring, and has changed even more to embrace informal shared leadership roles in which teachers influence others in an effort to improve teaching and learning. As the movement of "teacher as leader" continued into the 21st century, theoretical frameworks of teacher leadership were offered by Lieberman and Miller (2004), and Danielson (2006) and Sato (2005). While Lieberman and Miller and Danielson focus on areas of teacher influence that include the school, community and the profession Sato's concept of practical leadership focuses on the school level, with teachers' "deliberative acts" influencing other teachers' instructional practices as a means to enhance students' learning. These actions are taken in response to the teachers' situations encountered in their everyday work with students.

In this chapter we focus on the leadership experiences of two elementary teachers as they continue classroom teaching. Using the framework of practical leadership (Sato, 2005) we investigate the teachers' *deliberative acts* (Sato, 2005, p. 58) and how these acts influence other teachers' instructional practices and enhance students' learning in local contexts. The practical leadership framework is predicated on the idea that "actions rather than roles or functions" (Sato, 2005, p. 70) identify teacher leaders. Deliberation, as in making choices regarding one's actions, is also a key element in practical leadership. As Sato (2005) writes, one "who implements the edicts or protocols of others is *not* engaging in deliberation and is *not* engaged in practical leadership" (emphasis added, p. 58).

In this chapter we illustrate how acts such as conducting research, attending conferences, and sustained relationships with university faculty influence the teachers' action and their local contexts. The two teachers we describe in our cases, Katie and Madeline, are teachers who we have worked with extensively over the last several years in varied capacities. We recognized that Katie and Madeline fit the characteristics of teacher leaders (see York-Barr & Duke, 2004 for full list), including the following:

- Significant teaching experience
- Deep knowledge of the field of teaching and learning
- Risk-taking lifelong learners with a passion for teaching
- Hard workers with the ability to manage their workload
- Effective communicators
- Collaborative

We first present each teacher as a case that was created from analysis of interviews, field notes, and collected documents such as presentation materials and articles co-authored by these teachers. We then share a cross-case analysis to determine commonalities that allow these teachers to lead and influence while remaining classroom teachers.

KATIE: ENACTING TEACHER LEADERSHIP AS A FIFTH GRADE TEACHER

Across her 16-year teaching career, Katie has taught multiple grades from third to eighth. During the time of this study, she was in her second year of teaching fifth grade at a rural, Title I school serving about 600 students in kindergarten through eighth grade. As a fifth grade teacher, Katie is part of a three-person team. She is responsible for teaching all students social studies (three classes for a one hour block each), as well as teaching language arts to her homeroom class.

Katie is deeply invested in her own education and in continuing to develop her expertise as a teacher. She earned a master's degree in elementary education and her National Board Certification as a Middle Childhood Generalist. Additionally, she has hosted several student teachers and worked as an adjunct faculty member at a local university. Katie describes herself as a life-long learner and is continuously looking for new ideas and ways to collaborate.

This willingness to learn and collaborate led Katie and Kelly (second author of this chapter) to develop a close research partnership during the previous three years. Their work typically focuses on integrating literacy into social studies and developing students' critical thinking skills. This partnership has included several hours of observation in Katie's classroom, co-planning, and co-teaching. Katie explains the benefit of this relationship.

> It's really awesome to have a partner in crime, someone to share things with. I just obsessively read stuff anyway so it is fun to have someone who is also reading because not everyone is like that. It is exhausting to people who don't do that so it's nice to have someone to share ideas with.

While the sharing between Katie and Kelly is important, their collaboration has extended well beyond Katie's classroom, leading to other opportunities such as attending and presenting at a professional conference together. Multiple years of budget cuts across the state have led to far fewer opportunities for professional development outside of the school, so it had been a few years since Katie had been able to attend a conference. She described herself as "re-energized and affirmed" afterward. A small grant from the University paid for part of the conference expenses and the school's Parent-Teacher Association (PTA) paid the difference. While Katie felt overwhelmingly positive about the opportunity to attend the conference, she also shared her feelings of guilt because there were other teachers who did not get the same chance. She worried some about the perception of special treatment, but in the end decided that the positive aspects of attending far outweighed the negative. She openly shared what she learned with her colleagues upon her return, noting that she felt "empowered" by the knowledge.

Beyond sharing instructional practices at this conference and with her colleagues, Katie has also co-led professional development sessions with Kelly on their work with teachers from across the state. She has co-authored a manuscript and has helped prepare presentations for other audiences. Each of these sharing opportunities has increased Katie's sphere of influence. The pre-service teachers in Kelly's classes also feel Katie's influence as she uses many examples from her class to help ground her instruction in the "real world" of the classroom. Interestingly, Katie saw this element of their collaboration more as an opportunity for her students to have influence rather than for her.

> When I introduced Kelly, I said, "You might affect kids in college! They could be your teachers by eighth grade so you might actually have a voice on your lessons in eighth grade. This is your chance to show what you like and don't like."

Katie's willingness to open her classroom to an outside researcher and to share her practices with others, demonstrates a willingness to be vulnerable. Rather than worrying about what others might think of her teaching, Katie chooses to view observers this way.

> I've always tried to embrace even a one-day observer or someone who is there for a long period of time, embrace the idea that it is extra attention, and we are welcoming that person as a guest. It is nice to have an extra person who is invested in the kids as part of the collaboration. It has also been positive for people to come in and see the growth of the students. The outside perspective is refreshing.

This sort of positive outlook and propensity toward learning from experiences is typical of Katie. She is action-oriented, believing that she and others have the ability to affect change. For Katie, this action is two-fold: 1. Problem solving as a teacher and helping her colleagues do the same, and 2. Centering her teaching on helping students understand how to take action.

In her own classroom, Katie is presented with regular opportunities to problem solve. She often finds herself working to balance new initiatives, expectations, or requirements with what is best for her students and the realities of her classroom.

> Last year we planned this big text set unit and the principal was like great, but you have to stick to something out of this Common Core Curriculum Map book. It is a really great book but we didn't have most of the resources in the book ... We had spent the spring planning and were ready to go live and then had to switch to this. Then we found this courage unit in the book that fit with [our goals] so I took some of the ideas it had, used the text set I created and modified some of the assignments. So it wasn't really the blueprint from that book, but it did have some of the deeper thinking questions from the unit.

When deciding how to approach these types of challenges, Katie thoughtfully considers multiple sources of information, including what she learned in graduate school, current readings, and other professional experiences. "What you can't do is throw out all the good things that you used to do when new things come along. You have to constantly balance that."

Katie's desire for action and problem solving does not end in her own classroom. When other teachers share concerns, she looks for solutions.

> In our Professional Learning Community (plc) for grades fifth through eighth, there were a lot of complaints that students were not doing enough writing in the lower grades, that the kids' grammar just wasn't there and they didn't know how to write a research paper. So I thought, "Let's have some solutions with this." [The teachers] were not moving forward. They were just having complaints that didn't seem to be going anywhere. I had been to a conference and really wanted to get on the agenda to share some things I had learned there. I feel like my ideas were a lot better received because I could explain where the idea came from rather than if it had just been my own personal perspective. That was the first time since I had been at this school where this one particular teacher tried something new. It had always been, "Oh, that won't work here or who's got time for that."

Katie explains that social justice is important to her and often guides her instructional decisions. Her stance on taking action extends into her classroom where she often focuses on helping students become self-directed problem solvers and discovering what issues about which they care. She explains, "The kids are more engaged with challenging tasks when they have something they really care about." Katie sees teaching as an opportunity to bring about change in the world and to help students understand their role in that change. She describes her hope for students this way.

> I hope they will ask questions. I hope that they will think open-mindedly and consider that there might be experience they haven't had in life, that someone else might have a different perspective. Maybe they agree with it or disagree with it and maybe their circumstances are different, but I hope they try to seek understanding and see the bigger picture of what might be there … I want them to know that you can make a difference.

Katie feels a sense of responsibility in helping empower students, solve problems, and bring about social change. This responsibility guides her decision making and drives her as a teacher-leader.

MADELINE: ENACTING TEACHER LEADERSHIP AS A FIRST GRADE TEACHER

Madeline has taught for 12 years and is a recent regional teacher of the year. Her rural southeastern school is designated as Title 1 due to the high percentage of children from low-income families. She currently teaches first grade, along with four other teachers, and works with a part-time teacher assistant, although recent statewide changes have led to decreased teacher assistant time. Having been at her school for many years, Madeline has developed positive relationships with colleagues and administrators and feels that she is supported, trusted, and treated as a professional. She has mentored many preservice teachers in early field experiences as well as yearlong internships.

Madeline earned her bachelor's degree in elementary education and has worked with Patricia (first author of this chapter) since she was an undergraduate student. At that time she eagerly accepted an open invitation to all students to present their experiences with science inquiries and lessons with Patricia at a national science educational conference. Five years into her teaching career, Madeline began work on her elementary education master's degree at the same university. She completed her master's degree four years later.

Always looking for ways to improve her teaching, Madeline regularly takes on new projects and challenges in her classroom. They typically focus on creating, implementing, and researching student-centered, engaging curriculum that meaningfully integrates required content across disciplines. One example stems from a self-designed project Madeline completed in a graduate course, a yearlong plan for integrating science and literacy in her first grade classroom. The plan closely connected to Patricia's research interests and they decided to collaborate again. The following school year they worked together to refine the initial plan, co-teach, reflect, and research. While they had known each other for quite some time and were excited about this work and about learning together, it still took time to establish trust and comfort.

> We had to get over that embarrassment factor and the fear of not knowing what you would expect of my teaching. Then we would talk and she would say I am more nervous than you are. I haven't taught young children in a long time. That kind of embarrassment, of feeling each other out, of stepping in and helping out … Co-teaching takes some time.

One part of the science curriculum focused on the needs of plants. While Madeline had grown plants from seeds in her classroom in the past, she decided that year she would take another step and have her class plant a garden. After getting permission from the principal to dig up part of the schoolyard, she called on class parents and her own family to help with initial garden preparation. As she puts it, she sometimes finds herself begging, borrowing, and stealing to make things happen. This first gardening season her students grew and ate lettuce, spinach, and radishes while learning about plant needs, reading informational texts including seed packets, using math to plan and plant, and writing observations in their journals.

When Madeline discusses this and other projects, she talks about letting go, taking risks, being flexible, and stepping up and doing what needs to be done, even when it is stressful. While acknowledging that it can be time consuming and grueling, she says taking the time to think, reflect, and discuss is critical. She emphasizes the value of meetings with Patricia, Kelly (second author), and Nancy (another teacher education faculty member), sharing that this helps her dig deep into the matter of things. These conversations encourage her to look at different perspectives and help her access new materials and research. They provide encouragement and constructive feedback. She feels that the partnerships make a huge difference.

> I was getting very down. It is hard not to be down with the way things have been in our state. Having something else to focus on that says okay I am not going to worry about the politics, I am going to work on what is best for kids. Any time you try something new, especially when you are successful, it really motivates you to go forward with it and do it again. Not getting stuck in a rut for me is a very important thing because if I'm bored the kids are going to be bored. I really like to challenge and to try new things. It really impacted me greatly … I can draw a direct line from my graduate program to me becoming a better teacher, and a direct line from these partnerships and collaborations too.

Through the years, the collaborative projects have continued and all have focused on an aspect of integrating science and literacy. Madeline has continued to independently teach and refine topics from previous years and team efforts have focused on adding new layers such as science-related poetry and digital storytelling. The long-term collaboration has decreased the nervousness and increased the trust and comfort.

These projects are intrinsically interesting to other teachers and Madeline is very willing to share with her school colleagues. As she began to further develop the idea of a school garden, she invited teachers in her school to come to meetings to develop a plan. There were at least 10 teachers who attended the planning meetings and people began to take on different roles to help make the garden happen. Madeline shared:

> We all worked together to make a blueprint for the garden and to figure out how to pay for materials on a limited budget. A fourth grade teacher had her students measure out the space for the garden beds and other kindergarten and first grade teachers helped to spread the mulch and plant new vegetables. A teacher assistant offered to bring her compost from home to mix in with the garden soil. Later, one of our EC teachers had her students pick the vegetables to share with families during the summer break. It was truly a great collaborative project. I was amazed how one idea could bring so many teachers together. Now we have teachers that are planning flower and herb garden beds in other parts of the school as well as teachers planning on incorporating worm composting bins.

Madeline's excitement for teaching science and literacy also influenced some of her colleagues. As she began to share and others began to see her students in action, they began to ask for some materials she had used and they were able to work together to plan new activities as a team. She uses the baseline of what was done in the past, including student work samples, to encourage other teachers and to help them see that even young students are capable of great things such as writing poetry and creating digital stories. Realizing that certain teachers have no interest, she chooses to work closely with colleagues who are excited about trying something new. They share ideas but are not required to do the same thing.

Madeline believes that she has very limited influence on school level issues. However, she does think she has influenced a few items, such as mandated use of a new district-wide reading program, through candid and honest discussions with her administrators. Whenever she is asked for input, she researches thoroughly and that can be a challenge given the many different tasks teachers juggle both professionally and personally. She emphasizes the need to set priorities and to earn the respect and trust of other teachers and administrators.

> It is easy to always have an opinion. It is much harder to be reserved and try to affect change in a different manner of problem solving and offering solutions.

Over the years, Madeline's work has been recognized and her scope of influence has expanded beyond her school. Many examples from her classroom are used in teacher education courses taught by Patricia and her colleagues. They help both preservice and in-service teachers see how the theory looks in real practice, in a nearby school, with a teacher who once sat in the same seats they do. The collaboration also helps Patricia stay current and realistic in her teaching. Their partnership has led to multiple presentations at professional conferences and a published article for elementary teachers.

Madeline's selection as a regional teacher of the year has led to more formal leadership roles. She has presented professional development related to her literacy work at the district level and at a regional education alliance. She feels this has given her the best opportunities to influence other teachers. She enjoys leading professional development in this setting because she believes that the teachers who attend have chosen to participate and are invested in implementing new ideas in their classrooms. She feels like she makes a difference when she receives follow-up emails and calls asking for more information and that leading professional development is a learning experience for her. "It reminds me how we are able to spread best practices from classroom to classroom through the simple act of sharing." Madeline has spoken at several education forums, advocating for public schools, teachers, and students. She also serves as a teacher voice fellow, working to inform education policy in order to improve the education of children and the working conditions of educators.

Madeline's disposition toward growth and inquiry has helped her become a leader through her actions within her own classroom as well as through these formal roles.

DISCUSSION

When considering both Katie and Madeline, we see many of the characteristics Sato (2005) describes in her framework of practical leadership. Neither Katie nor Madeline has had formal leadership roles within their schools. As classroom teachers, they both engage in *deliberative acts*. Instead of simply following mandates, doing what has always been done, or doing what everyone else is doing, they make decisions based upon the best interests of students and their education. As part of this process, they work to offer solutions when problems are encountered. They frequently use their funds of knowledge, referring to professional books and articles, graduate courses, classroom stories, and student work samples. They clearly exhibit a sense of agency in which they use their professional knowledge to voice, enact, and model best practices and new possibilities within their classrooms. A sincere spirit of collegiality that allows them to influence others within their everyday actions accompanies Katie and Madeline's deliberative acts. They are willing to be vulnerable, to let people into their classrooms, and to intimately discuss and share their teaching practices. Sometimes their colleagues ask them to share and other times they initiate sharing of their ideas with others.

While influence beyond their own schools is not addressed in Sato's framework for practical leadership, clearly Katie and Madeline's spheres of influence do extend beyond their own classrooms and schools. As previously noted, in Madeline's case, some of this influence is due to formal roles connected to her selection as a regional teacher of the year. It is likely that strong practical leadership leads to opportunities for recognition and more formal leadership roles that might be done alongside classroom teaching or might paradoxically draw these teacher leaders to roles outside their classrooms. In fact, Madeline has recently taken a one-year leave to work at a university as a teacher education visiting faculty member.

Both Katie and Madeline have been influenced by their sustained research-related relationships with university faculty. They both value collaboration, lifelong learning, and being connected rather than isolated. They also seem to have a predisposition to engage in research, present, and write. As can be seen in these cases, this type of collaboration can be beneficial for both the teacher and teacher educator/researcher. Hedges (2010) describes the role of a "critical friend" and "blurring the boundaries" of the teacher-researcher relationship to bring mutual benefits. Teacher educator practice is grounded in the realities of the classroom, teachers and researchers become advocates for each other and their students, and teachers are supported in trying new ideas and locating resources. Such collaboration is not without challenges such as scheduling, finding time, and overcoming the sense of vulnerability. Building a strong and trusting relationship between the teacher and teacher educators is essential to success. Both partners must be willing to consider the needs of each other and to be flexible. Being involved for an extended period of time can enable a deeper relationship, help shape the collaboration, and support teachers in their practical leadership.

Ironically, Katie and Madeline are hesitant to call themselves teacher leaders. We need to help teachers understand practical leadership so they can develop their sense of agency, become leaders, and see themselves as leaders. To be a good teacher, especially when school systems are faced with numerous challenges, a person needs to be a leader who advocates for what is in the best interest of the children she teaches as well as the profession and the greater good.

DISCUSSION QUESTIONS

1. Do you see yourself as a practical leader? Why or why not?
2. How might you grow as a practical leader?

3. What impedes teachers' ability to demonstrate practical leadership in schools? How can these challenges be addressed?
4. How are teachers currently supported or rewarded for participating in practical leadership in schools? How might they be?
5. How can we help preservice educators and new teachers understand and become practical leaders?
6. Discuss some potential benefits of teachers working with teacher education faculty as discussed in this chapter.

REFERENCES

Danielson, C. (2006). *Teacher leadership that strengthens professional practice.* Alexandria, VA: ASCD.

Hedges, H. (2010). Blurring the boundaries: Connecting research, practice and professional learning. *Cambridge Journal of Education, 40*(3), 299–314.

Lieberman, A., & Miller, L. (2004). *Teacher leadership.* San Francisco, CA: Jossey-Bass.

Sato, M. (2005). Practical leadership: Conceptualizing the everyday leadership work of teachers. *The New Educator, 1*(1), 55–71.

York-Barr, J., & Duke, K. (2004). What do we know about teacher leadership? Findings from two decades of scholarship. *Review of Educational Research, 74*(3), 255–316.

CHAPTER SEVEN

Culturally Responsive Principal Leadership

A Case Study

KENDRA LOWERY AND KOFI LOMOTEY

Kamau Nkrumah, the principal of Shirley Chisholm Elementary School (SCEC), located in a northeastern city, was celebrating, having recently received the Johnson Family Award. He won the award for being designated as the outstanding educator of the year. This national award is given annually to two educators who have demonstrated exceptional commitment to the students and families in their community, contributing to their pre-collegiate and postsecondary success. Recipients receive $10,000 and a community celebration. During the award ceremony, three former and three current Chisholm students stood up to talk about how Principal Nkrumah had changed their lives.

The occasion prompted Principal Nkrumah to reflect on the rich experiences and continuing challenges he faced at Chisholm. He and his staff had developed close relationships with members of the community over the past 10 years. Several of the staff who had been with the principal throughout his entire tenure grew up in the community and had established trusting relationships with students and families—a crucial component of culturally responsive leadership. Many of his senior staff had been leaders in the building. They were considered respected elders and were mentors to the younger staff.

Over the past three years more than a third of his senior staff had retired, necessitating the hiring of several new faculty and staff. The district entered into an agreement to hire new staff who were graduates of an alternative licensing program and who had not taken any coursework in key administrator standards, including culturally responsive teaching and engagement with families and communities. Nkrumah immediately saw this as a challenge as he knew the importance of culturally responsive leadership—particularly with the population of students at SCES. Principal Nkrumah set up collaborative interviews for the selection of new teachers and he implemented a mentoring system; he felt confident in the potential his young hires demonstrated in their interviews and teaching demonstrations.

The successful candidates appeared to have confidence in the SCES students, a strong desire to work these students and their families and a deep commitment to the education of the students. Midway through the current academic year, Nkrumah began to sense concerns—not just from the new staff, but also from some veterans who were becoming disillusioned about educating students in their underserved, urban community of predominately African Americans. During some classroom walkthroughs, Principal Nkrumah began to notice what appeared to be a lack of commitment to providing rigorous academic instruction. This was of concern to Nkrumah, as he had dedicated his tenure at SCES to making sure that each student left the school with a deep confidence in their ability to achieve excellence wherever they went.

Several occurrences motivated Principal Nkrumah to think more deeply about changes occurring at SCES. They encouraged him to think about the degree to which he and his staff were continuing to provide a culturally responsive education for the students at SCES. On the Monday morning following the awards ceremony, Principal Nkrumah walked past George Burrell, a fifth grade student with whom he had an especially close relationship. George's three older siblings had matriculated through Chisholm Elementary and their life stories resonated with Principal Nkrumah. George's father and mother were both college-educated. His father had recently been laid off from his job and the family was struggling to make ends meet. Mr. Burrell suspected that his layoff was racially motivated; some recent hires who were all white, kept their jobs and were given raises while he—an African American—was let go. Principal Nkrumah could relate to those feelings and reflected on his own father's feelings when he went through something similar decades prior. However, just as Nkrumah's father encouraged him to get his education and focus on his school and career goals, Mr. Burrell assured Principal Nkrumah that he did not want his son to become discouraged and give up on his own dreams. On this particular morning, Principal Nkrumah stopped and spoke to George, who was wearing a t-shirt that said, "Ivy League bound … Yeah right!" Principal Nkrumah shook George's hand and said,

Principal: Good morning, George.
George: Hi, Principal Nkrumah. What's up?
Principal: Life is good. It's better because you are the first person I see on my way to my office. … Explain your motivation for wearing that shirt.

George rolled his eyes ever so slightly as to avoid appearing totally disrespectful.

George: Man—

Principal: Principal or Mister. *Principal Nkrumah reminded the young student.*

George: My bad. Principal Nkrumah, I know what you're going to say. Some of my friends in the middle school got this shirt and I think it's hilarious. I mean, come on. Everybody knows you have to be super smart to get into Harvard or Princeton or Yale. Plus, now with my dad being laid off, man, I mean, Principal Nkrumah, you know we can't afford anything. I'll probably be working odd jobs for the rest of my life.

Principal: George, where have you learned that you can't go to any school you choose?

George thought for about 10 seconds.

George: Well, it's not like anybody's ever told me. I just have to face reality. All the college pennants that you put up in that school can't change my reality. I love my dad and I think I need to work to support him. I'm just preparing for it.

Principal: Even though that's not what your dad has told you or me?

George: Principal Nkrumah, I think Ivy League is a joke. It's only for the rich. I know you believe in me. But, I got other things to worry about now.

Principal: George, this conversation is to be continued. *All of the students knew that when Principal Nkrumah wanted to make a point but knew the students needed some space to think about it he told them, "to be continued." George shook Principal Nkrumah's hand and wandered off.*

This conversation frustrated Principal Nkrumah, as he was committed to insuring that all students felt able to do whatever they chose to do. George—and increasingly other students—was questioning his own potential. Nkrumah was spending much of his time reflecting on ways to reverse the discouraging trend.

Principal Nkrumah knew the importance of enabling students to "see themselves in the curriculum" in order for them to feel sufficiently motivated to excel academically (Lomotey, 1989). He was pleased with the way his staff had imaged his school with inspirational posters telling students they could be whomever they choose to be. But when he looked at the many posters showing racially diverse images of scientists, politicians, athletes, businesspeople and educators who broke barriers along with inspirational quotes, and the college pennants George referred to, he entered the building with new eyes. He was challenged to re-think this strategy. *Were these posters really sending the message he and his staff intended?* Some of them had been hanging in the same spot for over three years, he thought, as he uncurled a frayed corner of a President Obama poster that had been hanging in the same spot since 2009. *Maybe the students don't even notice them anymore.* "Even the best of us need to revisit some things," he sighed as he entered his office. As he sat down, he dialed Mr. Burrell's phone number and prepared to make a purchase.

Typical of school principals, Nkrumah was compelled by circumstances to shift from one agenda item to another throughout the school day. He knew he could not spend the entire morning focused solely on George Burrell. He prepared to begin his regular classroom walk-throughs.

CLASSROOM 1

While in Ms. Noble's first grade reading class, Principal Nkrumah observed three African American students, two boys and one girl, with their heads down while Ms. Noble was doing a think-aloud activity to model how the students were to engage in the morning's lesson. At first, he started to call them out by name, but remembered that the boys had told him they hated it when a teacher called them out; it made them feel like the teacher did not want them in the class. Principal Nkrumah walked over to the students and gently nudged them. He whispered, "What is the expectation about posture while in class?" They looked at him, mouthed "Sorry" in unison and sat up. On his way out of the classroom, he glanced back to the students and saw that although they were complying and had their heads up from their desks, their heads were in their hands and they looked thoroughly disengaged—bored.

After school, Principal Nkrumah asked Ms. Noble why she allowed the students to keep their heads down when the school-wide expectation is that all students are to demonstrate they are engaged in the lesson with their heads up. Ms. Noble looked down nervously and said, "Mr. Nkrumah, can I tell you honestly why I allow that to happen?"

"Of course."

"I know it goes against what you say, but honestly, I feel like it's easier to say it when you're not confronted daily with these students' behaviors during a lesson that you've spent hours preparing. First of all, it's better than them talking back or yelling at me and ruining the education for the other students. Second of all, I know Martin and Keisha have been struggling at home and are probably hungry. All three of them are behind grade level anyways, so it's not like they can really ever get caught up. But don't get me wrong. I'm trying my best with them. I don't want to push them too hard—because I feel bad for them." This exchange reinforced for Nkrumah that the focus on success for all was not being internalized by all of his teachers. He reflected for a few moments more and went to his next walk-through.

CLASSROOM TWO

Principal Nkrumah entered the second classroom while the fifth grade math teacher, Mr. Anderson, was reviewing simple addition flash cards and giving students candy for getting the right answers. The students were laughing and having a great time. When Principal Nkrumah walked in the room, some of the students smiled and said, "We love Mr. Anderson. He's great! He gives us candy!" Principal Nkrumah asked Mr. Anderson to speak with him after school. In that afterschool meeting, the following exchange occurred.

Principal: Mr. Anderson, I see that the students like you. I am concerned that you are teaching them far below the age and grade-appropriate level for fifth grade.

Mr. Anderson replied,

Anderson: Trust me, I know. But, I know you know some of the families these students come from. I've called home but don't get an answer when I try to talk about their skills. This is the only way I know how to keep them engaged and motivated to keep trying. Plus, I know you tell us that all students are capable of achieving, but this class is just a low bunch. Normally I wouldn't say that, but this is a unique class. I try to give them homework but it comes back not done. The parents aren't helping. Plus, you know the Latino students who barely speak any English! It's a challenge to talk to them or their parents. I don't know what their skills are.

Principal Nkrumah replied after thinking deeply,

Principal: Mr. Anderson, it has always and continues to be my expectation that those who teach in this building teach our students in a way that demonstrates we believe they can achieve. We do not decide who is capable and who is not. It is clear that we need to strategize about what resources or support you need to uphold this expectation in your classroom.

CLASSROOM THREE

Principal Nkrumah went to Mr. Grange's social studies class. Mr. Grange had requested additional support the previous academic year because he did not think he was reaching the students. Principal Nkrumah coached him on creating student-centered lessons, got a teacher leader from the district office to help go over lesson plans and suggested some webinars for increasing student engagement. At the beginning of the current school year, Mr. Grange caught up with Principal Nkrumah and told him he was confident this year would be better. The most important thing was how Principal Nkrumah kept asking him the same questions in their coaching sessions: "What is the purpose of your lessons? Why should the students care about this? How does this connect to their daily lives?"

Principal Nkrumah entered the classroom at the end of the class, and saw students reviewing the lesson. In teams of two, students were sharing a sentence about how the lesson about the Revolutionary War was important to them.

Mr. Grange asked for two volunteers to share with the class why the lesson was important to them. Jerry Thomas said, "This lesson was important because I didn't know there were Black people who were not slaves during the Revolutionary War times. I want to learn more about them." The other students nodded their heads. Mr. Grange invited students to write questions on the board that they wanted to explore about the Revolutionary War. More than half of the class rushed up to the board to write their questions. Mr. Grange noticed two students in the back who did not look engaged and was on his way over to them when Principal Nkrumah nodded with approval. As he left the room, he heard Mr. Grange telling one of the students that he just talked to his mother the previous night and she said that her son seemed to like military history, so he wondered why he appeared to show a lack of interest.

CLASSROOM FOUR

Principal Nkrumah walked through Mrs. Foxwood's general music class because he wanted to see if she was implementing any of the strategies he had discussed with her to help with the management of the discipline problems she was continuously having. When he entered the classroom, he stood behind a filing cabinet so the students could not readily see him. Mrs. Foxwood was working with one section of the classroom with her back turned to the other students. She was intently trying to get the students to learn a particular melody. When Peter Sherwin got up to sharpen his pencil, she yelled, "You! You over there! Sit down. How many times do I have to tell you to sit down?" Several other students started laughing and said, "Yeah You! Sit down." Peter threw his pencil at them and they all started laughing.

Mrs. Foxwood stopped the class and said, "You guys are ruining this class. I'm trying to teach you good music. Please cooperate." Harley, who was a gifted musician who played the piano offered to help. "Mrs. Foxwood, I can play the piano while you teach them the notes," she offered. Mrs. Fox wood looked up and seemed surprised. "That's okay, Harley. Thank you, though. I can handle it. You all just wait patiently."

One of the girls, Aisha, attended church with Principal Nkrumah and he knew her to be a very polite student. Aisha said, "You know, Mrs. Foxwood, these songs are horrible. Who are these people who wrote them? We don't know any of this music. Why should we care?" Mrs. Foxwood responded, "Because these are the classics." The students let out a collective groan. After 20 minutes of observing Mrs. Foxwood work with the students in groups while the other students waited with nothing to do, Principal Nkrumah moved to the next class. While he walked, he reflected on how much more effective Mrs. Foxwood might be if she tried harder to engage students in all facets of her lessons.

Mr. Nkrumah asked himself how Chisholm Elementary School got to this point. How was it, he wondered, that too many teachers seemed less concerned about the success of all students, less engaged with students' families and generally, less creative in the classroom. Sure, he could focus on the other classrooms like Mr. Grange's where he observed teachers working individually with students in small groups and then transitioning to whole group instruction, or where the students were learning about a culturally and racially diverse set of inventors, or where the teachers greeted students by name in the hallway and welcomed them into their classrooms with an engaging activity. Those best practices were important to continually uplift. It was clear that the mentoring program that he had implemented for new faculty was not working as effectively as it was in the beginning.

Nkrumah knew he had to address the dangerous practices and thinking that were creeping into his building. *How could these negative and harmful ways of thinking infiltrate the inner workings of his school? How could he stop the harm being done to the students on a daily basis?* He longed for the days when he and his staff were of the same mind. He realized, however, that in the past three years he had become more focused on advocating for resources to keep up with 21st century technology, making sure that testing occurred when it should, making sure that students were present on testing days, and making sure that he followed up on any discipline infractions. He realized that he was taking for granted the basic tenets of cultural proficiency because he trusted the staff that he had grown with over the past 10 years and assumed that they would stay the course and the new teachers would inherit the culture created in the building. Principal Nkrumah realized that he needed to reassess his effectiveness as a leader, reinforce the critical aspects of cultural responsiveness, and create an Action Plan to develop cultural responsiveness and collaboration with families and the community.

That evening, Nkrumah attended the district-wide History Bowl and saw the Chisholm team, made up of white, Latino, and African American students win first place. They would receive scholarships to attend a college tour and trip to Washington D.C. the following summer. Principal Nkrumah knew he had done the right thing by pushing his social studies teachers to promote the study of history and to encourage the students to set the goal of competing in the bowl.

Principal Nkrumah surveyed this success and the many other positive things he had in place already that could be leveraged to reinforce cultural competency among his staff. Chisholm's school-wide leadership team had been established two years ago and met bi-weekly to assess progress toward school goals. This was the first year parents and a community member were included on the team. Everyone thought this was an important addition but also recognized some challenges.

Principal Nkrumah decided to start discussing what he noticed with the staff; he called a faculty meeting for the next day. After shaking everyone's hand as they entered the room and asking for any celebrations, as was his customary start to his meetings, Principal Nkrumah began. "I have been thinking, reflecting and observing our school's operations—how we do business—how we interact with each other, our students and caregivers, and I've noticed that we need some fine-tuning and some re-teaching and teaching on our core principles. We begin every year by recommitting ourselves to these core principles. Some of them include valuing each student as a capable and valuable person in our class. We believe that all students are capable of achieving academic excellence and pursuing their dreams. We believe that we should cultivate students' interests and expose them to other content that extends their thinking about the world around them. We believe that students are educated in order to discover the world. The other point I want to stress is that we believe that families and parents are assets to us. They are our partners and we welcome them in our endeavor to educate their children. Think about these beliefs to which you have committed. How well are you upholding them? How well are *we* upholding them? What are your thoughts?" Mrs. Reyes, a veteran teacher who has been at Chisholm longer than even Principal Nkrumah started by asking, "What happened to the days when we partnered with the Arbor Hills Nursing Home and brought seniors in to discuss history with our students?"

Other veteran teachers chimed in and bemoaned the "good old days" when community members were interested in their students and activities. Tracy Goldberg, one of the new teachers hired this year said, "Oh! That's a cool idea! How come we don't do that anymore? My students would love that!"

"Well, back in the old days you could just invite people in. Now, everyone has to have a background check and sign away their life in order to interact with students."

"Yeah; times have really changed." Mrs. Reyes added, "We stopped asking for an area business to adopt our school about three years ago because Mr. Jackson (the literacy specialist) just couldn't coordinate it on top of all of his other duties. It burned him out." Principal Nkrumah interjected, "Okay. Even though times have changed and we have security requirements in place to protect our students, we can still revisit how to interact with people in the community in order to make our curriculum come alive."

Mrs. Foxwood, the music teacher, complained, "Many of our students don't feel like what we teach matters to them. They only want to be basketball players or the next hot rap star!" Ms. Noble said, "I'm sorry but I don't even know why the curriculum matters. I'm just following along with the curriculum map so I don't get in trouble for not complying with our national and state standards."

Ms. DeJean stated that she just did not see how she could focus on science all the time when she knew some of her students were hungry, or were going home at night where the heat wasn't working. She said, "I read about Maslow's hierarchy and how students can't learn if they are hungry. I don't want to push them too hard. I feel bad that they have so many strikes against them in society and I want to support them."

Principal Nkrumah gently reminded Ms. DeJean, "Remember, our job is to go beyond feeding and clothing students in poverty. We must uphold high academic standards and support them to reach those standards."

Mr. Jackson, the literacy specialist, stood up and said, "Exactly! So, how is babying them going to help? What are you teaching them? To give up? You can't be part of the solution if you're just going to treat them like a bunch of babies." The room fell silent as people looked dejected and worn out.

Principal Nkrumah asked, "What about what we are doing? What can we control that we are not doing to the best of our ability? Are you calling parents when there are discipline issues? Do we know our students and their families? Think about this. How often do you take time to get to know your students and their families? In what are they interested? What are their hopes and dreams? How can we connect that to their learning? We are going to reconsider our school improvement plan with these issues in mind. The next time we meet we will establish some new goals for cultural responsiveness.

Three days later, after school, Principal Nkrumah asked George Burrell to stop by and see him in his office.

George: What's up, Principal?

Principal: I had a conversation with your dad the other day after our talk about your t-shirt. The one that, coincidentally, you are wearing today.

George: Yeah; he told me that you called him and said you were concerned that I didn't believe I could attend Harvard, or something like that.

George shrugged and smiled.

Principal: Well, that's it. I want you to choose your own path, but I want you to choose it without limitations. If you decide to attend the local state school, or travel in Africa for a year after graduation, it's your choice, but my mission is to provide as much opportunity for all of my students to see they are not limited by anything other than what they want to do.

George: Okay; no disrespect, but what does that have to do with my t-shirt?

Principal: Your dad and I talked about how this could be a fad or a joke, but it seems like you are sending a message that you aren't good enough or capable enough to do anything you want.

George: Yeah; my mom said the same thing.

Principal: Great. Three very important adults in your life agree. What does that mean to you?

George: I mean, I don't think the shirt means all that, but I respect your opinion.

Principal: Well, I didn't want to tear down your choice without offering you an alternative. Check out what's in the bag. Your parents and I agree that this is something you can wear with pride.

George opened the bag and pulled out a Columbia Law School t-shirt. He smiled.

Principal: I remember last year you gave a report on Eric Holder and said you admired him. I thought you might want to go to his alma mater. Of course, you don't have to go there, but I don't want the reason to be because you don't see yourself there.

George was silent. Then he said,

George: Thank you, Principal Nkrumah. This means a lot. And thank you for listening to me.

Principal: Oh. I would also like to get your input—maybe you and some of your friends—on some new empowering posters for the hallways. What do you think?

George: Sure, Principal Nkrumah. Thank you. *George put the new shirt on and stuffed the other one in his backpack. Well, it's a start, thought the Principal.*

These interactions had Nkrumah thinking more and more about the mounting challenges at SCES associated with a lack of respect for parents by teachers and an unwillingness on the part of many teachers to commit to bringing about success for all students. Even though Mr. Nkrumah set the expectation that teachers will call parents any time they experience discipline issues, he personally called the Sherwin home because he wanted them to know that he was concerned about Jeff's behavior and that he was working to figure out how to support him and Mrs. Foxwood. During the phone conversation, Mr. Sherwin committed to holding Jeff accountable for anything he was doing wrong, but he just did not know that he could trust Ms. Foxwood's interpretation of her son's behavior. "Look, Mr. Nkrumah, three of my four children have been through your school in the past 10 years and you know that I hold them accountable and expect them to be on their best behavior. The thing is, when Jeff comes home sometimes he says that Ms. Foxwood doesn't like him. He says that she picks on him. He says they created classroom rules, but she only picks out certain ones to enforce. She's only called our house twice and she didn't have anything positive to say." The concern for the increasing divide between teachers and parents was growing.

During the monthly Parent Association meeting, Ms. Brown, the mother of a second grader and a set of fourth grade twins, asked, "How come so few of the teachers seem to live in our community anymore? It's hard to see an investment in our school and families when they don't even live around here. I mean, people have a right to live where they want to, but the reason so many of us believe in you is because we see you in our community. I mean, do your new teachers even know anything about us?"

Mr. Konkel, the parent of a fifth grade student, chimed in. "And why did one of your staff sound so surprised when I answered the phone? He asked for my son's parent, but it sounded like he thought he would talk to his mother—like there are no fathers in the homes around here."

Mrs. Burrell stated, "We believe in you and we want to stay committed to this school. But, we want to be assured that our students continue to get the best education at this school.

We see we need to be more of a part of the school, but we can't come to school during the business day. It doesn't mean we don't care about our children. Yeah, I know everybody here doesn't work two jobs, but I do. I don't want you or your staff to think I don't care just because I don't come to listen to student's speeches or to chaperone field trips."

It wasn't just at parent meetings where Principal Nkrumah heard the concerns of the mothers and fathers of SCES students. Principal Nkrumah had promised a group of 4th grade girls that he would attend one of their Saturday basketball games before the semester ended, so he took the opportunity to attend one on Saturday morning. After the game, Lucy Parker, the mother of one of the student-athletes, waited for Principal Nkrumah to finish shaking hands and exchanging greetings with the other parents from both teams. It took a while because Principal Nkrumah had a story to share and a question to catch up on about the students of practically every family in attendance. Ms. Parker finally approached him.

Parker: Mr. Nkrumah I'm glad I caught up with you today. Can I get your ear for a few minutes?

Principal: Of course, what's going on?

Parker: You know, I love sending my kids to your school—really our school—but my biggest issue is that the math is so different from when I was a kid. I don't know how to do this math. My daughter, Stephanie, comes home and asks for help on her homework and I don't know how to do it. And I'm not illiterate or dumb. I didn't learn math that way. "How come the teacher can't teach her how to do the math in the class? Why do I have to re-teach it?"

Principal: That's a good question, Ms. Parker. We are examining some of our practices and this is an important one to add. Our teachers have to remember that instructional time is to teach the content and homework is to extend and apply what has been taught. Thank you for this reminder.

Principal Nkrumah realized how important it was to revisit what some of the veteran staff may consider the basics of communicating and connecting to students and families. But, he also realized that he and many of the veteran staff had not necessarily been *taught* how to relate to the students and families in the school community, because they either grew up in that community or in a similar urban environment. He decided that the best way to identify the needs of everyone—the students, staff, families and community members—was to create an action plan that placed several core ideas at the center: building cultural responsiveness, examining beliefs about the students and families, teaching, communication and relationships.

Principal Nkrumah developed an outline of essential points to be explored and presented them at the next school leadership team meeting. For this meeting, he issued an open call to any staff who wanted to come, stating that they were developing a new plan to foster increased cultural responsiveness at Chisholm. He emphasized the importance of (1) teachers being self reflective in terms of their own cultural identity and in terms of how they feel about the students with who they work, (2) believing that all students can be successful, (3) parents being encouraged to play a key role in the education of their children and, perhaps most importantly, (4) realizing that cultural responsive education requires enabling students to see themselves in the curriculum.

At the next school leadership team meeting, Principal Nkrumah was surprised to see an increased number of teachers in attendance, all displaying high levels of energy. Principal Nkrumah asked for their feedback on his preliminary questions about the central points for inquiry. He stated their task was to brainstorm questions and ideas followed by developing a plan to present to the staff. He started:

- How do we examine our beliefs and expectations about what students can achieve?
- What data will we use? How do we measure progress?
- What do we know about our students, families and the community?

Some of the teachers agreed that it was important to start by placing the students at the center. They added:

- Getting to know or refamiliarize ourselves with the families and community—What can we learn from them? How might we include them in school decision making?

Two of the parents thought it might be interesting to encourage some activities:

- Encourage staff to do partner visits to homes.
- Get to know the community. Attend a worship service. Attend a community sports event.

The teachers were very excited about the prospect of a community partnership. Principal Nkrumah asked them what they were specifically excited about. One of the teachers responded, "Maybe they can help us by donating materials and paying for field trips and extracurricular activities." Another teacher added,

"Maybe they can help us with some job shadowing and some career exploration, like maybe help us with a career fair!" Mr. Grange asked, "How do these activities help us learn though? We're benefiting from their services, but I think we need to remember that a partnership works two ways."

The teachers continued to problem solve around what it means to be collaborators with families and community organizations. After an hour, they presented a five-point plan to present to the rest of the staff. The group agreed to introduce the plan based on the following two questions:

- How will we transform our learning about culturally responsive education into goals and action steps for improving our relationships, instruction and interactions with students?
- What resources should be at the center of our learning?
- How will we monitor and assess progress toward those goals?

At the end of the staff meeting where the leadership team presented and discussed the professional development plan, two veteran staff, Mr. Nickels and Mrs. Goldsby, approached Principal Nkrumah. Mrs. Goldsby said,

> Principal Nkrumah, you know we have been here with you from the beginning and we believe in your mission. But we both will retire at the end of next year. We just don't have the energy to do all of this. We put our time in and got to know the community back when we started. We've built relationships with students' families who have all gone on and graduated from high school. We don't want to go out anymore. I just don't see how we can sustain all of this action. Plus, you know they just rezoned that low-income housing development within our service area next year; that's going to be a whole new set of issues.

Mr. Nickels added, "Besides, we're not getting paid for any of this extra time, so we respectfully decline to participate. We think we're naturally culturally responsive, anyway. We'll do our part during the school day."

Although the planning meeting ended on a discouraging note, when he stopped at the grocery store, Principal Nkrumah ran into Doris Christiansen, the mother of one of Ms. Noble's students who the principal witnessed in class with his head down, unengaged.

She said to him, "Hi Principal Nkrumah! Andre has been coming home a little more excited about his class. He even told me what he was learning even though he didn't really know much about it. And, Ms. Noble called me yesterday to let me know he's improving. She seemed a little uncomfortable, but I appreciated the effort."

The exchange encouraged Principal Nkrumah to keep forging ahead to pave the way for academic excellence for all of the students in his building. Nkrumah knew, however, that much more effort would be needed to provide a truly culturally responsive learning environment at Shirley Chisholm Elementary School. He was committed to providing the necessary leadership to take the school where it needed to go to be all that it could be for every student.

DISCUSSION QUESTIONS

1. In what ways did Principal Nkrumah demonstrate confidence that all of his students could achieve?
2. Explain how Principal Nkrumah's ethic of caring for students and the community went beyond empathizing with them, or feeling sorry for them.
3. How did Principal Nkrumah establish trusting relationships with his staff? students? families?
4. How did Principal Nkrumah promote culturally responsive instruction in his role as an instructional leader?
5. What questions would you use to review the lesson with Mrs. Foxwood?
6. How did Principal Nkrumah interact with families? How did he view them as assets?
7. Knowing that the goal of the school's new professional development plan is to build capacity to be culturally responsive educators, what action steps are critical for the faculty and staff at Chisholm Elementary? What lessons can the staff take from Principal Nkrumah's modeling to form their plan?
8. How might Principal Nkrumah address Mr. Nickels and Mrs. Goldsby?
9. What do you think were the most impactful culturally responsive strategies or actions Principal Nkrumah employed with students, staff, and/or families?
10. What actions raised questions for you?

REFERENCE

Lomotey, K. (1989). Cultural diversity in the urban school: Implications for principals. *NASSP Bulletin*, *73*(521), 81–85.

CHAPTER EIGHT

Developing Effective Learning Communities

The Power of Principal and PLC Leadership Team Collaboration

JESSICA R. WEILER AND KATHLEEN TOPOLKA-JORISSEN

COLLABORATIVE LEADERSHIP FOR THE DEVELOPMENT OF EFFECTIVE LEARNING COMMUNITIES

In recent years, many principals have assumed the challenge of implementing professional learning communities (PLCs) to foster school improvement. Whether motivated by the reported benefits of learning communities (Annenberg Institute for School Reform 2005; Carroll, Fulton, & Doerr, 2010; Gupton, 2003; Holland, 2005; Jaquith, 2013; Louis, Leithwood, Wahlstrom, & Anderson, 2010; Newmann & Wehlage, 1995; Vescio, Ross, & Adams, 2008) or by a district mandate, principals have been widening the scope of leadership to include teachers in collaborative efforts to improve student achievement. In many cases, they do so without a clear understanding of their own leadership role in this process or the critical steps needed to implement learning communities successfully.

Professional learning communities engage educators in working collaboratively to increase student achievement (DuFour, DuFour, Eaker, & Many, 2006; Hord, 2008). Although the concepts and processes of the PLC have been evolving in schools for over 20 years, definitive research on the supports needed for PLC success has been limited. Consensus on the key role played by the principal is strong, but specifics about what that role entails are somewhat limited, and even more scarce is research on strategies principals should use to ensure that PLCs achieve maximum effectiveness. In this chapter, we draw upon the research that *does* exist, in addition to our own experiences working with school leaders to implement learning communities. We identify four *critical leadership steps* for principals and other school leaders who seek to build effective PLCs. These four steps suggest a model for collaborative leadership—a novel concept in an era when educators are still trying to break strong norms of privacy (Elmore, 2003a, 2003b; Fulton, Yoon, & Lee, 2005; Little, 1990; Louis, Leithwood, Wahlstrom, & Anderson, 2010) and to act, instead, from a belief in collaboration to improve teaching and learning (Conzemius & O'Neill, 2001; Drago-Severson & Pinto, 2006). Moving from individual to collaborative work, however, calls upon educators to move from comfort zones into new professional social territory. That includes principals, all of whom are cognizant of expectations that they demonstrate results.

Seeking to increase the capacity of educators to engage in collaborative work, namely the development of effective PLCs, principals must take each step outlined below, with the understanding that the steps are not sequential but rather iterative, with tasks of some steps supporting the accomplishment of other steps. It is critical, though, to address each of the steps thoroughly and strategically, working with the leadership team to ensure that, over time, each phase of the process is strengthened as steps are revisited, responding to emerging needs of the leadership team as it facilitates PLC work. Principals often minimize or skip these steps entirely, for a variety of reasons. They may not understand the purpose of each step or how to accomplish them. Frequently, they feel under the gun to show results quickly, and they may be inclined to rush the process. Recent literature substantiates the pressure to move quickly to demonstrate improvement in the face of accountability standards that require rapid change (Fuhrman & Elmore, 2004). At the same time, research suggests that large scale improvement initiatives do, indeed, take a significant amount of time (Louis, 1994) and that the long-term sustainability of effective PLCs requires a paradigm shift from a compliance stance to one of ongoing capacity building (Mitchell & Sackney, 2009). In reading this chapter, principals and district leaders interested in sustained school improvement, rather than a quick fix, will gain knowledge of four steps to lay the foundation for sustained productive professional learning communities.

STEP ONE: BUILD A STRONG, COLLABORATIVE PLC LEADERSHIP TEAM

The first step in the process is to begin to build an organizational structure that supports and fosters a collaborative school culture. Creating a strong, collaborative PLC Leadership Team is essential for PLCs to be successful (Herrity & Morales, 2004). The PLC Leadership Team must clearly be defined as an enabling structure, rather than a part of a new level of the school hierarchy. This structure facilitates teacher problem-solving in an environment where expertise and professional judgment are valued, where teachers are empowered (DiPaola & Hoy, 2008, p. 37) and where teachers "exercise leadership within a coherent collegial framework rather than as a response to the exercise of power applied from the top down" (Frost & Durrant, 2004, p. 310). Schools and districts give their PLC Leadership Teams a variety of titles to fit their cultures and norms, but whatever the title, this leadership team works together to provide sustained support to the rest of the school community in developing PLCs. Although the principal provides developmental support for the leadership team, particularly in its initial stages, the strength of a team in which multiple leaders enter into interdependent relationships to achieve a collective goal or purpose has been firmly established in the literature (Gardner, 1993; Kouzes & Posner, 2008; Yukl, 2009). Just as the principal provides developmental support for the leadership team, the team itself provides developmental support necessary to build the capacity of all of the PLCs within the school.

Rationale for Building a Leadership Team

The importance of starting the process by building a leadership team cannot be overstated. Research has substantiated causal relationships between educator collaboration and student achievement (Goddard, Goddard, & Tschannen-Moran, 2007; Louis, Leithwood, Wahlstrom, & Anderson, 2010), the development of leadership capacity among teachers (Rasberry & Mahajan, 2008), and "a vehicle that allows principals to execute a number of the responsibilities of school leadership in an integrated and focused fashion" (DuFour & Marzano, 2011, p. 52). Most importantly, the leadership team serves the pivotal role in coordinating information gathering, guiding the vision-making process, and facilitating communication within the school community (Burke & Cavalier, 2004).

Identifying PLC Leadership Team Members

Because one of the primary roles of the leadership team is to communicate with others in the school community, including disseminating information to and assessing the progress of all PLCs in the school, the members of the leadership team should represent the key stakeholders. For example, one school may have a leadership team with a principal, assistant principal, instructional coach, and classroom teachers representing each grade-level or content area. Another school's leadership team may have a principal, lead teacher, math coach, literacy coach, and representative classroom teachers. Some schools also include parent or community representation, student representatives, and representatives from the support staff. Although team make-up can vary, it is critical that classroom teachers be included and serve as both equal leaders and representatives of *their* teacher-team (McLaughlin, 1991). In some schools, each teacher-team has a leader who also serves as a member of the school-wide PLC Leadership Team. In other schools (typically large schools) the teachers who serve on the PLC Leadership Team represent multiple teacher-teams within a department.

To ensure that the PLC Leadership Team members are well qualified for their role, principals should consider asking teachers to apply to serve on the leadership team and develop a process to provide the principal and other leaders with a clear picture of the applicant's qualifications. Qualifications desirable in team members include a range of beliefs, knowledge and skills, including a commitment to building knowledge, practice, and leadership through professional learning (Mitchell & Sackney, 2009) a commitment to the PLC process (DuFour and Marzano, 2011), a sense of self and team efficacy (DuFour and Marzano, 2011; Mitchell & Sackney, 2009) an ability to inspire and influence others (DuFour and Marzano, 2011; Mitchell & Sackney, 2009) and skill in systems thinking (Isaacson & Bamburg, 1992; Martin & Chrispeels, 2004;) Example interview questions and prompts for applicants might include: (1) Why have you decided to apply for this position, (2) What is your vision for our school's PLC, (3) Include a description of what our PLC will look like and the outcomes it will produce, (4) Describe your leadership experiences in education and outside of the field of education, (5) Describe the training/professional learning opportunities you have experienced related to learning communities, and (6) Are you prepared to lead your peers through this process, even when conflict arises?

Many schools struggle to build a qualified leadership team when resources are scarce. Asking teachers to complete this important, challenging work in addition to the work they are already doing, without additional compensation through time and/or money, may be met with resistance in many schools. However, creative principals develop ways to compensate teacher leaders for such extra responsibilities. For example, principals may hire a team of substitutes for one day a month to sub for a half-day leadership teamwork session. Another strategy is to regroup classes, so that teams cover for a colleague's time while they are working with the leadership team. Most importantly, the principal does not have to work alone to solve this dilemma; leadership teams have proven very effective in developing creative ways to carve out the needed time for accomplishing the work.

STEP TWO: INCREASE THE LEADERSHIP CAPACITY OF PLC LEADERSHIP TEAM MEMBERS

Capacity building for leadership team members increases not only their effectiveness within the leadership team, but also prepares them for fostering collegial learning. In fact, all effective learning communities provide continuous, job-embedded learning opportunities for educators. The research-based connection between teacher learning and student learning (Annenberg Institute for School Reform, 2005; DuFour &

Marzano, 2011; Goddard et al., 2007; Holland, 2005; Vescio et al., 2008) supports the need for school leaders to embrace their role as a capacity builder and to make it a top priority.

The principal's responsibility is to work with the PLC Leadership Team to: (1) identify the desired learning outcomes for its members, (2) choose and/or develop professional learning opportunities for the accomplishment of those outcomes, (3) develop a comprehensive plan for building the capacity of faculty to perform effectively within a learning community, and (4) facilitate and support the success of the PLC Leadership Team members. These four tasks are iterative, with each supporting the accomplishment of the others. For example, while engaged in the process of identifying team learning outcomes, the members of the team will also practice many of the process skills they need to function well as a team. This section details these four responsibilities as they relate to the capacity development of the PLC Leadership Team members. In Step 4, *Build the Infrastructure to Operationalize your PLC*, we will return to these responsibilities with a different lens—capacity development for teachers on teacher-teams.

Identify the Desired Learning Outcomes

In order to identify the desired learning outcomes for PLC Leadership Team members, the team must begin by creating a collective vision for their school's PLC. (See Step 3: Collectively Define and Create a Vision.) With a shared vision, the team will be able to identify the roles and responsibilities they must assume and the skills they need to facilitate achievement of the vision. Examples of primary responsibilities in the initial stages of PLC Leadership Team development often include, but are not limited to:

- Developing a collective vision, goals and an action plan for implementing the PLC and facilitating or participating in those activities
- Building an infrastructure that supports teacher-collaboration (See Step 4: Build the Infrastructure to Operationalize your PLC)
- Serving as capacity builders: helping teachers, faculty, staff, and students understand the PLC construct and the expectations for moving forward
- Serving as team support providers to help build strong teams or intervene when teams experience conflict

In the table below, these four roles and responsibilities are paired with possible desired learning outcomes. Although PLC Leadership Teams might choose to use, adjust, or expand upon some of these examples when determining their responsibilities, teams must collectively construct their own roles/responsibilities and desired learning outcomes as a processes for learning and collective sense-making (Coburn, 2001).

Table 8.1. Connecting PLC Leadership Team Roles and Responsibilities with Learning Outcome.

Possible Roles and Responsibilities of the PLC Leadership Team Members	Possible Desired Learning Outcomes for the PLC Leadership Team Members
Develop collective vision, goals and an action plan for implementation of the PLC and facilitate or participate in those activities Collectively develop the expectations for faculty and teacher-team behavior/ performance within the PLC	1. PLC Leadership Team members will gain common, foundational knowledge of the PLC construct and PLC leadership. 2. PLC Leadership Team members will increase their understanding of a variety of functioning PLCs across their district, region, state, and/or country.
Build an infrastructure that supports teacher-collaboration (e.g. changing the master schedule)	PLC Leadership Team members will increase their understanding of the literature supporting effective PLC infrastructure, as well as, a variety of functioning PLCs across their district, region, state, and/or country.
Serve as capacity builders, helping teachers, faculty, staff, and students understand the PLC construct and the leadership's expectations for moving forward	1. PLC Leadership Team members will gain common, foundational knowledge of the PLC construct and PLC leadership. 2. PLC Leadership Team members will build their capacity to identify criteria for team success and communicate this criteria to teacher-teams. Members will build their capacity to: (1) identify teacher-teams that are performing with fidelity, (doing "the right work" as identified by the leadership team) and (2) support teacher-teams who are struggling, or not meeting the fidelity requirements.
Serve as team support providers to help develop strong teams or intervene when teams experience conflict	PLC Leadership Team members will increase their capacity to build and maintain strong teams, as well as, intervene when teams experience conflict

Choose and/or Develop Professional Learning Opportunities

As the leadership team works together to identify desired learning outcomes, the members will also learn and practice skills needed to function effectively on a team, such as establishing trust (Annenberg Institute for School Reform, 2005; Herrity & Morales, 2004), maintaining effective communications (Mitchell & Sackney, 2009; Roberts & Pruitt, 2009), consensus building and conflict resolution (Martin & Chrispeels, 2004; Mitchell & Sackney, 2009), and celebrating their achievements (Cziko, 2008; Louis, 2008; Mitchell & Sackney, 2009; Pascal & Blankstein, 2008; Roberts & Pruitt, 2009). This type of job-embedded professional development not only builds the capacity of the leadership team members but also prepares them for choosing and/or developing appropriate professional learning opportunities for the accomplishment of their identified goals. The team's familiarity with the school culture and the readiness of teachers to engage in collaborative learning will enable them to choose or develop learning activities along a continuum ranging from novice to advanced (Allen & Topolka-Jorissen, 2016), grounded in the experiential knowledge of the power of job-embedded learning. Another table is provided below. The first two columns repeat the information in the table provided above. A third column (shaded) connects team purpose and desired learning outcomes with possible professional learning opportunities.

Table 8.2. Template for Professional Development to Build PLC Leadership Team Capacity.

Possible Roles and Responsibilities of the PLC Leadership Team Members	Possible Desired Learning Outcomes of the PLC Leadership Team Members	Possible Professional Learning Opportunities for the PLC Leadership Team Members.
Developing collective vision, goals and an action plan for implementation of the PLC and facilitating or participating in those activities Collectively develop the expectations for faculty and teacher-team behavior/performance within the PLC	1. PLC Leadership Team members will gain common, foundational knowledge of the PLC construct and PLC leadership. 2. PLC Leadership Team members will increase their understanding of a variety of functioning PLCs across their district, region, state, and/or country.	• Attend workshops, seminars, or conferences that provide foundational knowledge for implementing and leading learning communities in schools. Ensure opportunities for the team to discuss what they are learning and achieve a collective understanding. • Book group using a text or texts that provide foundational knowledge • Webinars and other on-line presentations • Literature reviews

(*Continued*)

Table 8.2. (*Continued*)

Possible Roles and Responsibilities of the PLC Leadership Team Members	Possible Desired Learning Outcomes of the PLC Leadership Team Members	Possible Professional Learning Opportunities for the PLC Leadership Team Members.
		• University courses • Work with a learning communities consultant who can provide trainings specific to the educational context • Visits to functioning PLCs across the district, region, state, and/or country.
Building an infrastructure that supports teacher-collaboration (e.g. changing the master schedule)	PLC Leadership Team members will increase their understanding of the literature supporting effective PLC infrastructure, as well as, a variety of functioning PLCs across their district, region, state, and/or country.	• Visits to functioning PLCs across the district, region, state, and/or country. • Attend workshops, seminars, or conferences that provide foundational knowledge for implementing and leading learning communities in schools • Work with a learning communities consultant who can provide trainings specific to the educational context
Serving as capacity builders, helping teachers, faculty, staff, and students understand the PLC construct and the leadership's expectations for moving forward	1. PLC Leadership Team members will gain common, foundational knowledge of the PLC construct and PLC leadership. 2. PLC Leadership Team members will build their capacity to identify criteria for team success and communicate this criteria to teacher-teams. Members will build their capacity to: (1) identify teacher-teams that are performing with fidelity, (doing "the right work" as identified by the leadership team) and (2) support teacher-teams who are struggling, or not meeting the fidelity requirements.	• Attend workshops, seminars, or conferences that provide foundational knowledge for implementing and leading learning communities in schools, as well as knowledge regarding team productivity and effectiveness • Book group using a text or texts that provide foundational knowledge • Webinars and other on-line presentations • Literature reviews • University courses • Work with a learning communities consultant who can provide trainings specific to the educational context and assist with identifying criteria for team success • Observations of effective teacher-teams across the district, region, state, and/or country.

(*Continued*)

Possible Roles and Responsibilities of the PLC Leadership Team Members	Possible Desired Learning Outcomes of the PLC Leadership Team Members	Possible Professional Learning Opportunities for the PLC Leadership Team Members.
Serving as team support providers to help develop strong teams or intervene when teams experience conflict	PLC Leadership Team members will increase their capacity to build and maintain strong teams, as well as, intervene when teams experience conflict	• Attend workshops, seminars, or conferences that target effective team building and team conflict resolution • The lists of learning opportunities above could be repeated here, with an emphasis on learning opportunities related to team development, growth and sustainability.

Develop a Comprehensive Plan for Building the Capacity of Faculty

As teachers begin to transform the school culture into a collaborative one, they also redefine their roles as teachers. Capacity building, then, is needed to support the development of professional identity. Areas for development include the capacities for honest dialogue, for generating new knowledge, for applying new learning to professional practice, and for publically sharing practice (Lieberman & Miller, 2008). Understanding the principles of adult learning is important in developing a comprehensive professional development plan. Many resources are available (see Drago-Severson, 2009; Katzenmeyer & Moller, 2001; Learning Forward, 2011; Roberts & Pruitt, 2009). Learning Forward (https://learningforward.org), an association that focuses on the professional development of educators has developed seven research-based professional development standards that connect educator learning to student learning (Learning Forward, 2011). Those standards (learning in PLCs, strong leadership, allocation of resources, focus on student learning outcomes, use of data, effective learning designs, and implementation that addresses and supports the complexity of change) are reflected in the model presented here. We encourage PLC Leadership Teams to review these standards in detail when designing professional development plans for capacity building. Using the standards as part of a planning template will ensure that plans will engage and prepare the professional community to apply their learning to achieve the intended outcomes.

Although plans may reflect a range of formats and components, depending on the needs of the organization, leaders should include a time frame and ensure the adequacy of resources necessary to make the chosen learning opportunity happen.

For example, when will the team members attend a seminar or work session? How much will it cost? Will we need to pay for substitute teachers? What are the funding sources? Is there an approval process with district leaders? The plan should also include documentation describing how the learning outcomes will be measured and assessed. For example, did all team members attend the seminar? How did the team members apply what they learned? Did the team achieve the desired learning outcomes? How do we know? A comprehensive capacity building plan underscores the leader's commitment to the application and long-term sustainability of professional learning.

Facilitate and Support the PLC Leadership Team Members

Although the PLC Leadership Team should execute the three responsibilities described above collaboratively, each requires principal facilitation and support. The PLC Leadership Team must have a leader. In most cases, this would be the principal or an assistant principal. We have seen some teams choose an administrator and a teacher to co-lead, so that responsibilities are shared and school leaders and teachers are represented. This also helps when the leaders need to assess the progress of the PLC Leadership Team. Co-leadership sets up a forum for idea exchange and collaborative problem solving when the PLC Leadership Team is struggling to move forward. Co-leadership also serves as a safeguard when one leader is unexpectedly unavailable to lead. We have also encouraged principals to (re)allocate resources in a way that allows someone to serve *solely* as the leader of the school's PLCs and the PLC Leadership Team. In other words, that person has no other responsibilities outside of PLC leadership.

Beyond facilitation of team meetings, action plans, and the formative assessment of team and PLC performance, leaders, including PLC Leadership Team members, should look for ways to support leadership teams both directly and indirectly. Support includes resources such as time, direct and indirect compensation, access to data, technology, school and district experts and support staff, and on- and off-site meeting space. Most importantly, teams need time to collaborate. With respect to time, team members must be given a sufficient amount of time outside of their regular classroom duties to do the work of the PLC Leadership Team and to do it well. Principals who value the work of the PLC Leadership Team will work with the leadership team to find ways to clear the members' plates of extraneous duties to focus on the critical work of the team. Step Four provides additional information on how principals and PLC Leadership Teams build a supportive infrastructure including time (re) allocation.

STEP THREE: COLLECTIVELY DEFINE AND CREATE A VISION

Collectively defining a vision to serve as a beacon for the leadership team and the school's PLCs is widely acknowledged as an essential initial task (DuFour, DuFour, & Eaker, 2008; Harris, 2004; Hord & Sommers, 2008; Isaacson & Bamburg, 1992). Yet, we have noticed great variations in how school leaders define, envision and operationalize the learning community model within their school. These differences stem from disparate "sense-making" (Weick, 1995) on the part of school leaders. School leaders make sense of improvement initiatives, in this case the learning community construct, by integrating their interpretation of both the information received from professional learning opportunities and instructions provided by their district leaders (Coburn, 2005; Rigby, 2015). Since PLC Leadership Team members arrive with different interpretations of the PLC construct, the team must commit to and work toward collective sense-making that often occurs when the team defines and creates a vision for their PLC. Our experiences suggest that the work of collaboratively defining and envisioning a context-specific learning community is challenging and often mitigated when teams begin with a shared, desired outcome or aim. What is the goal of the learning community? What are the outcomes we seek from the creation of our PLC? We do not argue in support of one, single definition or promote one, ideal vision. We do, however, support definitions and visions that connect the work of teacher-teams to the advancement of student learning.

A wide range of definitions exists for the term professional learning community (PLC) within the educational field. In 1997, Shirley Hord extracted a definition from the work of earlier scholars, "The professional community of learners in which the teachers in a school and its administrators continuously seek and share learning, and act on their learning. The goal of their actions is to enhance their effectiveness as professionals for the students' benefit" (Hord, 1997, p. 10). Hargreaves and Fullan suggested:

> They are places where teachers [and teams of teachers] constantly inquire into learning and problems together, drawing on their different experiences of particular children or strategies, and on what the evidence they can collect is telling them—about the best way to approach a child, a different curriculum concept, an unfamiliar innovation, or a group of learners who are falling behind. And they are places where teachers don't just endure but actively enjoy challenging and being challenged by their colleagues and their administrators [in a spirit of continuous improvement]. (Hargreaves & Fullan, 2012, p. 143)

Other leaders and scholars at the forefront of the PLC movement suggests that a PLC is:

> An ongoing process in which educators work collaboratively in recurring cycles of collective inquiry and action research to achieve better results for the students they

> serve. Professional learning communities operate under the assumption that the key to improved learning for students is continuous job-embedded learning for educators. (DuFour et al., 2006, p. 2)

These three definitions present common terminology that teams might reference to refine their collective definition including: *collaboration, teams, student learning, teacher learning, inquiry, and improvement.* Unfortunately, a common definition does not provide a common vision. We often ask leadership teams working toward a collective vision, "What would guests, coming to visit your PLC, *observe* as components or characteristics of your PLC?" Much of the resulting discussion focuses upon the performance of teacher-teams. More specifically, what would guests observe teacher-teams doing? In our view, effective teacher-teams are the engine of strong, effective learning communities, underscoring the need for school leaders to provide both a clear vision of, and clear expectations for, the work of teacher-teams. Other potential questions we have asked to prompt collective sense-making include: How would this look inside and outside of the classroom with respect to teacher and student behavior? Scholars and educators alike continue to build on the literature describing teacher-teams and detailing their work. As with the definition of a school-wide learning community, educators do not have one common definition, view or understanding of teacher-teams and the work they *should* do to advance student learning. David Jacobsen (2010) articulated three approaches for teacher-team work. The first, or "inquiry oriented" approach describes school leaders with minimal involvement in team decision making or efforts. School leaders direct teacher-teams to lead themselves through an inquiry process for improved teaching and learning. Alternatively, the "results-oriented approach" describes school leaders as heavily involved in determining the team's work, often focusing the team on assessment. Seeing benefits and flaws to both approaches, Jacobson promotes a third avenue, which he calls the "common priorities" approach, defining it as a blend of the first two. He further illustrates this model as a cycle of continuous activity starting with assessment and moving toward data analysis, goal development and refinement, collaborative lesson design and execution, and a return to assessment (Jacobson, 2010).

We support these activities and have included a framework we designed, that provides additional specificity. Our framework has helped school leaders guide the work of their teacher-teams, especially those who are new to the collaborative process. Although we believe much of the work of the teacher-teams is cyclical, we chose a linear, step-wise orientation to help leaders and teams new to the process: (1) understand the essential components of the team work, (2) set goals for achieving the work and moving forward, (3) provide markers for determining team progress, and (4) suggest areas for team capacity development.

Table 8.3. Results-Oriented Framework for Teacher-Team Work.

Same-Subject or Grade-Level Teacher-Team Work that Advances Student Learning

Step #1: →	**Step #2:** →	**Step #3:** →	**Step #4:** →	**Step #5:** →	**Step #6:**
Teams collaborate to choose common, essential standards.	Teams collaborate to develop common, student-friendly learning goals that stem directly from the chosen standards. **—AND—** The development of common learning goals accompanies a collective determination and development of performance/ success criteria for goal achievement.	Teams collaborate to develop a common pacing guide that includes time-frame targets for: (1) coverage of standards/content, (2) learning goal achievement, and (3) administration of common formative assessments.	Teams collaborate to develop common formative assessments that assess student progress toward achievement of the learning goals. **—AND—** Teams will need to develop or access a system for collecting and sharing common formative assessment data.	Teams collectively analyze common formative assessment data and common student work to: (1) Identify which students have met, not met, or exceeded the learning goal for targeted intervention or enrichment, (2) Identify and share instructional practices that are working, and (3) Identify potentially flawed assessment items and refine assessments in response	(In conjunction with a school-wide, systematic process for responding to student learning) provide timely, targeted intervention and enrichment based upon assessment results.

Teams often choose to complete steps 2–4 in a synchronous fashion--completing steps 2, 3, *and* 4 across a unit or across a standard, as opposed to completing one step before moving on to the next step.

Both of these frameworks can serve as road maps or guides for determining the work of teacher-teams. Both encourage teamwork that connects to the same desired outcome: the advancement of student learning. Although PLC Leadership Teams can certainly construct their own frameworks as guides, we continually emphasize the need for school leaders and teams to collectively commit to a model in order to: (1) ensure a shared understanding of the expectations for team performance, and (2) assist the PLC Leadership Team in its subsequent efforts to operationalize the PLC.

STEP 4: BUILD THE INFRASTRUCTURE TO OPERATIONALIZE YOUR PLC

As with any developing system or organization, new learning communities will fail if the infrastructure is inadequate. Infrastructure is an important consideration, because "the structural arrangements in a school serve as the institutional scaffold on which educational activities are staged, and different sorts of scaffolds enable and anchor different kinds of activity" (Mitchell & Sackney, 2009, p. 133). Although multiple supports are important for both successful PLC implementation and sustainability, four foundational pillars are necessary: (1) adequate time for teacher-team collaboration and response to student learning needs, (2) high levels of teacher-team capacity, (3) leadership focusing on accountability and fidelity, and (4) adequate funding to ensure allocation of the first three. Principals who attend to these pillars will ensure that PLCs have access to resources essential to success.

Adequate Time for Teacher-Team Collaboration and Response to Student Learning Needs

Essential to a supportive infrastructure is the allocation of time for collaboration (Harris, 2004; Lambert, 2003). DuFour and his colleagues stress, "We believe it is insincere and disingenuous for any school district or any school principal to stress the importance of collaboration, and then fail to provide time for collaboration" (DuFour et al., 2006, pp. 95–97). Yet, school leaders continue to struggle to find/allocate adequate amounts of time for collaboration, in part because of the increased emphasis on testing and accountability. School leaders and teachers alike are concerned about reducing the amount of instructional time (time working with students) in order to make time available for collaboration. This concern suggests two underlying assumptions: (1) more instructional time improves student performance on tests, and (2) teacher-collaboration does not necessarily improve student performance on tests. In a report released in February 2009, by researchers from Stanford University and the National Staff Development Council (now *Learning Forward*) these assumptions were debunked. Nations performing at significantly higher levels in educational outcomes were providing less instructional time and more collaborative time than U.S. schools. The Stanford Center for Opportunity Policy in Education detailed the report in an online news release (2009):

> In most countries, about 15 to 20 hours per week is spent on tasks related to teaching, such as preparing lessons, meeting with students and parents, and working with colleagues. By contrast, U.S. teachers generally have from 3 to 5 hours a week for lesson planning, which is done independently. (What Other Nations Do, para 15)

> While rigorous studies indicate that intensive professional development efforts that offer an average of about 50 hours of support a year can make a significant impact on student achievement, raising test scores by an average of 21 percentage points, the majority of teachers in the United States (57 percent) receives no more than about two days (16 hours) of training in their subject areas. Less than one-quarter (23 percent) of all teachers receive more than 36 hours of professional learning in their subject areas. (Progress & Challenges, para 10)

Other common hurdles to increasing collaborative time include state policies requiring schools to schedule a particular amount of instructional time, multiple conflicting priorities (e.g. teachers who advise athletics and extracurricular activities may have little available time outside of student contact hours for meeting with their colleagues), and/or teacher planning periods that vary to accommodate course availability for students. Because of these conflicts, leaders often choose to compromise—requiring only short and/or infrequent collaborative sessions, accepting less than 100% participation (excusing some teachers from participating on their team) or resisting schedule changes entirely and, instead, inappropriately asking teachers to collaborate outside of their contractual or compensated time (e.g., before school, after school, or during their designated lunch period). The result of such compromises: less productivity, discontent, and/or ineffective teacher-teams (Weiler, 2013).

Given the benefit of teacher collaboration, principals and PLC Leadership Teams should commit to finding collaborative time, despite the present challenges they face. Leaders who believe ... are *committed* to teacher-team collaboration for the advancement of student learning, will establish collaborative time as a priority—"a non-negotiable."

We are often asked, "How much time is enough time for teacher-team collaboration?" Not surprisingly, there isn't *one* recommended amount of time. The amount of time needed is dependent on the cohesiveness of the team, the newness and the complexity of the team's task. Leaders often find and/or create large blocks of time (e.g. half and full days) especially for beginning teams, to allow them to dive deeply into the work, which also includes, for many, learning how to collaborate and work on a team. Leaders who monitor the progress of their teams will notice that team performance varies much like student performance in a classroom. Some teams need additional time and support to be successful, and some teams need less. As with excellent teachers, excellent leaders must respond to this variation with differentiated support. Our observations support the need to provide regular collaborative time embedded within the school day as well as compensated collaborative time outside of the school day (e.g. "professional development days" or "teacher work days").

PLC Leadership Teams must also find/create/allocate time in the schedule for teachers to respond to student learning needs. As the two frameworks above suggest, teacher-collaboration alone will not advance student learning. DuFour and colleagues assert that the collaborative teams must go beyond the mere identification of struggling learners and work with school leaders to provide, "… a coordinated intervention plan that ensures that students who struggle receive additional time and support for learning in a way that is timely, directive, diagnostic, precise, and most important, systematic" (DuFour & Mattos, 2013, p. 39). During "results-oriented" collaborative sessions, teachers identify student performance levels in order to determine who is struggling, who is proficient, and who is exceeding expectations for specific learning goals/outcomes. This determination must be followed by opportunities for intervention or enrichment that target the students' areas of need. For example, if a team determines that a student does not meet the success criteria for a learning outcome, the intervention should be provided to help the student achieve the learning outcome. If a student has achieved the outcome, enrichment opportunities should be considered. If school leaders do not provide sufficient opportunities for intervention and enrichment in response to student learning needs they have encouraged collaboration for the sake of collaboration, not for the advancement of student learning/achievement. Unfortunately, the limited amount of time imposed by the master schedule and often dictated by state policies for both teacher-collaboration *and* intervention/enrichment opportunities has encouraged many school leaders to choose one over the other, or to severely limit the time allotted to both, bringing into question whether the collaboration or intervention/enrichment time provided is sufficient enough to have an impact. As with collaborative time, there is not *one* model for how to structure intervention/enrichment time. Individual contextual needs often drive scheduling conversations. Examples of how the master schedule can be adjusted exist at many individual school sites and across the web (e.g. allthingsPLC.info). Once PLC Leadership Teams commit to the need for both collaborative time and intervention/enrichment time, they can begin looking at sample schedules, considering the needs of their community, and working together with all stakeholders to create a new schedule that reflects a commitment to collaborative learning.

High Levels of Teacher-Team Capacity

Not only is individual teacher leadership capacity important, but also the development of team capacity is a required piece of the PLC foundation. Learning sessions for teacher-teams should focus on desired learning outcomes, determined by assessing the collaboration skills of the teachers and targeting areas for development. Useful questions include:

- What do you want your teacher-teams to learn?
- What do you want your teacher-teams to be able to do?
- What is your success criteria? What will successful teacher-teams look like?
- What are your specific expectations for what your teams will do?

Critical content for team learning—content that teams must learn to have a successful start—includes: (1) foundational knowledge of the PLC construct, (2) foundational knowledge for teacher-team collaboration and the characteristics of high-performing teams, (3) an understanding of the PLC model chosen by school leaders as the guide or road-map for team-work, and (4) clear expectations for team-productivity that ensure both fidelity and accountability to the chosen PLC model. Beyond content, format and frequency are key components of a capacity building plan. It is not sufficient to provide one learning opportunity, perhaps in the form of a beginning-of-the-school-year, school-wide in-service. School leaders must consider ways to provide ongoing learning opportunities in an effort to reach: (1) new teachers or other faculty who were not present at the time of the school-wide in-service, (2) faculty who attended but did not fully engage in the learning or understand part or all of the content, and (3) teams who need to re-visit information during team meetings to engage in collective sense-making and planning. As we all know, attendees of a learning session often leave that session with different levels or types of understanding. In order to mitigate the variance and create common understanding, leaders must be willing to provide a variety of ongoing learning opportunities which might include: (1) workshops or seminars provided by PLC Leadership Team members (and/or others with expertise), (2) shared textbooks, (3) guiding frameworks and artifacts developed by the leadership team and/or teacher-teams, (4) digital learning platforms with learning materials, artifacts, video examples or illustrations, and other guiding information, (5) school-wide repository for team constructed artifacts, (6) faculty meetings with embedded learning sessions led by successful teacher-teams, or (7) targeted trainings for specific teacher-teams needing specific capacity development.

Leadership Focusing on Accountability and Fidelity

Another critical piece of the infrastructure is leadership, specifically, ongoing leadership support from school leaders, the PLC Leadership Team, and/or teacher-team leaders that ensures both *accountability* and *fidelity*. Leaders of effective learning communities deliberately participate in specific leadership behaviors to ensure the success of their teams. Unfortunately, school leaders are often expected to develop and lead learning communities without sufficiently building their awareness, understanding, or capacity to perform the necessary leadership behaviors. Certainly, more research is required. In our work with school leaders, however, we have focused on two areas for leadership: *accountability* and *fidelity*. We chose these areas in response to research by Weiler (2013), exploring the perceptions of teachers and teacher-teams of leadership throughout the first year of their school's learning community. Team success was largely dependent on these two variables.

Accountability

A team will not be successful if its members do not consistently meet, follow the co-constructed norms of behavior and actively engage in collaboration for a shared goal. Simply put, teachers/team members must show up and participate. Unfortunately, this seemingly easy directive often produces defiance because of the many barriers facing new teams, including, but not limited to: (1) strong norms of privacy and an unwillingness to share one's educational practices, (2) reduced levels of "buy-in" to the PLC construct and the suggested impact on students, and (3) an unwillingness to give up one's individual planning time or other non-student contact time. It is the leader's responsibility to understand these challenges and work with the PLC Leadership Team to mitigate them over time. In the interim, leaders must demonstrate their commitment to learning communities/teacher-teams by creating accountability systems that ensure all team members are meeting and contributing to the work of the team. Accountability systems should include three components: (1) a way to document participation (amount and type), (2) a process for leadership review of member participation, (3) an opportunity for leaders to communicate with members about their participation, and (4) clear consequences for non-compliance. To be clear, all four components are necessary. Leaders who require only that a team submit an agenda each week cannot claim that teams are being held accountable. We have seen many leaders stop at the first requirement, because they simply do not have the time to follow-up with a review of the documentation and/or communication with members regarding the documentation. We encourage leaders to think creatively about how they can allocate time or other individuals to help with this process. In our experience, it is more appropriate for school administrators (or others positioned in supervisory/evaluative roles) to take on the responsibility of leadership for teacher-team accountability. Leaders without this designation (e.g. teacher leaders, instructional coaches) are better positioned for leadership that ensures fidelity.

Fidelity

Merriam Webster (http://www.merriam-webster.com) provides a definition of fidelity as "the degree to which something matches or copies something else" or "accuracy in details." Extending from this terminology, we suggest that leaders who ensure fidelity in a learning community demand that teams do *the right work*, and support them in ways that allow them to do it. What does "the right work" entail? In Step 3, we recommended that school leaders choose a guiding framework. This framework, in part, can help illustrate "the right work" or, in other words, the work that is believed to be connected to the desired outcome or aim: the advancement of student learning. Not surprisingly, school leaders must participate in specific leadership behaviors to ensure fidelity to the chosen framework. In our experiences, fidelity is breeched when team members do not understand the framework or the tasks required to support the framework. In other cases, teams breech fidelity by participating in activities other than those suggested by the framework because they do not "buy into" the framework or its purported effects. In the latter case, we encourage leaders to see this as an issue of accountability—teams deciding not to follow the expectations of leaders. Leaders must work with these teams to agree on the negotiability of team behavior and performance.

In the case of teams who do not fully understand the framework, we suggest leadership/assistance from PLC Leadership Team members who understand what "the right work" looks like for both teams and individual teacher/team-members who must apply the team's work into the classroom to affect student learning. In many cases, these leaders (fidelity supporters) are teacher-leaders, lead-teachers, and/or instructional coaches who have demonstrated high levels of pedagogical expertise. These leaders must spend time with teams, build positive relationships, and offer support to the team as they work to accomplish their goals. For example, a team may be struggling to create common formative assessments for data analysis. A fidelity coach could provide sample assessments, facilitate a team discussion on formative assessment, or provide resources to encourage a collective understanding of formative assessment. Another approach to leadership for fidelity is asking teams who have demonstrated an ability to do "the right work" to assist teams who need additional support. When successful teams emerge, leaders must celebrate those teams, share their work, and tap into their potential to help build the capacity of other teams.

Adequate Funding to Ensure SUFFICIENT Time, Capacity, and Leadership

We recognize that many leaders reading this chapter may feel great concern for their inability or limited ability to provide the resources necessary for ensuring the right amount, type and quality of leadership that successful learning communities demand. We, too, are concerned that the lack of resources (for some) will produce ineffective teacher-teams, resulting in the eventual abandonment of the learning community construct. As stated earlier, and supported by our observations in the field, leaders who are truly committed to the development of a collaborative culture will find ways to re-allocate the time, money, and people necessary for its success. In our discussions with school leaders committed to building PLCs, we have heard many comments about the increase in costs related to professional development/capacity building. Leaders tell us they are allocating or re-allocating significantly more funding to professional learning opportunities than they had in the period before PLCs. When asked where the monies go, popular examples include funding for: (1) substitute teachers—allowing the regular teachers to receive PLC-related training or collaborate for longer periods of time, (2) stipends for *PLC Leadership Team Members*, (3) attendance at off-site institutes or workshops, (4) the creation of a PLC leadership position to facilitate the PLC, and (5) summer funding for professional development and team work sessions. We suspect there are a host of ways leaders are supporting PLC development and sustainability through financial (re)allocation. Determining a sufficient total amount differs, based upon the specific actions the school plans to take. However, if a PLC is not succeeding—the school has not been able to realize its vision for the PLC—it is entirely possible that leaders did not provided a sufficient amount of time, capacity-development or leadership that is often the result of inadequate funding or poor use of available resources.

CONCLUSION

It was not long ago that educational researchers began providing the rationale for shifting away from a system of "go-it-alone" teaching to a system of collaboration among educators. Now that educators have embraced collaborative learning, research on how to build and sustain effective learning communities, particularly with respect to leadership practices, has become an imperative. In essence:

> Principals are becoming dependent on teacher leaders. Improving student outcomes on a continuous and sustained basis requires partnerships with the school personnel who are closest to students—the teachers themselves—and who are directly responsible for student learning; as a result, principals must share school-level leadership decisions. (McDonald & Keedy, 2004, p. 220)

In addition, it is clear that districts must provide support for the capacity building essential to sustained PLC work, if PLCs are expected to be productive (Burke & Cavalier, 2004). In this chapter, we drew upon some of the research that *does* exist, in addition to our own experiences working with school leaders attempting to implement learning communities. We suggest that our four *critical leadership steps* for school leaders who seek to build effective PLCs serve as a potential model for collaborative leadership. Moreover, we believe that our articulation of and explanation of these steps contribute to the literature base for increasing the capacity of leaders to design, develop, grow, and sustain strong learning communities that lead school improvement for the benefit of all students

QUESTIONS FOR DISCUSSION

For principals and leadership team members

1. Develop a vision for teacher-teams in your school or, if you have already completed this process, review your vision. What evidence will you use to assess the degree to which you are achieving your vision for their performance? How will you (or have you) communicated your vision to the entire school community?
2. Review Table 8.1 together and determine at least three priority learning outcomes for your leadership team. Discuss strategies for achieving those learning outcomes and decide together on those your leadership team will use.
3. Spend a portion of one of your meetings discussing the key concepts in this chapter as they apply to your leadership team. Perhaps go around the group and have each team member share a concept that he/she thinks is particularly important for your team. List these as a way of identifying areas of agreement you might use for team planning.

For Superintendents and District Level Leaders

1. After reading this chapter, spend a portion of time at a work session or leadership council meeting sharing key concepts from this chapter. Identify how district level leaders might support school leadership teams and teacher-teams in their work.
2. In pairs or threes attend a leadership team meeting in one of your district's schools for the sole purpose of listening to the team members. Allocate time at a leadership council meeting to discuss the strengths of the teams and what district level leaders might do to assist in supporting the teams.

3. Review district data, or invite your assessment director to present data, in a way that might indicate the developing influence of PLCs in improving student achievement across the district. How can district level leaders use this information to support school leadership teams and PLCs?

REFERENCES

Allen, A. S., & Topolka-Jorissen, K. (2016). Teacher leadership continuum: How principals develop and support teacher leaders. In E. Blair (Ed.), *Teacher leadership: The "new" foundations of teacher education* (pp. 63–69). New York, NY: Peter Lang.

Annenberg Institute for School Reform. (2005). *Professional learning communities: Professional development strategies that improve instruction.* Providence, RI: Author. Retrieved from http://annenberginstitute.org/pdf/proflearning.pdf

Burke, P. H., & Cavalier, M. (2004). Changing the culture of a middle school: A narrative examination of a new principal's implementation of shared leadership. In J. H. Chrispeels (Ed.), *Learning to lead together: The promise and challenge of sharing leadership* (pp. 23–45). Thousand Oaks, CA: Sage.

Carroll, T., Fulton, K., & Doerr, H. (2010). *Team up for 21st century teaching and learning: What research and practice reveal about professional learning.* Washington, DC: National Commission on Teaching and America's Future.

Coburn, C. E. (2001). Collective sense-making about reading: How teachers mediate reading policy in their professional communities. *Educational Evaluation and Policy Analysis, 23*(2), 145–170.

Coburn C. E. (2005). Shaping teacher sensemaking: School leaders and the enactment of reading policy. *Educational Policy, 19*(3), 476–509.

Conzemius, A., & O'Neill, J. (2001). *Building shared responsibility for student learning.* Alexandria, VA: Association for Supervision and Curriculum Development.

Cziko, C. (2008). Meeting at the café to do teacherly things: Community and competence in a teacher reparation program. In A. Lieberman & L. Miller (Eds.), *Teachers in professional communities: Improving teaching and learning* (pp. 41–50). New York, NY: Teachers College Press.

DiPaola, M. F., & Hoy, W. K. (2008). *Principals improving instruction: Supervision, evaluation, and professional development.* Boston, MA: Pearson.

Drago-Severson, E. (2009). *Leading adult learning: Supporting adult development in our schools.* Thousand Oaks, CA: Corwin.

Drago-Severson, E., & Pinto, K. C. (2006). School leadership for reducing teacher isolation: Drawing from the well of human resources. *International Journal of Leadership in Education, 9*(2), 129–155.

DuFour, R., DuFour, R., & Eaker, R. (2008). *Revisiting professional learning communities at work: New insights for improving schools.* Bloomington, IN: Solution Tree.

DuFour, R., DuFour, R., Eaker, R., & Many, T. (2006). *Learning by doing: A handbook for professional learning communities at work*™. Bloomington, IN: Solution Tree.

DuFour, R., & Marzano, R. J. (2011). *Leaders of learning: How district, school, and classroom leaders improve student achievement.* Bloomington, IN: Solution Tree.

DuFour R., & Mattos, M. (2013). The Principalship. *Educational Leadership, 70*(7), 34–40.

Frost, D., & Durrant, J. (2004). Supporting teachers' leadership: What can principals do? A teachers' [*sic*] perspective from research. In J. H. Chrispeels (Ed.), *Learning to lead together: The promise and challenge of sharing leadership* (pp. 307–326). Thousand Oaks, CA: Sage.

Fuhrman, S. H., & Elmore, R. F. (Eds.). (2004). *Redesigning accountability systems for education.* New York, NY: Teachers College Press.

Fulton, K., Yoon, I., & Lee, C. (2005). *Induction into learning communities.* Washington, DC: National Commission on Teaching and America's Future.

Gardner, J. W. (1993). *On Leadership.* New York, NY: The Free Press.

Goddard, Y. L., Goddard, R. D., & Tschannen-Moran, M. (2007). A theoretical and empirical investigation of teacher collaboration for school improvement and student achievement in public elementary schools. *Teachers College Record, 109*(4), 877–896.

Gupton, S. L. (2003). *The instructional toolbox.* Thousand Oaks, CA: Corwin.

Hargreaves, A., & Fullan, M. (2012). *Professional capital: Transforming teaching in every school.* New York, NY: Teachers College Press.

Harris, A. (2004). Successful leadership in schools facing challenging circumstances: No panaceas or promises. In J. H. Chrispeels (Ed.), *Learning to lead together: The promise and challenge of sharing leadership* (pp. 282–304). Thousand Oaks, CA: Sage.

Herrity, V. A., & Morales, P. (2004). Creating meaningful opportunities for collaboration. In J. H. Chrispeels (Ed.), *Learning to lead together: The promise and challenge of sharing leadership* (pp. 46–79). Thousand Oaks, CA: Sage.

Holland, H. (2005). Teaching teachers: Professional development to improve student achievement. *Research Points: Essential Information for Educational Policy, 3*(1), 1–4. Washington, DC: American Educational Research Association.

Hord, S. M. (1997). *Professional learning communities: Communities of continuous inquiry and improvement.* (Contract RJ96006801). Austin, TX: Southwest Educational Development Lab.

Hord, S. M. (2008). Evolution of the professional learning community. *Journal of Staff Development, 29*(3), 10–13.

Hord, S. M., & Sommers, W. A. (2008). *Leading professional learning communities: Voices from research and practice.* Thousand Oaks, CA: Corwin.

Isaacson, N., & Bamburg, J. (1992). Can schools become learning organizations? *Educational Leadership, 50*(3), 42–44.

Jacobson, D. (2010). Coherent instructional improvement and PLCs: Is it possible to do both? *Phi Delta Kappan, 91*, 38–45.

Jaquith, A. (2013). Instructional capacity how to build it right. *Educational Leadership, 71*(2), 56–61.

Katzenmeyer, M., & Moller, G. (2001). *Awakening the sleeping giant: Helping teachers develop as leaders* (2nd ed.). Thousand Oaks, CA: Corwin.

Kouzes, J., & Posner, B. (2008). *The leadership challenge: How to keep getting extraordinary things done in organizations.* San Francisco, CA: Jossey-Bass Publishers.

Lambert, L. (2003). *Leadership capacity for lasting school improvement.* Alexandria, VA: Association for Supervision and Curriculum Development.

Learning Forward. (2011). *Standards for professional learning.* Oxford, OH: Author.

Lieberman, A., & Miller, L. (2008). Developing capacities. In A. Lieberman & L. Miller (Eds.), *Teachers in professional communities: Improving teaching and learning* (pp. 18–28). New York, NY: Teachers College Press.

Little, J. W. (1990). The persistence of privacy: Autonomy and initiative in teachers' professional relations. *Teachers College Record, 91*(4), 509–536.

Louis, K., Leithwood, K., Wahlstrom, K., & Anderson, S. (2010). *Learning from leadership: Investigating the links to improved student achievement.* Minneapolis, MN: University of Minnesota.

Louis, K. S. (1994). Beyond 'managed change': Rethinking how schools improve. *School Effectiveness and School Improvement, 5*(1), 2–24.

Louis, K. S. (2008). Creating and sustaining professional communities. In A. M. Blankstein, P. D. Houston, & R. W. Cole (Eds.), Sustaining professional learning communities (pp. 41–57). Thousand Oaks, CA: Corwin.

Martin, K. J., & Chrispeels, J. H. (2004). A middle school strives to achieve team leadership through opposition and uncertainty. In J. H. Chrispeels (Ed.), *Learning to lead together: The promise and challenge of sharing leadership* (pp. 104–131). Thousand Oaks, CA: Sage.

McDonald, D. H., & Keedy, J. L. (2004). Principals conceptualize the development of teacher leaders: A cross-case study of shared leadership in high-poverty Kentucky schools. In J. H. Chrispeels (Ed.), *Learning to lead together: The promise and challenge of sharing leadership* (pp. 219–254). Thousand Oaks, CA: Sage.

Mitchell, C., & Sackney, L. (2009). *Sustainable improvement: Building learning communities that endure.* Rotterdam: Sense Publishers.

Newmann, F., & Wehlage, G. (1995). *Successful school restructuring: A report to the public and educators by the Center on Organization and Restructuring of Schools.* Madison, WI: University of Wisconsin.

Pascal, N. S., & Blankstein, A. M. (2008). "Communities committed to learning": A case story of building sustainable success. In A. M. Blankstein, P. D. Houston, & R. W. Cole (Eds.), *Sustaining professional learning communities* (pp. 5–21). Thousand Oaks, CA: Corwin.

Rasberry, M. A., & Mahajan, G. (2008). *From isolation to collaboration: Promoting teacher leadership through PLCs.* Hillsborough, NC: Center for Teaching Quality.

Rigby, J. (2015). Principals' sensemaking and enactment of teacher evaluation. *Journal of Educational Administration, 53*(3), 374–392.

Roberts, S. M., & Pruitt, E. Z. (2009). *Schools as professional learning communities: Collaborative activities and strategies for professional development* (2nd ed.). Thousand Oaks, CA: Corwin.

Stanford Center for Opportunity Policy in Education. (2009). United States is substantially behind other nations in providing teacher professional development that improves student learning (Press release). Retrieved from https://edpolicy.stanford.edu/news/articles/197.

Vescio, V., Ross, D., & Adams, A. (2008). A review of the research on the impact of professional learning communities on teaching practice and student learning. *Teaching and Teacher Education, 24*(1), 80–91.

Weick, K. E. (1995). *Sensemaking in organizations.* Thousand Oaks, CA: Sage.

Weiler, J. R. (2013). *Coming to collaboration: A study of the factors contributing to the successful development of common learning targets and common formative assessments.* (Doctoral dissertation). Retrieved from Proquest LLC.

Yukl, G. (2009). *Leadership in organizations* (7th ed.). Upper Saddle River, NJ: Prentice-Hall.

CHAPTER NINE

Imaginative Action Research (IAR)

The Missing Element in Leadership Development

MICHELLE VAUGHAN AND IRA BOGOTCH

We are writing here as progressive educators who analytically and imaginatively see schools as they might be rather than as they currently are. That is not to deny that in pockets what happens inside individual classrooms and even within whole schools is not excellent, even joyful (see Gaines, Bogotch, & Salaam, 2015). Yet, institutionally, schools are conservative and inextricably tied to the prevailing structures of power that reproduce the values and structures of the existing social, economic and political order. To which we ask in this chapter, what is the proper role of the educational researcher in documenting and supporting school reforms and social change? For surely, describing again and again the managing of schools and classrooms as they are only supports a future already prescribed by dominant social forces, precluding the possibilities for teacher and administrator leadership, and trivializing the writings of researchers. We do not think that this assessment is too strong an indictment of school structures, practices and the state of educational research. The question is whether we are able—in this short chapter—to demonstrate a new way of thinking and acting as researchers for both teacher and leadership development.

What we propose is a method called *imaginative action research* (IAR), a methodology that moves from individualized conceptions of classroom and school problems and solutions to an analysis that systematically re-constructs individual problems into broader contexts requiring imaginative solutions beyond a single case study. In other words, the methods proposed allow individual researchers to examine documented cases not just for similarities and differences, as in cross-case analyses, but through applying action research methods to multiple cases simultaneously.

The individual cases used in this chapter were taken from traditionally constructed, short-term action research projects (N = 14), which were then integrated and analyzed critically. What this means is that we as researchers asked the data to reveal patterns aligned to (1) how data were originally presented to the researchers; (2) how the researchers supplemented the data with local knowledge, from students primarily, and (3) how the data were subsequently to be disseminated to administrators, parents, and students. The three-step process is meant to make the data relevant beyond a single classroom by imagining systemic change efforts. The analogous situation, if this is helpful, is similar to how quantitative researchers might engage in "goodness of fit" modeling as part of a meta-analysis. Yes, we are deliberately violating the major tenets of qualitative case study research, but one cannot engage in critical research, even critically pragmatic research, without advancing new methodologies for the fields of teacher education and educational leadership to consider.

TEACHER LEADERS AND ACTION RESEARCH

Lieberman and Miller (2004) argue that teachers can and should play an integral role in transforming schools. They call out three specific roles they can assume: (1) as advocates for new forms of accountability and assessment, (2) as innovators in the reconstruction of norms of achievement and expectations for students, and (3) as stewards for an invigorated profession (pp. 12–13). In today's climate of common assessments, high-stakes testing, and teacher evaluations based on student performance, the roles discussed over a decade ago by Lieberman and Miller seem farther away and more difficult to obtain for teachers—as well as principals. In order for teachers to embrace roles as advocates, innovators, and stewards, new definitions of what it means to be a leader inside a school need to be developed.

In contrast to the titular heads of schools and school systems, the leadership among teachers is by necessity, an activist, bottom-up intervention (Lopez, 2014, p. 466). It works around, not through, the general and theoretical studies of principal leadership. According to Insana, Johnson-Mardonnes, Welsh, and Johnston-Parsons (2014, pp. 448–449), the theories of educational leadership have taken "a narrow methodological approach, [...] ignoring the social context in which schooling and educational leadership takes place." Isana et al. include in their critique transactional leadership, distributed leadership, collaborative leadership, and transformational leadership—theories that comprise a large segment of the published literature. Bogotch and Shields (2014) explicitly called for a stronger advocacy role in educational leadership. The question is how can researchers engage the dominant discourses of traditional educational leadership and policymakers? The most obvious answer, the *lingua franca,* is to speak to those in power using the language of data. Thus, the teacher as researcher and researcher as leader have become the focus of many graduate teacher education programs across the country (Vaughan & Burnaford, 2015). Narrative inquiry, curriculum inquiry and action research are three of the research vehicles being used to develop skills and dispositions needed by future and current teacher leaders who can engage in school policy and enact needed school changes.

The movement to connect action research and teacher leadership is growing steadily in graduate coursework, school and district programs, and educational initiatives across the globe. Within the following discussion of teacher leadership programs, it is important to note the emphasis on advocacy and the use of collective research to inform policy. Adams et al. (2013) examined the impact of a job-embedded graduate program on the preparation of teacher leaders and their continued use of inquiry in their roles as teacher leaders within a university-district-school partnership. The Teacher Leadership for School Improvement (TLSI) program "aims to develop in teachers the skills of a master teacher, teacher leader, and teacher researcher" (p. 583) throughout their graduate program. With a designed focus on teachers working in high-need schools, the program builds leadership capacity through job-embedded research and inquiry experiences paired with authentic collaboration and schools that support the growth and development of teacher leaders and researchers. Results of a program evaluation indicated the "every teacher (100%) reported sustained inquiry use a year beyond graduation even when it was not required as part of TLSI coursework" (p. 591).

Similar initiatives and results are seen within the National College for School Leadership (NCSL), which was created to "support and develop England's 25,000 head teachers and thousands of other teachers with leadership roles and aspirations" (Coles, 2004, p. 11). Through the development of research associateships, the program funds time away from school administration responsibilities to carry out small-scale research projects in order to make research more meaningful for school leaders. Additionally, the program focuses on supporting school leaders in inquiry, as opposed to spending the majority of time analyzing standardized data, and giving practitioners a role in the research community. By elevating the research status of practitioners and supporting school leaders in more classroom-based inquiry, NCSL is attempting to bring both teachers and administrators together with meaningful data to build a group of school leaders. The reports from the research associateships are systematically synthesized and disseminated to every school in England as well as to those individuals involved in creating policy.

Lastly, the Teachers Leadership Network Institute (TLNI), an arm of Teachers Network, identifies "fellows" across the United States who apply to be part of this elite group armed with conducting action research and providing reports to impact policy. Reasons for applying and joining TLNI vary; however, research indicates that "action research is a critical draw for these teachers, as are the opportunities that TNLI provides for collegiality, for intellectual stimulation and for keeping up-to-date with current research and policy" (Rust & Meyers, 2006, p. 73). Through collaborative action research projects, another goal of the TLNI is to familiarize fellows with policy and use their research to engage in decision making. Through presentations to school boards and panels, meeting with state legislators, and serving on various task forces, the fellows are using their collective research to voice concerns from classrooms across the country.

This chapter makes the case that the data produced through action research projects are an integral element of decision making at the school, district, and state level. We will use our own illustrative cases to show the unique and valuable data obtained from action research conducted by teacher leaders and the potential impact it can have on school policy and curriculum. These cases tell stories of teachers using research and curricular processes to defend, advocate and innovate alternative ideas and decisions that administrators, teachers and students make in their classrooms and schools. Utilizing the current language of data in educational reforms, these teachers are preparing themselves to take back much of the power that neoliberal policies and high-stakes testing have taken from the profession. The shift of power back into the classroom, where teachers can make data-based decisions about their own students is one way to create a leadership community where teachers are the main players and stewards of the profession. Cochran-Smith and Lytle (2009) reflect on the role of research in schools in the preface of *Inquiry as Stance*:

> The knowledge needed for teachers to teach well and to enhance students' learning opportunities and life chances could not be generated solely by researchers who were centrally positioned outside of schools and classrooms and imported for implementation and use inside of schools.

In order to redefine what it means to be a teacher leader and consider how this role can carry real power in the school setting, it is necessary for teachers to become teacher researchers. Armed with research skills, teachers may once again reclaim the power to drive instruction and make significant curricular changes based on real-time data within their own classrooms—impacting schools and communities.

DEVELOPING THE CASE

In a typical classroom action research project, we have one teacher with 25 students. Here we have 14 teachers with approximately 350 students—which blurs the lines across classrooms, teachers and students. Our imaginative action research design (IAR) uses a traditionally qualitative design as a meta-analysis. Quite literally, IAR puts researchers into the shoes of the greatest number of students, his, hers and theirs, allowing for more intuitive sense-making than when conducting a single case study. Our approach is literary, not unlike the "cut-up" technique or montage invented by the painter Brion Gysin (1959) and the writer William Burroughs (1984/1991, p. 266). During the late 1950s and 1960s, Gysin collaborated with Burroughs on literary works and films using the "cutup method" in which excerpts from literature [from Kafka to Shakespeare] and pop culture were randomly pasted into Burroughs' stories. According to the critic, Skerl (1985), Burroughs developed a theory of the cutup as a way to liberate himself as well as the reader from the control that words and images have on the mind (p. 49). "For Burroughs as an artist, the cutup is an impersonal method of inspiration, invention, and an arrangement that redefines the work of art as a process that occurs in collaboration with others and is not the sole property of artists" (pp. 49–50). Piecing together findings from multiple action research projects creates the potential to see new realities beyond any one project or teacher or administrator.

What we seek are multiple and different mindsets and ways of teaching and learning that may lead to new and different futures—as yet unforeseen, as yet unempirical from any one case study. Our goal is to reach all children and all classrooms, and since traditional and predictable educational research—challenging correlational and causal approaches—has not led to new and exciting ideas, we are looking here for new methods for renewing hope for the future.

In doing quantitative research, statistical significance has become a proxy for judging whether the research designs, questions, and findings were valid. Researchers looked for statistical differences in every imaginable setting, controlling for or asserting away [e.g., claiming all things being equal, for purposes of this study only] other potential "causes" of differences. Yet, even with these methodological delimitations in place, published studies could not predict. In fact, like wisdom, the more we come to know about teaching, learning and leading, the more we realize how much we do not know. What we do not know in quantitative designs falls within categories of unexplained variance and probability values. Neither unexplained variance nor non-significant results are ever analyzed or critiqued with the same depth of scrutiny as we give to statistically significant findings. Yet, what we know tends to be quantitatively what we can measure. But what about unmeasured, unexplained as well as qualitative research?

What we are asking readers here is to pay attention to the contextual "storylines" (Bogotch, Keaster, Baldwin, & Wonycott, 1995). Inside of the storylines are influences and geopolitical interpretations of realities some educative, some miseducative. Once the doors to personal lived experiences are opened, then issues of power and knowledge come together and to the forefront of our data analysis. Our proposed methods seek to move from passive data analysis to active ownership of both data and the conditions that need to change in classrooms and schools all around the world. We are seeking to close the distance between school leadership and classrooms, curriculum and pedagogy.

Under traditional designs and methods, knowledge is often edited out of final drafts. Under traditional designs and methods, rules of logic prevail that do not necessarily fit the lived experiences of educators in schools. There are no rational rules of central tendency in education. There are only contextual differences, personal knowledge and experiences influencing attitudes and actions. No one case study is capable of revealing unknown truths. Our method here searches for truths between the lines, within the nagging concerns of teachers, and especially students.

A leadership response to research is to not pull back, but rather to persist and argue the consequences of destabilizing methods and traditions, knowledge and power. Why should educational leadership settle for what is already known? Should we wait for current school conditions to improve in order to reduce our risk of taking actions? Or, do we proceed imaginatively and intellectually through research and practice along uncertain paths? We are opting here for the latter pathway.

A MASTER CASE IN ACTION RESEARCH

Our *fictional* case begins with the research questions generated by teacher researchers. While student achievement is paramount to teachers, specifically if their evaluations are connected to it, within our cases, it was rarely the main focus of research. Perhaps because there are so much data already generated around that topic or perhaps teacher researchers recognize that the reasons students achieve or do not achieve is often tied to factors that are not easily measured in a standardized format. Some examples of individual action research topics were: Long-term retention of skills with the curriculum, Engagement with manipulative use in mathematics, Mentorship experience with new teachers in a district mentoring program, Impact of small group counseling on adolescent females in high school, Building empathy through the use of multicultural literature, Motivation through open assessment choice, Building awareness of the school-to-prison pipeline and Impact of phone calls on attendance and pace in online classrooms. Even though these topics became a focus for action research an argument can be made that all of these strategies could have an impact on student achievement, it is often secondary to the topics being focused on within their research. One teacher explained "the purpose in asking this question is to improve the educational experience for both students and teachers" while another said "in this study I will examine how the learning, lives and motivation of my eighth grade U.S. History students are impacted by student autonomy and choice." The need for research grows from the students, from the careful daily observation and interpretation of their actions and achievements. These teacher researchers focus on what standardized data are *not* telling them about their students.

The topics reflect teacher interventions to address and make sense of systemic policies foisted onto teachers and principals. Can a teacher find time to study a potential solution and still keep pace with instruction? Goals such as retention, engagement, mentoring, counseling, empathy, motivation, awareness, and impact are very different from the standardized data presented to these teachers and their principals.

After looking at what they are studying, it is important to understand *why* they are choosing to study these topics. Teacher leaders use research to embrace the roles of advocate and innovator (Lieberman & Miller, 2004), and when a gap exists between what they feel is important in their classroom and what they are being asked to do by administration or policy, the systematic collection of data is giving these teachers a voice and a vehicle to express their needs and perceptions. When discussing topic choices, one teacher leader explains how the focus on high stakes testing "causes many school boards, administrators, and teachers to implement pedagogical practices and content decisions that can alienate a diverse set of students such as mine." Teacher leaders are navigating the existing demands placed on them and their students to ultimately do what they feel is best for their students long-term. Another teacher researcher explains why she feels it is important to have data that support student choice.

> Inquiry into the impact of choice on motivation is important on many levels as students strive to meet the demands and high expectations put on them by their parents, teachers and administrators, all of which coexist with pressures they place on themselves. Understanding what motivates students and how they view themselves and their capabilities is crucial to being an effective educator.

Table 9.1 highlights some of the collective reasons the teachers used to support their topic choices and explain the content in which they were researching. It is clear these researchers are using their projects as a vehicle for change, pedagogically and managerially.

Table 9.1. Reasons teacher researchers choose their topics.

- There is a discrepancy between what they are asked to do and what they perceive to be needed by students
- In order to present documentation and evidence to administration to purchase needed materials
- There is a gap between what they learned in teacher education and the curriculum given when hired
- To increase confidence in their students in a given subject area
- To create changes in programs offered by the school district
- To spread instructional changes to surrounding schools

School systems are notorious for ignoring dilemmas and contradictions. Systems put so much time and effort into collecting standardized data across subjects, schools and other systems, that there is little to no time left beyond reporting out those data. The schools these teachers work in are filled with data, but these researchers did not make use of the data available to them. Instead, they created new data sources, ones that were closer to the students and more authentic in nature.

Through coursework and methodology texts in action research, teacher leaders embrace the role of researchers. The methods used to collect data vary based on the research question they design. Taking on the role of a participant observer can prove challenging; however, within all the exemplar cases reviewed, triangulation of data was essential in order to establish the validity of their findings. Additionally, teachers reported a deeper understanding of the interplay between quantitative and qualitative data.

> One thing which I learned from analyzing the data I obtained was the interdependence of qualitative and quantitative data. Before, I had a vague idea of how the two can supplement each other, but completing this project showed me how interrelated they really are, and how both are necessary to enhance our understanding of the topic being studied.

The types of data collected were: student interviews, survey data, classroom observations, student work, peer observations, and researcher journals but the lack of standardized achievement data should be noted.

Results of these action research projects often show an increase in achievement *and* something else, whether it is motivation, engagement, or attitude. It is interesting to note that while the researcher may intend to study the impact of a chosen strategy on attitude or engagement, they often find achievement goes up as an unintended outcome. This is a shift in understanding for teacher leaders, because they receive the validation that teaching to the needs of the student, even if their need is not explicitly academic in nature, does indeed impact their achievement and they now have the data to support those efforts. "I was able to see the direct results of a project-based strategy I chose to implement in my own math class this year. The data was eye-opening, and the experience was rewarding." Reflections on the application of these findings go beyond just their own classroom and reveal the connectedness between the needs of their students and the needs of teachers.

> Moreover, this study went beyond the scope of choice related to motivation and delved into other factors which can be applied to many other situations. These research results are valuable beyond the realm of education and can influence professional environments as well. Finding ways to increase motivation in the workplace can lead to higher productivity and potentially more enjoyment and thus feelings of fulfillment.

Teacher researchers report feeling empowered to continue to systematically collect data to support their instructional choices in the classroom. Making instructional decisions based on data is a common practice in schools today, but what data are we using to make those decisions? One teacher leader describes how a supportive environment can foster this behavior.

> Teachers, particularly when allowed to teach in an environment that permits decision making and creativity, are informal researchers, seeking to answer "what is the impact of ..." across a huge variety of topics, monitoring the effect of the changes, and determining the final implications of what occurred.

Teachers now have the skills and practice to create a new set of data, data that may either complement or contradict what we traditionally view as school data. Only when we bring both data sets together, can we get a full picture of what is going on in the classroom and what is working for both our students and their teachers.

> It was very interesting to be able to take what we are able to see in our everyday lives as professionals and design a study to address a particular aspect of our craft. This project has also been a welcome change from the traditional style of study by allowing an insider to be the researcher in order to fuel a positive change in a particular area of interest.

The hope for teacher researchers is that their data will result in change or perhaps result in preventing a change that may hinder student learning. Data are a source of power for decision makers and when teachers own a valuable piece of the data, the result is a stronger voice and a higher representation of student needs that may only be seen within the classroom. Following the dissemination of her own results, one of the researchers explained,

> After sharing my results with the faculty at my school, I hope to convince the teachers to support the effort needed to make these agendas for all the students at our school. My principal has tentatively agreed to try using the agenda with one grade level. I am interested if the same results can be replicated with a larger group.

Collectively, teacher researchers reported that they shared their results with peers first, hoping to elicit some volunteers to work together implementing their new strategy. As Table 9.2 shows, they also planned professional development sessions and made plans to share with their administration. No one in this group had plans to meet with policymakers, publish their work, or share outcomes with the district office. Moving the advocacy of their ideas beyond their own classroom and school could be a goal of future coursework.

Table 9.2. Examples of next steps for sharing action research results.

• Share results with colleagues
• Create professional development sessions for their schools
• Share results with administration
• Change instructional practices within their own classrooms

MOVING FORWARD

After reviewing the 14 cases collectively, we are confident that the data collected by these teacher researchers contain valuable information about student learning, motivation, and achievement. Their research is closely tied to the needs of diverse learners and often addresses areas that no standardized form of classroom research currently examines. However, what happens next for these data? As we saw in Table 9.2, teacher leaders do not have (or are not aware of) a path to follow to share their work with decision makers outside of their immediate administration. York-Barr and Duke (2004) outline some of the factors that can help facilitate the success of teacher leaders. To support and sustain teacher leaders, they must have "participatory decision-making structures and processes" within their school site and "hierarchal structures in schools and districts" (p. 271) should be removed. To move beyond an impact on one classroom or at one school, the value of these data must be recognized and sought after. We cannot learn what is best for our students if their voice is not represented in the data we are using to make decisions about them and for them.

CONCLUSION

The case data in this chapter were collected by teachers with the objective of improving the student experience within the classroom, but also to contribute meaningful data to the decision making process at their school site As we get closer to the student (student data), we get closer to authentic school experiences. Teacher or administrative interventions that ignore student data are unethical and unprofessional, but that is exactly what we do. The methodological question is how to get as close to the students (all students) as possible.

The power of IAR is that we can more clearly see the range of topics, questions, findings, and data uses than if we had analyzed these cases individually as stand-alone studies. True, we miss the rich, deep descriptions so typical of cases, but we would argue that for research to become an instrument for making changes, we need to provide qualitative evidence in a quasi-quantitative manner. Some readers may object to our extending the borders of case study research, but we believe that new case methods are needed if we want to transfer power and decision making to those closest to the work.

Why student data collected by teachers? This is fundamental to validity. The analyses of standardized tests or even just teacher tests alone cannot capture the lived experiences of the students. Understanding their orientations, their anxiety and stress is as important as assessing what they know. What a teacher or an administrator believes to be helpful is not the same as students telling researchers (teachers and administrators) what would be helpful. Instead of "good enough" or approximate levels of adult understanding, student voice reveals a closer and more valid perspective on feelings.

This chapter is unique in two respects. It demonstrates (1) how classroom action research designs and the data stand in opposition to routine public school practices based on administering standardized tests, and receiving unanalyzed data on both classroom and whole decisions; and (2) how multiple classroom action research, rather than single stand-alone cases, provides broader contexts, and actions. An error in judgement makes a single case appear as the total picture, when in fact it is simply a fragment and leads to narrative conclusions based on limited evidence. The so-called "real world" of classrooms is not one, but many configurations encompassing policymaker, administrator, teacher and student interpretations of experiences. Armed with these data, schools will improve.

DISCUSSION QUESTIONS

1. Why is it necessary to look across multiple action research cases as well as within them to gather data related to the impact of these action research studies?
2. How are the original teacher leadership roles defined by Lieberman and Miller (2004) represented within the fictional case presented?
3. How does the method of imaginative action research stretch the standards of qualitative research?
4. How does the data collected within the fictional case "fit" with the traditional standardized data collected at many school sites?
5. What challenges do teacher researchers face within the current context of schools?

REFERENCES

Adams, A., Ross, D., Swain, C., Dana, N., Leite, W., & Sandbach, R. (2013). Preparing teacher leaders in a job-embedded graduate program: Changes within and beyond the classroom walls. *Teacher Education and Practice, 26*(3), 581–597.

Bogotch, I., Keaster, R., Baldwin, B., & Wonycott, A. (1995). Exploring the influences of contextual variables on beginning principals. *Journal of School Leadership, 5*(2), 231–247.

Bogotch, I., & Shields, C. (2014). *International handbook of social [In]justice and educational leadership.* (Part IV, pp. 543–683). Dordrecht: Springer.

Burroughs, W. (1984/1991). *My purpose is to write for the space age.* New York Times Book Review. Reprinted in Skerl, J., & Lydenberg, R. (Eds.). (1991). *William S. Burroughs: At the front* (pp. 265–268). Carrbondale, IL: Southern Illinois University Press.

Cochran-Smith, M., & Lytle, S. L. (2009). *Inquiry as stance: Practitioner research for the next generation.* New York, NY: Teachers College Press.

Coles, M. (2004). Using enquiry to deliver change: The NCSL research associate programme. *Management in Education, 18*(2), 11–13.

Gaines, F., Bogotch, I., & Salaam, O. (2015). Destiny High School: A template for urban high schools. In M. Khalifa, S. Hornsford, & C. Grant (Eds.), *Handbook of urban school leadership.* New York, NY: Routledge.

Gysin, B. (1959). *Cut-up technique.* Retrieved May 24, 2016 from http://www.languageisavirus.com/articles/articles.php?subaction=showcomments&id=1099110964&archive=&start_from=&u-cat=&#.V0STx2f2bIU

Insana, A., Johnson-Mardones, D., Welsh, H., & Johnston-Parsons, M. (2014). Narrative dialogue and teacher leadership for social justice: Re-storying to understand. In I. Bogotch & C. Shields (Eds.), *International handbook of social [in]justice and educational leadership* (pp. 447–464). Dordrecht: Springer.

Lieberman, A., & Miller, L. (2004). *Teacher leadership.* San Francisco, CA: John Wiley & Sons, Inc.

Lopez, A. (2014). Re-conceptualizing teacher leadership through curriculum inquiry in pursuit of social justice: Case student for the Canadian context. In I. Bogotch & C. Shields (Eds.), *International handbook of social [in]justice and educational leadership* (pp. 465–468). Dordrecht: Springer.

Rust, F., & Meyers, E. (2006). The bright side: Teacher research in the context of educational reform and policy-making. *Teachers and Teaching: Theory and Practice, 12*(1), 69–86.

Skerl, J. (1985). *William S. Burroughs.* Boston, MA: Twayne Publishers.

Vaughan, M., & Burnaford, G. (2015). Action research in graduate teacher education: A review of the literature 2000–2015. *Educational Action Research,* doi: 10.1080/09650792.2015.1062408

York-Barr, J., & Duke, K. (2004). What do we know about teacher leadership? Findings from two decades of scholarship. *Review of Educational Research, 74*(3), 255–316.

CHAPTER TEN

Culturally Relevant Leadership in Practice

A Case Study of a Black Woman Principal in the West

LINDA C. TILLMAN AND SONYA DOUGLASS HORSFORD

As educational leaders in the U.S.A. grapple with the complexities of preparing today's students in racially and socioeconomically segregated schools and communities, research on culturally relevant leadership practices have gained increasing attention. The pressures of widening racial and economic inequality coupled with what has been a high-stakes, top-down accountability environment, have incentivized individualized competition and performance over more collective notions of collaboration and community. As a result, educational *outcomes*, measured almost exclusively by test scores and other narrowly constructed indicators of student achievement, are now central to the work of today's school leaders. Yet *process*, which is by definition central to leadership, has been largely ignored, resulting in even greater divides in not only achievement, but engagement by parents, families, and communities, which is key to educational access and opportunity. In the case of public school leaders serving large populations of poor, emergent bilingual, and racially minoritized children in resegregated schools and neighborhoods, the necessity to engage in culturally relevant practices becomes even more pronounced, especially for those educators whose background, lived experiences, and cultural norms contrast in important ways with those of their teachers and students.

Advancing high-quality educational experiences and opportunities for high-needs students in resegregated schools is no easy task. In fact, it requires additional knowledge concerning not only what leaders must do, but also *how* and *why* they do what they do. Given America's legacy of racial exclusion, segregation, and unequal opportunities emblematic of the nation's miseducation of Black children and youth, the cultural perspectives of African American school leaders afford valuable insight into how to effectively educate and meet the socioemotional and cultural needs of historically oppressed and disenfranchised students. As such, research on the leadership philosophies, perspectives, approaches, and outcomes of Black principals (c.f., Lomotey, 1989, 1993; Tillman, 2004a, 2004b; Walker, 1993) provides a strong foundation on which to theorize and consider the study and practice of culturally relevant leadership in increasingly diverse and/or resegregated schools.

In this case study we seek to demonstrate the ways in which Black principal leadership can inform and extend our understanding of culturally relevant leadership in racially segregated schools and communities. It features the leadership of Principal Daisy, the veteran Black principal of Sunshine Elementary School, a high-performing, low-income, historically Black, but increasingly Hispanic, elementary school in a large urban-suburban school district in the U.S. Mountain West. Principal Daisy is heralded for her ability to build and sustain authentic relationships with Sunshine Elementary School's historically disengaged parents, families, and community members and to respond positively to the rapid demographic changes occurring near the end of her principalship. The case analyzes her leadership according to Horsford, Grosland, and Gunn's (2011) framework for culturally relevant leadership (CRL), and its four dimensions: (a) political context, (b) pedagogical approach, (c) personal journey, and (d) professional duty.

The chapter concludes with new understandings and implications for leadership theory, preparation, and practice. By focusing on CRL's dimensions of political context, pedagogical approach, personal journey, and professional duty, we argue that culturally relevant leadership can serve as a powerful approach to leading schools in increasingly diverse and/or resegregated communities. In the next section, we begin with a selected review of the literature on Black principals and the linkages between the research on the leadership perspectives of African American school administrators and culturally relevant leadership in PK-12 schools.

BLACK PRINCIPALS AND CULTURALLY RELEVANT LEADERSHIP

Research on the education leadership of African Americans under school segregation, desegregation, and resegregation has made important contributions to the study and practice of school leadership and administration, especially in racially diverse and/or isolated contexts (Tillman, 2004b). According to Tillman (2004a), the cultural perspectives of Black principals inform the dedication of their personal and professional lives to educating Black children and preparing them for social, emotional, academic, economic and political success. During government-sanctioned segregation, although their primary duty was to lead and manage schools, which were often under-resourced and under-funded in comparison to schools for white children, Black principals worked against all odds to establish and maintain schools for Black children. They taught in and led all-Black schools, while also serving as the voice of the Black community on matters relating to the education of Black children (Walker, 1993).

Similarly, after the *Brown v. Board of Education* decision of 1954, Black principals played an instrumental role in leading desegregation efforts and ensuring that Black children were receiving access to a quality education in what were oftentimes hostile schooling environments. In most cases, whether before or after desegregation, their efforts were met with white resistance, to include parents, educators, policymakers, and the white community writ-large. Now, more than 60 years after *Brown*, Black principals continue to lead and manage schools in large, urban and suburban school districts, and much like their pre-*Brown* era predecessors, they are responsible for and committed to meeting the social, emotional, cultural, and academic needs of not only Black students, but students representing a diversity of racial, cultural, linguistic backgrounds and cognitive and emotional needs.

Black Principal Leadership: Personal, Professional, and Cultural Perspectives

The work of Lomotey (1989, 1993), Walker (1993), Dillard (1995), and Tillman (2004a, 2004b) strongly suggests the presence of a distinctly Black perspective in school leadership based largely on Black culture. In the segregated schooling of the South and in many single-race urban schools today, Black principals practiced leadership based on their insider status and their membership with a distinct Black culture. Same-race/cultural affiliation influenced decision making at the school site, as well as the selection of teachers and interactions with parents. Evidence suggests that many of these principals embodied Lomotey's (1993) ethno-humanist role identity characterized by a commitment to Black students, compassion for these students and their families, and confidence in their intellectual ability. Tillman (2004a) identified similar themes in her review of research on Black principals, namely:

(a) resistance to ideologies and individuals opposed to the education of African American students (African American principals resist deficit ideologies and individuals who seek to deny African American students an equitable and excellent education);
(b) the academic and social development of African American students as a priority (African American principals believe in and are committed to the total development of African American students);

(c) the importance of the cultural perspectives of African American principals (African American principals are central figures in the school and community and espouse the racial and cultural norms of the African American community); and
(d) leadership based on interpersonal caring (African American principals work to meet the psychological, sociological, and academic needs of students).

While the philosophies of Black principals in the pre and post-*Brown* eras of education may have differed, Black principal leaders espoused a collective vision to provide the best possible education for Black students. Pre and post-*Brown* Black principals can be considered change agents. They had a vision for Black students, resisted theories of inferiority that suggested Black students should pursue jobs in manual labor and service industries rather than attend colleges and universities—places intended for whites only—and challenged the prevailing system by instilling within Black students racial pride and self-esteem. In short, Black principals made sure Black students had access to highly qualified and committed Black teachers, rigorous and relevant educational materials, and a support system whereby all stakeholders worked collectively to ensure the effective education of Black children.

With respect to Black female principals, Lomotey and Lowery (2015) found four characteristics that were most prevalent in the studies they reviewed:

(a) nurturing or developing caring and personal relationships with students;
(b) a focus on community involvement or facilitating a mutually beneficial two-way relationship between community organizations and individuals and the school community;
(c) an emphasis on a culturally responsive educational experience or stressing an academic experience that draws upon the culture of students to enhance their learning experience, and
(d) a commitment to student academic performance or demonstrating a sincere concern for the academic success of their students (Lomotey & Lowery, 2014, p. 336).

Overall, Lomotey and Lowery (2014) concluded that the characteristics of successful Black principals are important to Black student success particularly in large urban schools with majority populations of students of color. Further, they argue that such findings are critically important to the preparation of education leaders, who must be increasingly proficient in their ability to hold high academic expectations for all students, foster and sustain a caring and supportive learning environment, and engage families and communities in ways that promote a positive school culture. Central to their analysis were the ways in which Black principal leadership in urban schools can help "determine how these leaders can assist in facilitating a culturally responsive educational experience for Black students" (p. 325). Given our shared interest in possible linkages between Black principal leadership and culturally relevant leadership practices, we turn our attention to selected literature on culturally relevant leadership in PK-12 schools.

Culturally Relevant Leadership: Four Dimensions

In their review of the literature on culturally responsive school leadership, Khalifa, Gooden, and Davis (2016) identified "four behaviors of Culturally Responsive School Leadership, which included practices, actions, mannerisms, policies, and discourses that influence school climate, school structure, teacher efficacy, or student outcomes" (p. 3). The four behaviors included: (a) critical self-awareness (awareness of self and his/her own values, beliefs and dispositions when it comes to serving poor children of color); (b) culturally responsive curricula and teacher preparation (ensuring that teachers are and remain culturally responsive); (c) culturally responsive and inclusive school environments (leaders promote culturally responsive school context with an emphasis on inclusivity); and (d) engaging students and parents in community contexts (leader engages students, families and communities in culturally appropriate ways).

In their framework for culturally relevant leadership (CRL), Horsford et al. (2011) identified four dimensions that were particularly important to the effective leadership of culturally diverse student populations and school communities: (a) political context, (b) pedagogical approach, (c) personal journey, and (d) professional duty, which we describe in the next section.

Political Context: Gaps, Divides, Disparities, and Deficiencies

The first dimension of CRL, political context, focuses on "the educational leader's consciousness of the political context in which they are operating" (Horsford et al., 2011, p. 595). According to the authors,

> As policy implementers, school and district leaders must not only be capable of administering federal, state, district, and school-based policies and procedures, but also equipped to discern and analyze the educational ideologies, philosophical assumptions, and political perspectives that both underlie and frame such policies and practices. (p. 595)

Although educators are typically averse to politics and would prefer to keep politics out of education, the reality is that schools are contested spaces that exist within a larger political system that holds tremendous influence over what life is like in schools. This includes not only the politics of school boards, state legislatures, and education associations, but also the politics of race, inequality, and school reform, which have become increasingly important given the new education landscape. School leaders must recognize these larger political forces and trends and be situationally aware, equipped to develop relationships and build coalitions with policymakers and community leaders, and serves as community leaders themselves (Green, 2015).

Pedagogical Approach: Cultural Relevance and Antiracism

In addition to being prepared to successfully navigate the political context of education in an era of resegregation, culturally relevant school leaders ground their leadership in what they know about how culture operates daily in the lives of children at home and in the classroom. As Horsford et al. (2011) explained,

> Just as teachers must understand how culture operates daily in the classroom, foster learning environments that value cultural and ethnic diversity, and understand how these environments inform student achievement, educational leaders must also gain this awareness to assist their teachers in establishing a school culture and climate that advances student learning and engagement through cultural affirmation and social support. (p. 597)

As instructional leaders, culturally relevant leaders, understand the significance of pedagogy and the implementation of research-based instructional practices in ways that support high quality, culturally relevant teaching and learning in the school building.

Personal Journey: The Path to Cultural Proficiency

The third dimension of CRL, the personal journey, focuses on the reflective nature of cultural proficiency (Terrell & Lindsey, 2009) and its usefulness as a tool for school leaders. According to Horsford et al. (2011), this component represents the extent to which the school leader is willing and able to engage in self-study and self-examination as it relates to their own cultural values, assumptions, and beliefs, and how they influence their leadership practice. It is a prerequisite to holding and demonstrating high expectations for all students and developing "an ethical and professional frame for effective cross-cultural communication and problem solving" (Terrell & Lindsey, 2009, p. 101). In addition to becoming self-aware and knowledgeable with respect to the histories, perspectives, narratives, and lived experiences of individuals with cultural backgrounds different from their own, culturally relevant leaders acknowledge the risks associated with culturally relevant and antiracist work, but much like Black principal leadership, recognize that what is most important is advocating on behalf of the social, emotional, and educational needs of students.

Professional Duty: Leadership for Equity, Engagement, and Excellence

Schools need leaders who are not only committed to leading for equity, engagement, and excellence, but who believe it is their professional duty to do so. According to Horsford et al. (2011), school leaders must be able to monitor, mediate, and model effective cross-cultural communication and conflict resolution through mediation and dialogue and feel proficient and comfortable in initiating and sustaining cross-cultural relationships. This commitment to equity and excellence should not be relegated to just one of several approaches to how a school leader should view her or his professional duty, but rather a guide to ensuring the institution of public education maintains its role in providing equal educational opportunity to all students.

THE CASE OF PRINCIPAL DAISY AND SUNSHINE ELEMENTARY SCHOOL

Grounded in the research literature on Black principals and drawn from a larger qualitative study of the leadership practices of Black principals in racially diverse contexts, the case of Principal Daisy illuminates Horsford et al. (2011) framework for culturally relevant leadership (CRL) in K-12 schools. Participants were selected based on community nomination with data sources including: principal interviews, researcher field observations, school and district-level data, documents, artifacts, and other relevant and publicly available data. Elements of Tillman's (2002) framework for culturally sensitive research, which includes (a) culturally congruent research methods; (b) culturally specific knowledge of the participants; and (c) culturally sensitive data interpretations and guided the research design and methods. Focusing on CRL's dimensions of political context, pedagogical approach, personal journey, and professional duty, we argue that informed largely by Black principal leadership, culturally relevant leadership can serve as a useful approach to leading schools in increasingly diverse and/or resegregated communities.

Sunshine Elementary School

Sunshine Elementary School is located in West Las Vegas, a historically Black neighborhood in Las Vegas, Nevada, in the Mountain West region of the U.S. As part of the Clark County School District (CCSD), which is the fifth-largest school district in the country, Sunshine Elementary serves a predominantly Black and Hispanic[1] PK-5 student population, in the site of Black settlement in Las Vegas, and thus, home to the District's all-Black segregated schools prior to Clark County's school desegregation case, *Kelly v. Guinn* (1972), which deemed the Westside schools intentionally segregated and led to the adoption of the District's mandatory desegregation plan—*The Sixth Grade Plan of Integration* (Horsford, Sampson, & Forletta, 2013). This plan converted West Las Vegas elementary schools, which were predominantly Black, into sixth grade centers to be attended by sixth graders from the neighborhood and those bused from areas outside West Las Vegas.

Roughly two decades later, parents, educators, and community members became fatigued with the disproportionate burden of busing and desegregation on the Black children living in West Las Vegas. They organized for the return to neighborhood schools, which ultimately resulted in approval and implementation of CCSD's *Prime 6 Schools Plan* (Horsford et al., 2013) —a voluntary desegregation plan that would replace the *Sixth Grade Center Plan* and convert the racially desegregated sixth grade centers back into predominately Black elementary schools. As Horsford et al. (2013) explained, "the Westside, which was historically African American and home to Black neighborhood schools, became a community that was roughly 45% Black and 45% Hispanic, adding further complexity to issues of demography and diversity in both the area's neighborhoods and schools." Sunshine Elementary was one of those neighborhood schools, and was led from day one by Principal Daisy who opened the school in 1994 and would witness firsthand the ways in which social, economic, demographic, and political forces would transform the school's population and needs over 16 years as principal.

Principal Daisy

The subject of this case is Principal Daisy who began her career as a school building principal in 1994 at Sunshine Elementary School and served in that position for 16 years until her retirement in 2011. Prior to taking the helm of Sunshine, she spent three years in Clark County School District as an assistant principal of an elementary school and another 16 years as a classroom teacher (ranging from grades K-8), although she began her teaching career in her home state of Tennessee. As an African American woman, Principal Daisy's personal and professional identity informed her leadership philosophy, particularly as it pertained to the children and families in the historic West Las Vegas community that she served, since she served as not only a school leader, but also a community leader (Green, 2015; Walker, 1993). In fact, she used the motto, "Beating the Odds", to motivate teachers, students, parents and others within the school community, and as principal, considered herself to be a critical link between the school and the community.

The majority of her students came from the surrounding neighborhood and she worked hard to build and maintain positive relationships with their parents and the community. She strongly believed that a major role in her many duties as principal was to make sure parents felt they were welcomed in the school and that teachers and all members of the school community provided a caring, nurturing environment for each and every child. Principal Daisy's used her vast community network, leadership profile, and credibility as a respected educator to leverages resources and support for Sunshine Elementary School, as well as broader community-based initiatives and reforms intended to improve educational opportunities in West Las Vegas, and students of color throughout the school district. Additionally, the community looked to Principal Daisy for advice and guidance on educational and social issues that would affect their children, demonstrating the ways in which her leadership went far beyond that of instruction.

As a result of her community involvement and leadership, Principal Daisy received numerous professional honors and awards from local, state and national education and civic organizations over the course of her career, including the local NAACP, Professional Black Women's Alliance, 100 Black Men of Las Vegas, Distinguished Women of Southern Nevada, as well as the School Administrator of the Year from the Nevada Association of School Boards, and Milken Educator Award from the Milken Family Foundation, which honors "early-to-mid career education professionals for their already impressive achievements and, more significantly, for the promise of what they will accomplish in the future" (Milken Educator Awards, 2016, para. 2).

Findings and Discussion

In this section, we present case study findings and analyze Principal Daisy's leadership perspectives and practices according to Horsford et al. (2011) framework for culturally relevant leadership (CRL), which includes: (a) political context, (b) pedagogical approach, (c) personal journey, and (d) professional duty. We begin with a discussion of the political context in which Principal Daisy's leadership was situated, which is an important component of culturally relevant leadership practice.

Political Context

Throughout her 16 years as principal of Sunshine Elementary School, Principal Daisy was always very aware of the political context in which she operated. As a school that had been a predominantly Black and located in a historically Black neighborhood with a rapidly growing Hispanic immigrant population, Principal Daisy reflected on how population growth in Las Vegas and shifting student enrollment patterns in West Las Vegas held important implications for her student population and school environment. She explained that three years prior to our interview, the school was all Black, just like it was when she opened the school in 1994 as part of the *Prime 6 Schools* voluntary desegregation plan, or at least

"99 percent African-American." She recalled, "We had one white family that had a child. Two children actually. Anyways, we were all black."

But in 2007, due to overcrowding at a nearby elementary school that was predominantly Hispanic, Sunshine Elementary received 200 new children—all of whom were Hispanic, to which Principal Daisy remembered saying,

> We have a new face. We're not Black anymore. Because we were an African American school. Because all of our children lived right here in the neighborhood. The 200 Hispanic children, the Hispanic children lived within this zone and most of them can walk to school.

At first glance, it might appear that the decision by the school district to send 200 Hispanic children to Sunshine Elementary was solely an issue of overcrowding. Yet, the decision was also political in that the student population would now become racially mixed rather than a single race neighborhood school where the educational ideologies, philosophical assumptions and political perspectives (Horsford et al., 2011) were geared to African American students and parents and the African American community. The new demographics of the student population would bring with it a different set of politics based on race, culture, class and socio-economic status. Principal Daisy's culturally relevant leadership style would also be adjusted to include attending to the social, emotional and academic needs of her Hispanic students as well as their parents and other stakeholders.

Consistent with the political dimension of the CRL framework Principal Daisy's new school context would require her to build relationships and coalitions with policymakers and leaders in the Hispanic community and more importantly to serve as a community leader for a group whose culture was different from her own. One of the ways that Principal Daisy established relationships was to always welcome the parents of her Hispanic students to the school. She made it a point to welcome parents when they walked their children to school, when they came to the monthly parent meeting and when they came to the school to visit and check on their children. She made herself available to parents and made them feel not only welcome but that they were a part of the school culture. Her willingness to engage with all parents helped her to also build positive relationships with community stakeholders.

Pedagogical Approach

Principal Daisy was very clear in her pedagogical philosophy and approach to teaching and learning. She understood that many of her African American and Hispanic students were performing below grade level in key academic subjects. She also understood that many of her students came from homes where parents did not or could not help their children and did not stress the importance of academic achievement. To address these issues Principal Daisy emphasized that school was the place where students came to learn and that school personnel were responsible for not only conveying the importance of school attendance but for conveying the importance of doing well in all academic areas. She explained what she tells students and parents,

> We're here to learn to read on grade level. We're here to learn to compute, so that we can count. We're here to learn to think. Period. Because when you say, 'Why are you at school today? Because my momma told me.' Well, that's why you used to be here, but now, you're here to learn to read on grade level, you're here to learn to compute, and you're here to learn to think. So, everybody knows. Everybody knows why they're here.

In reflecting on the enrollment of her new Hispanic students into the school, she shared her belief that "what took place at [Sunshine] proved to us that good teaching is good teaching is good teaching." She continued,

> Programs are good, but unless you have a great teacher to come with every strategy that he or she can possibly think of, and not allow yourself to get discouraged because a child is struggling, it shows that the bottom line is good teaching, good classroom instruction.

She goes on to explain,

> Our Hispanic population is struggling in reading, because of the language barrier. Well, what we do is we use the language program to help children understand visually. That's one thing. We make sure that we are a visual teaching school, because every child, regardless of whether they are Hispanic or not, they have to be taught visually. We use other strategies, but visual is the main thing. They have to see it. They have to see it before they can every try to understand. We use it at Sunshine because of the academic challenge, so we use graphic organizers. That's part of our full curriculum across the board. Everything we do, we use graphic organizers to explain it so that children can understand it.

Principal Daisy worked with her teaching and support staff to help them be aware of and understand the cultural aspects of students' lives. Based on their awareness and understanding she also wanted them to structure classroom instruction and interactions to be conducive to good teaching that would lead to positive student outcomes. Consistent with the pedagogical dimension of the CRL framework, Principal Daisy used her leadership skills to enhance both teaching and learning for all students and particularly those students who experienced language and cultural barriers.

Personal Journey

In reflecting on her ability to connect with students from different cultures and backgrounds, Principal Daisy noted that,

> But do we have to sometimes search harder, as we are teaching across the curriculum, for people to really bring to life for children? Yes. Textbook-wise. But we (school personnel)

> also need to be culturally talented. It is a blessing that everybody's not Black or everybody's not white. We need to make sure that children understand that everybody's important, and the only way we can do it is to live it. We have to live it. We have to show them.

For example, one wall in the school showed pictures of students and their academic and social accomplishments. Students took pride in seeing themselves and having their accomplishments recognized. Another wall in the school showed the pictures and accomplishments of famous individuals who students could relate to culturally and ethnically.

Principal Daisy also believed that it was important that every child felt pride in themselves and that school personnel were, at least in part, responsible for instilling that pride. She stated that teachers must not only teach children to take pride in themselves but also must demonstrate that Sunshine Elementary is a diverse school and that all human beings are important.

Principal Daisy's culturally relevant leadership included setting goals for herself in terms of working with students, teachers, parents and the community. She too wanted to be culturally talented—to understand her students, where they came from, what type of home life they had and what she and her staff could do to help every child. One of the goals she set for herself was to visit the home of every student in her school. She commented on this goal in the following statement:

> You know, this was my plan, my goal. It was just something that I needed to do for myself. I visited every child's home that I was blessed to work with in this school. I could leave during the day and come back or walk home with them after school, or visit their homes on Saturdays. Everywhere that a Sunshine child might be, I'm there.

Home visits also made Principal Daisy more aware of the social and economic living conditions of each child. That knowledge in turn helped her to work with parents and to make sure their children received whatever the school could provide in terms of food, clothing, healthcare, and academic assistance.

Consistent with the personal journey dimension of the CRL framework, Principal Daisy was able to understand the cultural backgrounds of the African American and Hispanic children in her school. This knowledge enabled her to use her leadership skills to determine what the school, as the site of teaching and learning, could and should do to advocate for children and to enhance their social, emotional, physical and academic well-being.

Professional Duty

Principal Daisy believed it was her professional duty to use her leadership skills to help every child "beat the odds." She comments on this duty in the following statement:

> We have to beat the odds because of where our children live in West Las Vegas, and because of the homes the children walk out of in West Las Vegas. The odds are that they are not going to make it. The odds are right in a sense, because the fact is they are three years behind the majority [of white students]. Out of the 559 children that we're blessed to work with, 400 of our children walked out of somebody's home, and they were just not making the grade. So our job is to prove that we can beat the odds.

Another example of how Principal Daisy viewed the education of all children as her professional duty was her direct engagement with students. She taught a 2nd grade class every day. In her teaching she encouraged all students to display their knowledge by asking them questions, providing positive feedback and by "telling them they are smart."

Despite the fact that life's circumstances suggested that these children would not "beat the odds", Principal Daisy was committed to putting in place policies, practices and procedures to ensure that every child at Sunshine Elementary would have the opportunity to "beat the odds." Additionally, her philosophy that every child must be educated compelled her to work with her teachers and other school personnel, reach out to parents and the community, and take a personal interest in every student. While she was aware of the odds that defined the lives of many of the children in her school, she did not let those odds define her leadership. She persisted in using a culturally relevant leadership style that allowed her to develop a mission and a vision for her school and for the children she served. For Principal Daisy, "beating the odds" was her professional duty.

IMPLICATIONS FOR EDUCATION LEADERSHIP

School leaders, especially those in diverse school contexts, will be presented with numerous opportunities to practice Culturally Relevant Leadership. Political issues such as Common Core, standardized testing, immigration and school choice are all issues that politicize education and influence how and under what circumstances children receive an education.

Thus, the one size fits all approach to leading schools and educating children has ceased to be a useful model for today's diverse schools.

The diversity in U.S. schools demands new schools of thought when considering and adopting pedagogical approaches to teaching and learning. School leaders will need to adopt pedagogical practices that are culturally inclusive and anti-racist. Principals must also take the lead in helping teachers and other school personnel to re-think their methods with respect to children whose cultures are different from their own. Additionally, the principal who adopts culturally relevant leadership practices must identify professional development opportunities that allow teachers to develop effective pedagogical practices that benefit all students and the school generally.

School leaders who adopt culturally relevant leadership practices must also work to enhance their own cultural proficiency. Given the increasing numbers of international students who enter U.S. schools, it is important that school leaders develop and implement strategies that will allow them to serve every student, no matter their racial, cultural or ethnic background. The culturally relevant school leader is critical to the social, emotional and academic success of every student.

Finally, school leaders who wish to adopt culturally relevant leadership practices must be committed to diversity, equity and excellence in education. Not only should school leaders make this commitment a part of their own professional duty, but they must make their commitment a part of the mission and vision of the school; that is, teachers and other school personnel should "buy into" the principal's vision for a school that is committed to educating every child no matter the odds.

DISCUSSION QUESTIONS

1. Principal Daisy placed a great deal of importance on welcoming parents and making them a part of the culture of the school. What strategies can principals use to engage parents in the teaching and learning process and the overall school culture?
2. Principal Daisy was the leader of a school where many children were not expected to "beat the odds." Issues that included poverty, homelessness, lack of parental guidance and low academic performance were just a few of the problems that many of her students brought to school. What strategies can school leaders use to help students "beat the odds"?
3. Existing research suggests the cultural background and identity of a principal is critical to informing her or his leadership, particularly as it relates to issues of culture in the school. What role do you believe Principal Daisy's identity as an African American and woman played in her ability to engage the parents and families of Sunshine Elementary students who were previously disengaged from the daily life of the school?
4. In less than 16 years, Sunshine Elementary School, a once predominately Black school, became roughly 45% Black and 45% Hispanic, including a large share of students and parents whose home language was Spanish. How does a principal practice culturally relevant leadership amid swift demographic change?
5. Immigration, ethnic succession, resegregation, and gentrification reflect demographic and economic trends with important implications for the cultural demography of school populations. How should principals respond to

larger societal trends given the cultural conflict that often results in affected schools?

6. Given the four dimensions outlined in Horsford, Grosland, and Gunn's framework for culturally relevant leadership, are there additional dimensions that might be added to reflect how principals might facilitate family and community engagement in ways that move beyond the political, pedagogical, personal, and professional?
7. The school district superintendent has just identified you as Principal Daisy's replacement upon her retirement. In light of Principal Daisy's great popularity as principal of Sunshine within her school community, district, and larger Las Vegas community; how might you use CRL to frame your introduction and integration into the existing school culture and community?

NOTE

1. We use the term Hispanic to be consistent with Principal Daisy's usage in describing a share of her students and members of her school community.

REFERENCES

About the Milken Educator Awards. (2016). Retrieved from http://www.milkeneducatorawards.org/about/home/

Green, T. L. (2015). Leading for urban school reform and community development. *Educational Administration Quarterly, 51*(5), 679–711.

Horsford, S. D., Grosland, T., & Gunn, K. M. (2011). Pedagogy of the personal and professional: Toward a framework for culturally relevant leadership. *Journal of School Leadership, 21*(4), 582–606.

Horsford, S. D., Sampson, C., & Forletta, F. M. (2013). School resegregation in the Mississippi of the West: Community counternarratives on the return to neighborhood schools in Las Vegas, Nevada, 1968–1994. *Teachers College Record, 115*(11), 1–28.

Khalifa, M. A., Gooden, M. A., & Davis, J. E. (2016). Culturally responsive school leadership: A synthesis of the literature. *Review of Educational Research, 86*(4), 1272–1311.

Lomotey, K. (1989). *African-American principals: School leadership and success.* Westport, CT: Greenwood Press.

Lomotey, K. (1993). African-American principals: Bureaucrat/administrators and ethno-humanists. *Urban Education, 27*, 394–412.

Lomotey, K., & Lowery, K. (2014). Black students, urban schools, and Black principals: Leadership practices that reduce disenfranchisement. In H. R. Milner, IV & K. Lomotey (Eds.), *Handbook of urban education* (pp. 325–349). England: Taylor and Francis.

Lomotey K., Lowery K. (2015). Urban schools, Black principals, and Black students culturally responsive education and the ethno-humanist role identity. In Khalifa M., Arnold N. W., Oslanloo A.

F., Grant C. M. (Eds.), Handbook of urban educational leadership (pp. 118–134). Lanham, MD: Rowman & Littlefield.

Terrell, R. D., & Lindsey, R. B. (2009). *Culturally proficient leadership: The personal journey begins within*. Thousand Oaks, CA: Corwin Press.

Tillman, L. C. (2002). Culturally sensitive research approaches: An African American perspective. *Educational Researcher, 31*(9), 185–202.

Tillman, L. C. (2004a). African American principals and the legacy of *Brown*. *Review of Research in Education, 28,* 101–146.

Tillman, L. C. (2004b). (Un)intended consequences?: The impact of the *Brown v. Board of Education* decision on the employment status of Black educators. *Education and Urban Society, 36*, 280–303.

Walker, E. V. S. (1993). Interpersonal caring in the "good" segregated schooling of African-American children: Evidence from the case of the Caswell County Training School. *Urban Review, 25*, 63–77.

CHAPTER ELEVEN

Developing Teacher-Leadership by Employing an Improvement Science Framework for Organizational Problem Solving

ROBERT CROW AND REBECCA ENSLEY

INTRODUCTION

Leaders, not just as problem solvers, but also as problem finders, are often not the ones traditionally carrying designated leadership titles such as school principal or district superintendent. Because of the frequency of this nontraditional trajectory, professional preparation of those occupying non-traditional educational leadership roles happens haphazardly. One approach for moving toward creating a more inclusive, decision making organization is to cultivate a culture of collaborative leadership. In the collaborative leadership model, those who occupy the system hold the most valuable insights and use them to provide guidance toward tangible organizational improvements.

State and district level mandates for continuous improvement and quality assurance, requisites for collaborative approaches to improvement across organizational contexts, and the demands for professional development, provide a trifecta that when combined creates opportunities for staff to learn about evidence-based organizational problem solving. This illustrative case study presents a description of rudimentary niches where non-traditional leadership roles and skills may be developed, and tells the story of a high school principal who seizes opportunities for leadership development by coupling authentic practice with state-of-the-art frameworks for improvement.

THE SCHOOL IMPROVEMENT INITIATIVE: AN OPPORTUNITY FOR LEADERSHIP DEVELOPMENT

At the secondary education level, Jackson County Early College (JCEC) is an example of a culture where collaborative leadership is intentionally propagated among those with non-leadership designations or titles. A high school of innovative design, JCEC is located on the Blue Ridge mountain campus of Southwest Community College. The school represents a unique arrangement, comprising the principal, four faculty members, one guidance counselor, and one liaison to the Community College leadership.

Seven in number, the group's inclination toward participation was excitement, especially toward the topic of school impact planning, and in particular, for being involved and given the opportunity to provide unique perspectives on the annual improvement plan (Pearce & Conger, 2002). Because this group had been involved in ongoing professional development with education partner, NC New Schools, their exposure provided them with many examples of models of practice. Influenced by their working partnership with the former NC New School's network, JCEC's school improvement planning process followed a much different path than those followed by most traditional high schools in other states.

JCEC's unique pathway entails using a protocol called an IMPACT plan (see Figure 11.1). To reduce the degree of redundancy, the District allows the IMPACT Plan to serve as the School Improvement Plan (SIP), noting that the arrangement is in the vein of working smarter. IMPACT planning belies a continuous improvement mantra, a model more complex than those used in typical SIPs. IMPACT necessitates a school's commitment to regular collection and evaluation of data, cycling through it in iterative, analytical cycles. Using quarterly benchmarks, updates to the structured continuous improvement model regularly incorporate ongoing school self-assessment metrics (Cooperative Innovative High Schools criteria) to guide purposeful, data-informed planning throughout the school year. And while the goal of school improvement is cyclical, the IMPACT project timeline "refreshes" on an annual cycle, where yearly foci are determined each summer season.

The IMPACT planning model is grounded in the research of continuous improvement planning cycles. There are five main phases of the process, and the work done at each phase is meant to inform the next phase in the cycle. The cycle begins by having the individuals involved gather data that will be used to inform their process of identifying an area of improvement needed in the organization's current practice.

Once data have been collected, the teacher-leaders engage in a self-assessment of the organization's practices, and collectively score each area on a self-assessment rubric. The leadership team can incorporate the use of the causal systems diagram, such as a fishbone, to help them visually break down low scoring areas and isolate problems contributing to lower scores. Once the rubric is complete and the team has determined which area(s) to focus upon as they develop ideas for improvement, the group can then make use of the driver diagram framework to outline their improvement ideas. After the improvement ideas related to the plan are developed, the implementation phase of the cycle begins.

During implementation, progress-monitoring activities should be conducted at least every 90 days to assess the effectiveness of the change ideas executed and to determine whether adjustments, continued adoption, or the need to abandon the idea is necessary. The frequency of monitoring practices could be determined by the nature of the improvement initiative being implemented. At the conclusion of each school year, the teacher leadership team revisits the entire plan and all progress monitoring data to inform the development of the next cycle of improvement.

The recursive nature of school improvement lends itself to the use of improvement science tools for continuous quality assurance. Addressing areas where organizational or institutional deficits exist provides opportunities for those in non-traditional leadership roles to develop and hone leadership skills. With this idea in mind, the principal convened an initial meeting with the JCEC teacher-leadership group to seize on such an opportunity. The purpose for the meeting was to begin initial thinking regarding project formulation for addressing the group's annual task, the School Improvement Project (SIP).

The principal uses the SIP as an opportunity for professional development in using tools and frameworks adopted from the field of improvement science. Because of the relative age of the developing field, she decides to conduct an informal check of the team's readiness to tackle the task at-hand—in this case, readiness to use improvement science frameworks as tools for school improvement. Formatively, the principal determines that the improvement team lacks foundational knowledge in the area of improvement science frameworks, tools and processes, and that front-loading foundational knowledge would be necessary for readying the group to move forward with their task of creating the SIP.

The professional development required was conducted so that the team could ratchet up their current level of foundational knowledge on improvement science topics. Part of the front-loading was in reading the publication, *Learning to Improve: How America's Schools Can Get Better at Getting Better* (Bryk, Gomez, Grunow, & LeMahieu, 2015). The text was later discussed as a "book club" activity prior to beginning planning for the school's annual improvement initiative.

A Collaborative Tool for Organizational Problem-Finding: the Fishbone Diagram

Throughout the leadership planning sessions, prior to the group jumping in to the task at-hand, the principal made regular use of what she called the *Cognitive Warm-Up*. The objective of this particular warm-up activity is to activate the group's problem finding thinking. Conducted in three rounds, this exercise entails each team member being proscribed the role of either drawer, timekeeper, quality analyst, or coach/recorder. Within a prescribed timeframe, the principal instructed the team to reconstruct an image she briefly projected on the whiteboard. Although the directions were supplied, they were brief and lacked specific detail. The group then collaborated, exchanged dialogue, encouraged each other, asked questions, and completed the exercise with humor and enthusiasm. Once the activity was complete, the group processed the experience through dialogue with the principal. An excerpt follows:

Principal: *How did you approach the task?*
Participants: We brainstormed answers, began encouraging each other to move forward in the work, questioning the results we observed.
Principal: *What worked well?*
Participants: Others obeying; input.
Principal: *What could you change to do it better next time?*
Participants: We need more description, a collaborative orientation where each member could focus on a separate piece of the puzzle.

The principal introduced two more rounds, and asked the participants to continually refine their thinking about the process. One volunteer was overheard offering to take a certain section, so that her recreation of the original image was more intentional and focused. She explains:

Principal: *How did you approach the task?*
Participants: This time, jobs/roles were explained/determined ahead of time; clarified/demonstrated; focused more on details; even divided up the responsibilities—we adjusted our process; used prompted and guided questions for clarity and elaboration of detail.
Principal: *What worked well? And, what could you change to do it better next time?*
Participants: We retained some of the strategies (role-taking; questioning; encouragement) from the second round—but remained open to flexibility.

The goal of this initial *Cognitive Warm-Up* activity was to orient the group to problem-directed thinking. A reflective activity affords an opportunity for intentional role examination, and for processing the idea that clear communication influences the success or failure of collaborative initiatives. Other insights elicited by the exercise—determining preferences for ways of working on part of the whole; the intentional focus on strategy development; representation of a problem in multiple ways—demonstrate the efficacy, if only anecdotally, of the approach for eliciting strategic thinking on the part of the participants.

At this initial stage in improvement initiative planning, the leadership team spends time discussing issues, dilemmas, and problems the school is currently facing. The discussion enables the group to compile a list of potential aims and goals for the upcoming school year. Setting clear aims for their potential improvement initiatives allows the group to move to the next step, conducting a root cause analysis for determining the causal factors responsible for the issues, dilemmas, or problems identified.

Root Cause Analysis

Often labeled a fishbone diagram, the causal systems map is a structural tool for collecting and organizing current knowledge about potential underlying causes for complex organizational problems (Langley et al., 2009). A causal systems analysis is a primary component when working in organizational improvement. In the early stage of any improvement initiative, a causal systems analysis should be conducted using current knowledge about potential causes for the identified problem. In doing so, barriers are identified that hamper achievement of an outcome. The fishbone diagram allows ideas to be visually represented, literally allowing one to see the system that creates the problem (Bryk et al., 2015).

Through discussion, the group determines that "school disconnectedness" and "lack of academic support structures" are the two primary obstacles blocking JCEC's overall improvement aim—personalization of the student experience. The fishbone diagram depicted in Figure 11.2 presents these two perceived hindrances hypothesized to hamper feelings of school connectedness. Specifically, students' lack of feelings of personalization are due to (1) a disconnect from the school and its culture, and (2) a perceived lack of academic supports in place for scaffolding academic success. Two other categories, purpose and time, are also identified as causes believed to contribute to students' feelings of a school depersonalization, but are not discussed in this narrative.

Constructing a Theory of Action for Problem Solving: The Driver Diagram

In order to prime the group's thinking on problem solving, the principal first shows the teacher-leaders a three-minute YouTube video (*Stranded on the Escalator*). The *Cognitive Warm-Up* activity is used to prime thinking about problem solving (Mumford, Feldman, Hein, & Nagao, 2011). Once the initial activity has

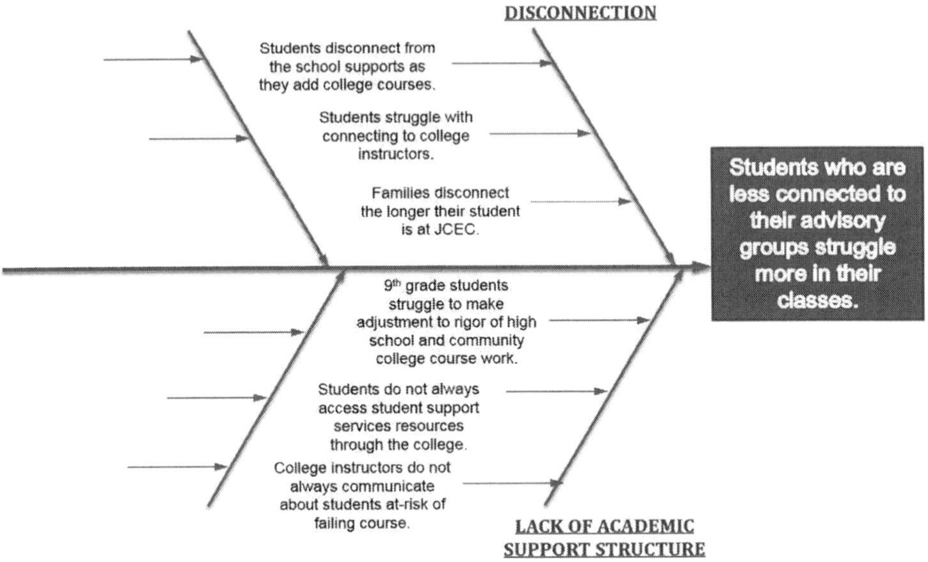

Fig 11.1. Causal systems analysis diagram.

been completed, the group begins to articulate a measurable aim, and to collaboratively respond to the questions, "What are you trying to accomplish?, How will you know that a chance is an improvement?, and What changes can you make that will result in an improvement?" (Langley et al., 2009, p. 9).

Once major causal factors have been determined, the next step in organizational improvement planning is to create a driver diagram. The learning arising from completing the causal systems analysis leads the group to work on the driver diagram. The driver diagram improvement framework allows participants to display their theory of improvement as well as to organize their ideas in order to answer the question, "What changes can we make that will result in improvement?"

The principal refers again to the New Schools rubric, pointing out the criteria of addressing "Personalization" as part of their school initiative. More closely, the principal directs the team's attention to the components describing the construct of 'personalization' and asks for feedback from the group about the choices of the two major problems facing JCEC student success being (1) feelings of disconnectedness from the school and its culture, and (2) the perceived lack of academic support structures to facilitate academic progress.

A synthesis of criteria arising from the work done with NC New Schools was elaborated upon and reworked for insertion into the driver diagram framework. Using the driver diagram description depicted in *Learning To Improve* (Bryk et al.,

2015), the principal reviews the diagram's components and orients the group in supplying the information called for by this particular framework.

Elements and Use of the Driver Diagram

As mentioned, a driver diagram is useful for articulating areas where change actions can be undertaken in an effort toward problem resolution. Driver diagrams are generally comprised of four elements, the first element being the outcome or aim of the overall improvement initiative. Once articulated, the aim statement guides all subsequent work. Second, primary drivers are crafted that represent major topical categories where, if changed or enhanced, would result in "moving the needle" toward achieving the project aim. In a typical project, 3–5 primary drivers are identified. Each of these drivers is subsequently broken down into a more granular subset of elements called secondary drivers. Aligned with each secondary driver are 2 to 3 change ideas written or stated in such a way that makes a change effort measurable.

Most often, improvement projects are framed within the iterative Plan-Do-Study-Act (PDSA) design for the cyclic exploration, testing and evaluation of improvement initiatives. Similar to the causal systems model, drivers in the model, and the change ideas associated with each driver, necessitate a determination as to which elements are the most attainable given contextual constraints. An analysis for choosing the highest leverage change ideas should be conducted for the expediency and impact of the project.

The group constructs the diagram's primary drivers depicting high leverage yet achievable actions believed to "move the needle" toward problem resolution. The principal includes the NC New School's criteria as a resource for aiding the group in fleshing out the primary drivers thought to contribute to achieving the ultimate aim; creating a feeling of connectedness among the student body (Figure 11.2). In our case, the primary drivers in the SIP are *relationships* and *academic supports*. Each topic represents a discrete category upon which improvement teams can focus. Often, each of the topics is assigned to a team or workgroup, so that several improvement initiatives may be conducted concurrently during a given year.

In order to articulate elements to serve as secondary drivers, the principal asks the group to identify "low hanging fruit." She asks, "What can we change most easily? Where can we get the most bang for the buck?" The group deliberates on her questions and then discussion ensues. One team member suggests the focus be on types of student support. Consensus leads the group to determine that the secondary drivers of student support, student ownership/leadership, and differentiated supports could be most readily addressed in the initiative.

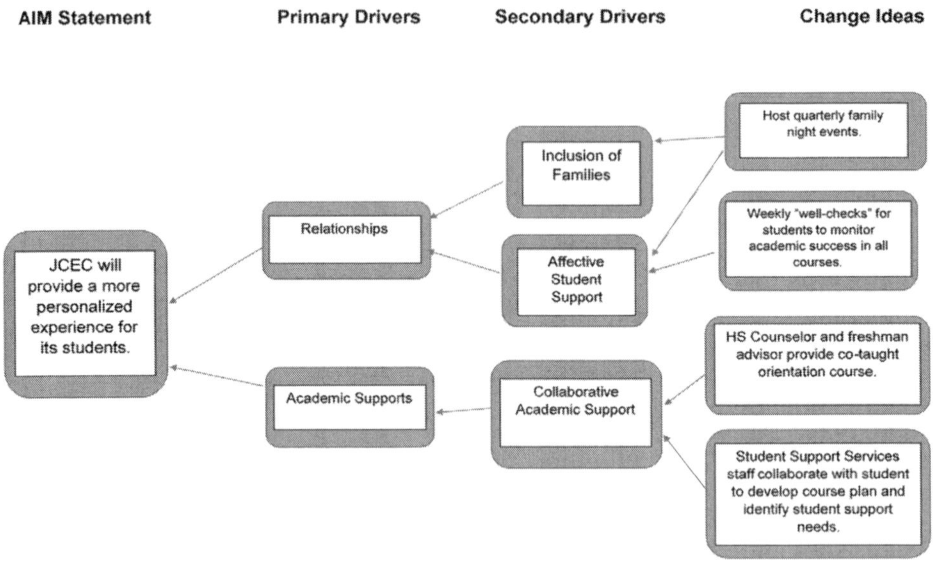

Fig 11.2. Example of a driver diagram model.

As the group began collaboration, a discussion ensued over elements of the driver diagram. In particular, one asks about the direction represented by the diagram, and what the direction implies for the change agents hypothesized to make a difference in achieving the overall aim. Other comments are exchanged in a dialogue theorizing about potential change ideas and their effect on the primary drivers.

In the final step of constructing the driver diagram the group crafts concrete, measurable change ideas to incorporate into the framework. The principal briefs the leadership team on "Big dot aims" versus "Little dot aims" and how achieving the aims will be related to the scope of the problem. In debriefing, the principal works with individuals to articulate change ideas logically aligned to their secondary driver counterparts. Because crafting descriptions of "means to ends" requires discussion and consensus building, dialoguing enables the group to establish a higher degree of shared understanding toward potential resolutions.

In the driver diagramming activity, teacher-leaders are learning to articulate responses to potential causes for the existence or perpetuation of problems identified. Flowing directly from the fishbone activity (i.e., the causal systems analysis), obstacles and hindrances thought to contribute to problem existence can be negated or have their impact lessened by crafting proactive responses. These responses, written in the form of action-oriented statements toward problem resolution, are depicted in the driver diagram in Figure 11.2.

Reflectively, the team mentions that, based on last year's work, more intentionality should be focused on a primary driver and more systematic focus on each of the major drivers. Lessons learned indicate that too many change agents loosely focused on an aim leads to frustration and exhaustion on the part of the teacher-leaders. More discussion ensued about the goals/aims, and the suggestions for change. The leadership group then engaged in weighing the relative merit of each change idea and the extent to which each is logistically attainable. The principal remarks, "The driver diagram is a graphic organizer for our work—it is a living breathing document."

Upon reflecting on the activity, it was clear that the group was at a novice level regarding their understanding and application of improvement science frameworks. How can we elevate their level of expertise is a question in preparing teacher-leaders to function as school leaders. Can simply reading about the topics—in this case, of improvement science—allow one to confidently apply the principles in the context of school leadership? Or, is a more comprehensive approach to professional development for school-based leadership by non-traditional leaders, such as teachers, necessary?

The group suggests that more information about the aim is needed. The group needed more consensus about the particulars of the initiative—What is it?, What we are aiming for?, etc. The group determines that more planning is needed and more debriefing considered in order to move forward with the improvement initiative. Some group members mention that it would help to (1) focus more on process, i.e., focus on the clarity of the end goal, (2) provide time to discuss notes, and (3) provide more devotion to develop the plan of action.

Testing Theories of Action: The Plan-Do-Study-Act Cycle

Using PDSA cycles to collect measurable data allows participants to determine whether an improvement effort really resulted in an improvement. Respectively, the PDSA cycle moves from plan to action (Langley et al., 2009) and is based on iterative learning arising from the completion of the cycle. The PDSA cycle (Figure 11.3) generally begins with devising a plan for achieving the aim.

Our aim to increase students' perceptions of personalization leads the leadership group to search for strategies and tactics deemed to be beneficial toward achieving that aim. The search for relevant information might entail locating published articles or books on the subject, consultation with experts and others related to the topic at-hand, and/or assessing the status quo on both the national and local levels regarding resources focused upon the topic at-hand. In essence, the plan phase of the cycle entails a good amount of investigative work.

The second, or do phase of the cycle, requires that improvement elements be tested. In our case, interventions in the form of family night, special orientation

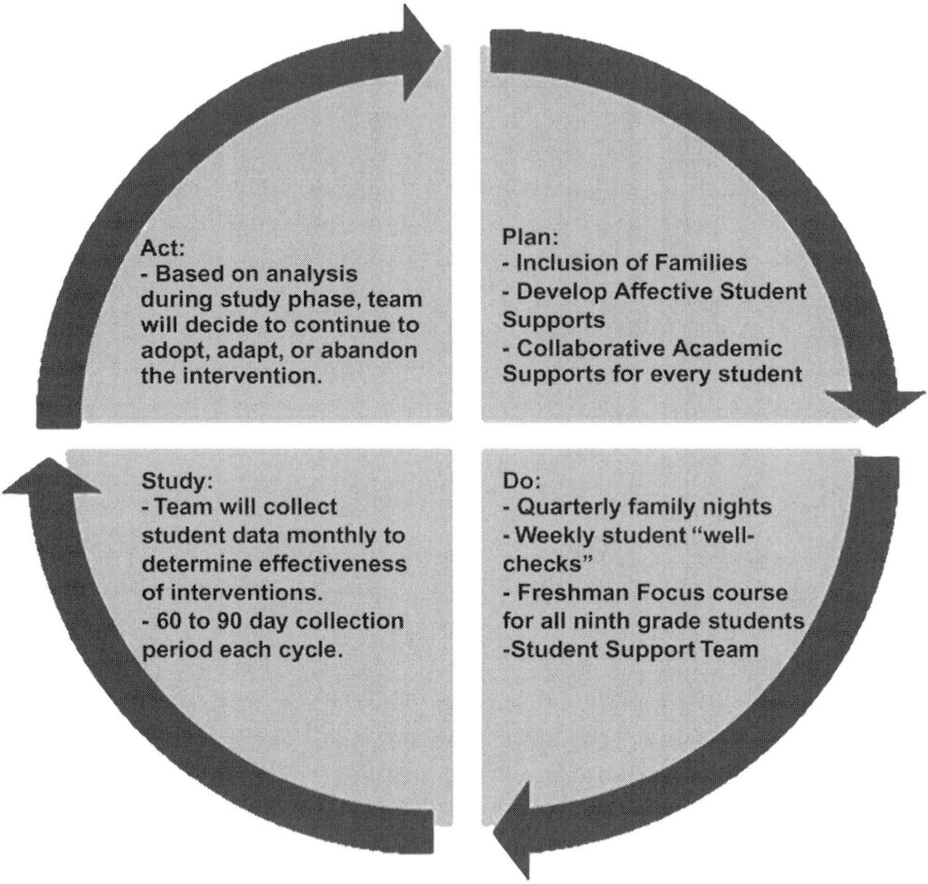

Fig 11.3. The Plan-Do-Study-Act cycle.

programming, and student wellness checks are examples where implementation teams can test actual efforts and their relative efficacy in "moving the needle" toward problem resolution.

Study, the third phase in the PDSA cycle, requires the evaluation of each of the change elements implemented. The team draws upon data collected during the previous phase, and makes judgments relative to progress. The trial-and-error nature of the PDSA cycle uses information, positive and negative, to make determinations regarding the improvement design's "next steps."

Due to the nature of the PDSA framework, "the models do not require [researchers] to specify ahead of time all the elements of an intervention, since practitioners participate in design, and implementation data inform an iterative design process that often transforms interventions" (Gutiérrez & Penuel, 2014,

p. 21). The final phase, act, is to put into action not only what is learned from the data presented, but to focus, as well, on the impact that new learning arising from conducting a trial-and-error approach, such as a PDSA cycle, assumes.

CONCLUSION

On the surface, what we see playing out in this illustrative case is that staff are leading an improvement initiative in their school. But what we do not see is the deep cognitive underpinning of leadership development: teachers "becoming" leaders through knowledge/skills development in using improvement science for organizational improvement. The ability to solve "problems of practice" is a skill not normally developed in either teacher-preparatory programs or other graduate coursework in education.

The unique expertise being developed at JCEC can happen in all schools. While covert in her implicit actions and embedded within the project, the principal of JCEC is integrating several major educational leadership outcomes into the experience:

- Transformational education leaders manage and develop staff members' professional skills and practices in order to drive student learning and achievement.
- Transformational education leaders cultivate a caring and inclusive school community dedicated to student learning, academic success and the personal well-being of every student.
- Transformational education leaders coordinate resources, time, structures and roles effectively to build the instructional capacity of teachers and other staff.

  (*Interstate School Leaders Licensure Consortium Standards for School Leaders*, 2015)

As a Cooperative Innovative High School (CIHS) team, JCEC has been engaging in continuous improvement planning for several years. The state model for school improvement planning being recommended to districts is formed directly from the iterative cycle processes that CIHS teachers have been engaging in for years. This trend makes the work teacher-leaders are doing at JCEC very relevant for other teacher leadership teams across the state to look to as exemplars to inform their own practice. This kind of collaboration leads to a network of improvement communities that can find strength in one another.

Collaborative leadership by those in non-designated or titled leadership roles cannot occur spontaneously. Specific opportunities must be created so that skills can be modeled and then practiced. The case presented here offers some insight about the type of professional development context in which these skills could be developed. The context must be intentional, that is, concrete projects serve as the site where theoretical constructs may be practiced on real-world problems. Annual school initiatives are particularly well suited for affording opportunities to practice leadership skills development. Opportunities for leadership development must be meaningful. Meaningful collaborations do not happen spontaneously, and trust- and team-building are necessary prerequisites for building foundational skills and dispositions.

The leadership goal is in providing opportunities for teachers to see themselves as action researchers. As leaders in decision making, the improvement project lends itself as a window of opportunity for teachers to learn and use improvement- and quality-oriented tools and frameworks as methods for making evidence-based decisions. We know that collaborative leadership skills must be intentionally developed, especially in those who occupy leadership niches that lack formal educational leadership titles, such as school principal or district supervisor. Often, the professional development of nontraditional leaders happens by chance, and unless intentional, these nontraditional leaders are often left powerless due to a lack of foundational leadership knowledge for practice.

This case presents a scenario where a principal leads her faculty and staff to occupy nontraditional leadership roles. Highlighting a case where the opportunity for leadership development centers around a school improvement initiative, this case presents the use of three different improvement science frameworks—the causal systems diagram, the driver diagram, and the Plan-Do-Study-Act Cycle. Empowering would-be leaders to actually lead by providing them a toolkit for evidence-based improvements leads to a new epistemology for sources of practical knowledge, in our case, the type of professional learning arising when evoking improvement science frameworks. The flow of practical knowledge will yield innovative thinking about practical solutions to pressing problems. With the ability to literally transform schools, improvement science frameworks should transfer to areas other than school improvement. Our hope is that these external frameworks, once internalized, open up opportunities for meaningful communication and shared ideas for improvement across all educational contexts.

DISCUSSION QUESTIONS

1. How might this collaborative experience transfer to the case of an individual teacher who is conducting classroom action research using the Plan-Do-Study-Act process?

2. Where are opportunities for "new learning" in improvement science processes?
3. What training or development should be included in teacher preparation programs related to organizational improvement?
4. How can classroom teachers use these tools to strengthen and improve classroom instructional practice?
5. What existing constructs or collaborative team models in education could be enhanced and improved by using Improvement Science frameworks as their guide?

REFERENCES

Bryk, A., Gomez, L., Grunow, A., & LeMahieu, P. (2015). *Learning to improve: How America's schools can be better at getting better.* Cambridge, MA: Harvard Education Press.

Gutiérrez, K., & Penuel, W. (2014). Relevance to practice as a criterion for rigor. *Educational Researcher, 43*(1), 19–23.

Langley, G., Moen, R., Nolan, K., Nolan, T., Norman, C., & Provost, L. (2009). *The Improvement guide: A practical approach to enhancing organizational performance.* San Francisco, CA: Jossey-Bass.

Mumford, M., Feldman, J., Hein, M., & Nagao, D. (2011). Tradeoffs between ideas and structure: Individual versus group performance in creative problem solving. *The Journal of Creative Behavior, 35*(1), 1–23.

Pearce, C. L., & Conger, J. A. (2002). *Shared leadership: Reframing the hows and whys of leadership.* Los Angeles, CA: Sage Publications.

Professional Standards for Educational Leaders. (ISLCC, 2015). Retrieved from http://www.ccsso.org/Documents/2015/ProfessionalStandardsforEducationalLeaders2015forNPBEAFINAL.pdf

SECTION THREE

Cases in Higher Education Leadership

CHAPTER TWELVE

Paul Quinn College's Michael J. Sorrell

A Case Study in Servant Leadership and Urban Renewal

AMANDA WASHINGTON, LEVON ESTERS,
AND MARYBETH GASMAN

Paul Quinn College is a private, faith-based, four-year liberal arts-inspired college that was founded on April 4, 1872 by a group of African Methodist Episcopal Church preachers in Austin, Texas. Today, the college boasts accolades that praise everything from its student leadership style to its institutional motto. Many of Paul Quinn College's accomplishments are the result of its faculty, students, and the dynamic leadership of President Michael Sorrell. Since 2007, under the presidency of Sorrell, Paul Quinn College has grown substantially. His leadership has focused on entrepreneurship, empowerment, and student engagement. With the implementation of the institutional ethos, "WE over me," President Michael Sorrell has proven that his unique leadership style is helping to revitalize Paul Quinn College while also instituting innovative and strategic developments for the small college's continued progress and evolution (Conrad & Gasman, 2015).

SERVANT LEADERSHIP

President Sorrell's motto of "We Over Me" is emblematic of the core principles of servant leadership, which emphasize increased service to others, a holistic approach to work, promoting a sense of community and the sharing of power in decision-making (Greenleaf & Spears, 2002; Spears, 2004; Spears & Schmader, 2014). Sorrell's commitment to the art and practice of relationship management has been effective in creating a culture at Paul Quinn where serving and empowering others is a natural way of life (Greenleaf & Spears, 2002). Also contributing to Sorrell's effectiveness as a servant leader is his strong moral compass, disdain for selfishness and aversion to mediocrity (Spears, 2004).

As is the case for most individuals who engage in servant leadership, Sorrell's approach to leading Paul Quinn has made a positive impact on faculty, staff and students. For example, Sorrell has made it a priority to serve the community in which Paul Quinn resides. Paul Quinn's approach to community engagement, which will be discussed later in this chapter, allows students to engage in efforts that are larger than themselves. Various community engagement activities allow students to build their servant leadership skills and participate in learning experiences that are transformational in nature. More importantly, exposing students to hands-on servant leadership opportunities helps build their leadership skill tool kit, which can contribute to their becoming more well-rounded individuals.

Another by-product of President Sorrell's commitment to servant leadership has been his influence on the level of accountability that students have for themselves and their peers. For example, the notion of accountability is so pervasive at Paul Quinn that students who do not buy-in to the "we over me" mantra typically do not last very long and usually end up leaving the college. Without question retention is important and taken very seriously at Paul Quinn, however, the institution wants to retain students who care about one another and the institution as a whole (Conrad & Gasman, 2015).

President Sorrell has made it a priority for the faculty, staff and students to engage with the local community through a variety of activities. Interestingly, Paul Quinn's focus on community engagement, which is a by-product of Sorrell's commitment to servant leadership reflects several of Wheeler's (2012) ten principles of servant leadership such as service to others being the highest priority, modeling servant leadership, and the development of more servant leaders. Many of the Paul Quinn's community engagement activities involve students' contributing to long-term service learning projects such as the school's recently created organic farm, which provides fresh produce to the local community.

President Sorrell's unwavering commitment to being an innovative servant leader has garnered the attention of individuals across all levels of higher education. His leadership style has empowered faculty, staff and students, all of which have contributed to Paul Quinn fast becoming recognized as an innovative urban liberal arts institution that serves students from underserved, underprivileged and low-income backgrounds. There is much to learn from Sorrell's approach to servant leadership and a good amount of evidence already suggests that his focus of serving others first has been a major factor in helping elevate Paul Quinn into national conversations of HBCUs that are making a comeback (Freemark, 2015).

Community Engagement

HBCUs have a strong history of community and civic engagement (Gasman, Spencer, & Orphan, 2015) and President Sorrell has been instrumental in elevating Paul Quinn as a national model because of his approach to engaging students in innovative community-based activities. Students attending Paul Quinn have opportunities to participate in a variety of community engagement activities, which focus primarily on service learning and civic participation. It is worth noting that a major outcome of engaging students in community engagement activities is that it provides them with opportunities for transformational learning experiences. In large measure, a driving force behind Paul Quinn's focus on community engagement is President Sorrell's commitment to servant leadership not to mention the institution's location in the middle of a food desert in South Dallas, TX, which provides opportunities for faculty, staff and students to serve the local residents, many of whom are from surrounding low income and under-resourced communities (Michael J. Sorrell, personal communication, fall 2015).

President Sorrell believes that small urban colleges have a moral and legal responsibility to address the needs of the community to which they reside and in many ways, Paul Quinn has been a shining example to this ideal. Sorrell has worked tirelessly to ensure that Paul Quinn serves as the impetus for economic development for the surrounding community by initiating an innovative community engagement model. Through various community engagement development efforts, Paul Quinn has been able to address the issues and needs important to the community it serves. These efforts have resulted in Paul Quinn serving as an anchor institution for the community. Sorrell's approach to community engagement focuses on serving others, especially those from the inner city and has helped create a unique institutional niche for Paul Quinn.

President Sorrell's innovative approach to community engagement has resulted in the development of the "We Over Me" organic farm. Much has been written about the farm and how it was borne into existence (Conrad & Gasman, 2015; Freemark, 2015). In short, Sorrell eliminated Paul Quinn's football team and decided to turn the football field into an organic farm. The farm serves multiple purposes: (1) as a source of fresh food for students and the local community, (2) as a lab for students to learn about entrepreneurship, nutrition, work, activism and community politics, and (3) as a source of funding to help reduce student debt and defray the cost of attending Paul Quinn College. A major benefit of having the farm has been that students learn about the role of work, job creation and most importantly, the role that service to others can play for individuals who are from under-resourced communities. Without question, the "We Over Me" farm has been one of Sorrell's most innovative ideas and can serve as a model for other urban, liberal arts colleges that are looking for ways to engage with their local community, expand student learning opportunities and create new revenue streams for their institution.

President Sorrell's focus on community engagement has resulted in faculty, staff, and most prominently, students participating in student activism efforts. In particular, students from Paul Quinn participated in a protest movement in response to the City of Dallas' decision to expand a landfill in the Highland Hills/ Paul Quinn College neighborhood. The movement, which became known as "I Am Not Trash," engaged more than eighty students, many of whom were members of the student government association. Faculty and staff were also involved in several protests. In short, the protests, which included numerous marches, resulted in the landfill expansion project being blocked. Interestingly, the idea of activist leadership, which was shown by the students' actions, permeates the entire campus and students see being civically engaged within the local community as vitally important. Clearly, Sorrell's vision for Paul Quinn's involvement in community engagement activities is very much related to his commitment to servant leadership.

It is clear that President Sorrell has focused much effort on expanding Paul Quinn's footprint within the community engagement movement. The "We Over Me" farm has provided students with a variety of quality learning experiences with the major outcome being that they learn the art and practice of being servant leaders. Sorrell's commitment to community engagement also continues to fuel his vision of creating a new urban college model. Other urban-based institutions can replicate many aspects of Paul Quinn's model, such as how the institution engages with the community. Finally, President Sorrel has plans to further expand Paul Quinn's community engagement through the development of a grocery store and "pop-up" restaurant that will further contribute to Paul Quinn's status as a premier urban liberal arts institution (Michael J. Sorrell, personal communication, fall 2015).

Branding

Twenty-first century HBCU presidents who recognize the importance of institutional branding and marketing and who are willing to make it a priority will better enable their institutions to thrive and expand their reach across the higher education landscape (Esters et al., 2016). To this point, there is little doubt that President Sorrell has been highly effective in branding, and in many ways, re-branding Paul Quinn College. President Sorrell has had a significant presence across social and print media and during every public speaking opportunity he makes it a priority to share the "Quinnite" nation story to whoever will listen. Sorrell is exceptional at sharing the successes of current students, alumni, faculty and staff. He is also well adept at highlighting various academic programs, curriculum offerings, as well as recruitment and fundraising events. A common thread among Sorrell's branding efforts is his commitment to the "We Over Me" mantra whereby the successes of others are first and foremost in his messaging (Michael J. Sorrell, personal communication, fall 2015).

President Sorrell has prioritized three distinct areas in his re-branding of Paul Quinn and includes a focus on: (1) Servant leadership, (2) Entrepreneurship and (3) Academic excellence. Regarding servant leadership, Sorrell highlights the "We Over Me" mantra, which reflects his commitment and expectation of others to put the needs of others first. Sorrell's actions speak louder than words. He puts the needs of others, namely students, first and expects that faculty and staff does the same. Most impressive is that a culture of peer accountability is pervasive throughout Paul Quinn whereby students hold each other accountable to the "We Over Me" philosophy (Conrad & Gasman, 2015).

President Sorrell has also made significant progress in taking an innovative approach to using entrepreneurship as a mechanism to create opportunities for the institution. As discussed previously, the "We Over Me" farm has been a shining example of Sorrell's vision on how to create a new funding model for Paul Quinn. Sorrell's vision to develop an innovative urban liberal arts institution is being achieved through the farm as it has contributed to Paul Quinn being recognized as a "work college" whereby student debt has been reduced and other costs of attending have been defrayed, resulting in students graduating with less than $10,000 in debt. The farm has also enabled students to gain valuable skills that contribute to them being ready for the workforce.

Perhaps the most important branding effort pursued by President Sorrell is his emphasis on establishing Paul Quinn as a place where academic excellence is integrated within the fabric of the entire institution. On any given day of the week, you will see President Sorrell highlighting the accomplishments of faculty, staff and students and the growth being achieved by each of these groups. Under President Sorrell's leadership, not only have enrollment, retention and graduation rates increased; the academic profile of Paul Quinn has been enhanced. For example, the average ACT and SAT scores of incoming students are within one point and 100 points respectively of the national average for African-American students. Other accomplishments include the creation of a Presidential Scholars Program, a robust online degree program, a summer internship program and a student track record of obtaining jobs in highly respected companies (Michael J. Sorrell, personal communication, fall 2015).

Sorrell's commitment to enhancing the academic profile of Paul Quinn has also afforded opportunities for faculty and staff to engage in professional development opportunities that allow them to enhance their course content and learn new and innovative teaching and learning techniques. Paul Quinn's enhanced academic profile has resulted in the development of partnerships with institutions such as

Duke, Yale, the University of Pennsylvania, and with business and industry. Study abroad, which was not a part of the Paul Quinn culture prior to Sorrell's tenure, is now embedded within the institution, which provides students with an expanded set of transformational learning experiences. Sorrell's commitment to academic excellence has resulted in numerous opportunities that will continue to raise the profile of Paul Quinn as a premier urban liberal arts institution.

HBCU presidents who are committed to enhancing the public image of their institutions through innovative branding approaches provide opportunities to build stronger support among current students, faculty, staff, alumni, and parents (Esters et al., 2016). What most contributes to President Sorrell's success is his use of consistent, distinctive and attractive messaging in concert with the strategic use of social media. It should also be noted that President Sorrell's approach to institutional branding and marketing as a serious undertaking has resulted in an uptick in the philanthropic support of Paul Quinn with two of the largest donor gifts being given during his tenure as president. President Sorrell's focusing his branding efforts on servant leadership, entrepreneurship and academic excellence has done much to elevate Paul Quinn into the national spotlight of institutions that have been able to create a culture of sustained growth and success (Michael J. Sorrell, personal communication, fall 2015).

Entrepreneurship

President Michael Sorrell's entrepreneurial spirit is both a driving force in his leadership style and a premiere reason for Paul Quinn College's success. Prior to President Sorrell's appointment, like many HBCUs across the nation, Paul Quinn College faced waning financial support, a limited endowment, and less state support than many of the surrounding larger majority serving institutions (Matthews, 2012). Such limitations can hinder faculty development and stifle new academic programs for students. In fact, in 2007, the Boston Consulting Group predicted that unless drastic measures were taken to address declining student enrollment, low campus morale and a lack of financial resources, the college would likely be forced to close it doors for good (Watson, 2014). President Sorrell has put entrepreneurship at the crux of his leadership style—a strategy that has proven successful. His entrepreneurial efforts have innovatively garnered additional academic, extracurricular, and financial resources for his students, the institution, and the surrounding Dallas community.

In an interview, President Sorrell noted, "our whole model is built on helping and building the community around us." In the nine years that he has served as President, Sorrell has undergone several entrepreneurial ventures that have raised Paul Quinn College's visibility and provided additional funding (Michael J. Sorrell, personal communication, fall 2015). Several years ago and as noted earlier in this paper, recognizing that his college was located in a food dessert, he led an initiative to turn the football field into a community farm. Since its 2010 inception, Paul Quinn College's "We Over Me Farm," has supported not only the college but also community members, restaurants and grocers with over 30,000 pounds of organic produce. As the mission of the farm is steeped in empowerment and service, ten percent of the produce has also been donated to neighborhood charitable organizations.

Continuing to channel his entrepreneurial leadership style, President Sorrell has helped the college and surrounding community access Dallas' vast performing art offerings. Years ago, he convinced the Dallas symphony to play three concerts on the college's campus every summer. President Sorrell opens the concert to the students, faculty, staff, and general public and builds a stage in one of the student parking lots. He admitted that the first few years were rough as many critics doubted student and community interest in classical music. Despite this opposition, Sorrell boasts that the college's Dallas symphony concert following has grown from a mere 250 to well over 2,500 audience members from all over the city.

The "We over Me Farm" and the Dallas Symphony concerts are just two of the many ways that President Sorrell's innovative and entrepreneurial spirit have profoundly shaped his leadership style. He urges fellow college presidents to lean into the risk of entrepreneurship and nontraditional innovation. His leadership style not only allows him to implement entrepreneurial ventures, but it also inspires him as he continues to uplift Paul Quinn College and the larger higher education community.

Empowerment

Another powerful component of President Sorrell's leadership style is his ability to empower and inspire those around him. He attributes much of his desire to inspire his students to his own upbringing in the rural South. The product of a father who did not go to college and of a mother who was second-generation college graduate, President Sorrell wholeheartedly believes in creating equally supportive environments for *all* students—those who were raised with "love" and those who were raised with "tough love" (Michael J. Sorrell, personal communication, fall 2015).

As he leads the faculty and staff of Paul Quinn College, he tries to lean into what he jokingly coins as "organized chaos." He empowers his faculty and staff by attempting to hire the smartest and most entrepreneurial people he can find, giving them a goal, and then,—after coaching—turning them loose to accomplish the goal. As he leads in this way, he aims to continually push the faculty at Paul Quinn College to adapt to the circumstances that are before them.

His advice for fellow college presidents is embedded in a phrase often used by his grandmother—"*you've gotta give them what the hand calls for.*" He hopes to empower college presidents with his personal leadership philosophy of "*giving what the hand calls for*" (Michael J. Sorrell, personal communication, fall 2015).

> In [my personal circumstance at Paul Quinn College], what the hand called for was crises management and in crises management you don't have time to worry about how people's feelings are going to be impacted. We were looking at the extinction of a 135 year old institution. Effectively, the school would have been able to survive post-slavery South but not us. That is a damning statement and it is also an incredibly embarrassing reality. When I looked at all of this and took it into account and tried to rationalize the place that we were in, it was clear that we were in extreme circumstances and in those extreme circumstances we were either going to evolve or perish. There were a lot of people that had bought into the narrative of 'we're a struggling HBCU and that's all we've ever been and all we're capable of.' They were wrong and I took refuge in the knowledge that there's not permanence in struggle—struggle is merely a state of transition on your way to not struggling. You have to acknowledge your circumstances and also acknowledge that your today will not be your tomorrow. (Michael J. Sorrell, personal communication, fall 2015)

Student Support

Paul Quinn College has soared under the leadership of President Sorrell. Another notable feature of his leadership style is his emphasis on student leadership. Students are at the crux of the Paul Quinn College mission so much so that the college won the "HBCU Student Government Association of the Year."

As a college athlete who was heavily recruited, Sorrell understands that recruiting is an important key to the success of students at the college. As he recruits students to Paul Quinn College, he messages that students will be a part of accomplishing something bigger than themselves because the college is centered on the mission of "WE over me."

He notes that he has successfully attracted students for a few reasons. One of those reasons is that he has created a financial structure that allows students to graduate with less than $10,000 dollars in debt. Additionally, he has worked tirelessly for Paul Quinn College's visibility and opportunities to balloon over the last nine years. Students never know what's coming next and "students like to win … you come to Paul Quinn if you want to win" (Michael J. Sorrell, personal communication, fall 2015).

As he engages with and produces exceptional student leaders, he suggests that the single best advice is that all leaders have to lead with love. This lesson has taught him that he needs to be more human and that the best way to get through to students is to let them know that they have a support system and, if they choose to come to Paul Quinn College, he will lead in love as he helps them get through the toughest times of their academic and life experiences.

CONCLUSION

In a time of leadership uncertainty and turmoil at Historically Black Colleges and Universities, Michael Sorrell's example is a crucial one. Presidents inheriting institutions that are teetering on extinction and even those in much better shape would do well to look to his lead and follow his example. With a combination of drive, bravery, integrity, and perseverance in the midst of ridicule and laughter from many inside and outside the HBCU world, Sorrell has transformed Paul Quinn College into a viable player in American higher education.

DISCUSSION QUESTIONS

1. What does a leader gain from using a servant leadership approach? What does s/he gain?
2. How does a leader foster entrepreneurship and servant leadership among his/her team?

REFERENCES

Conrad, C., & Gasman, M. (2015). *Educating a diverse nation: Lessons from Minority Serving Institutions.* Cambridge, MA: Harvard University Press.

Esters, L., Washington, A., Gasman, M., O'Neal, B, Commodore, F., Freeman, S., & Carter, C. (2016). *The 21st century HBCU president.* Philadelphia, PA: Penn Center for Minority Serving Institutions.

Freemark, S. (August 20, 2015). *The reinvention of Paul Quinn College. American Radio Works.* Retrieved from http://www.americanradioworks.org/segments/reinvention-paul-quinn-college.

Gasman, M., Spencer, D., & Orphan, C. (2015). Building bridges, not fences: A history of civic engagement at private Black colleges and universities. *History of Education Quarterly, 55*(3), 346–379.

Greenleaf, R., & Spears, L. (2002). *Servant leadership: A journey into the nature of legitimate power.* New York, NY: Paulis Press.

Matthews, C. M. (2012). *Federal support for academic research.* Washington, DC: Congressional Research Service, Library of Congress.

Spears, L. (2004). *Practicing servant leadership: Succeeding through trust, bravery, and forgiveness.* San Francisco, CA: Jossey-Bass.

Spears, T., & Schmader, W. (2014). *What exceptional leaders know: High impact skills, strategies & ideas for leaders.* New York, NY: Motivational Press.

Watson, J. (2014). Paul Quinn College sharing story of turn around with world. *Diverse Issues in Education,* http://diverseeducation.com/article/67362.

Wheeler, D. (2012). *Servant leadership for higher education: Principles and practices.* San Francisco, CA: Jossey-Bass.

CHAPTER THIRTEEN

Exploring Preservice Teachers', Novice Teachers', and Teacher Education Faculty Perceptions of Teacher Leadership

CARRIE ROGERS AND ROYA Q. SCALES

Teacher leadership, the concept and the multiple formal and informal roles that illustrate the concept within schools, is not new but as Lieberman (2013) writes, "Its purposes and definitions have changed continually revealing its complexities and conundrums" (p. 169). Teacher involvement in school reform and the improvement of teaching and learning in schools is often referred to as teacher leadership. The opportunities for teachers to become leaders varies greatly within contexts and norms of schools and districts, yet it is an expectation of most state and national organizations that teachers demonstrate leadership. In the state of North Carolina there are six standards for teachers, and standard one is "Teachers Demonstrate Leadership" (North Carolina State Board of Education, 2013). Now, not only are in-service teachers evaluated on leadership but preservice teachers, in North Carolina at least, are required to document and reflect on their leadership activities within student teaching as a part of their licensure requirements.

In a previous study (Rogers & Scales, 2013) we analyzed this licensure component and findings indicated that the preservice teachers expressed a wide variety of definitions of teacher leadership. Next, program graduates were followed to investigate their leadership activities and perceptions of themselves as teacher leaders while in their first year of teaching (Scales & Rogers, 2017). Those combined

service and novice teachers led us to survey our teacher edu-
ıbers to determine their ideas and definitions of teacher lead-
y for preservice teachers. In this chapter we review theories of
p, as well as our findings to explore the similarities and differences among p- ce, novice, and teacher education faculty ideas about teacher leadership. We offer this chapter as a case of varied perceptions of teacher leadership, and the significance these perceptions have on the preparation of teacher leadership in preservice teacher education are discussed.

WHAT IS TEACHER LEADERSHIP?

Leadership is an idea that most people understand in some way. But like other concepts such as love or democracy, leadership can be defined quite differently by people in different contexts. Who is a leader and what constitutes leadership is often in the eye of the beholder. While leadership is a complex concept with many different theoretical approaches, Northouse (2016) describes four components as central to any theory of leadership: process, influence, groups, and common goals. Northouse (2016) uses this as the guiding definition of leadership, "Leadership is a process whereby an individual influences a group of individuals to achieve a common goal" (p. 6). Similarly, the definition of teacher leadership that is most commonly used in teacher leadership research is, "Teacher leadership is the process by which teachers, individually or collectively, influence their colleagues, principals, and other members of school community to improve teaching and learning practices with the aim of increased student learning and achievement" (York-Barr & Duke, 2004, pp. 287–288). From this definition we can see that the goal to be achieved in teacher leadership is increased student learning. Other conceptions of teacher leadership exist, such as Lieberman and Miller's (2004), that breaks down York-Barr and Duke's definition into three separate roles teachers can take: advocates who concern themselves with student learning; innovators who are the change agents; and stewards who are the models of continued improvement of the profession. The concept of teacher leadership is a robust field of study, which focuses on (1) the roles and areas of influence that teachers have in their schools, (2) the larger educational community's research advocating distinct formal roles and differentiated paths (Margolis & Huggins, 2012), as well as (3) subtle acts of leadership in interpersonal relationships (Sato, 2005). Regardless of the nuances in definitions, the idea that teachers should engage in processes that guide policies that impact the school and students has been around for at least 70 years (i.e., Dewey, 1946).

The idea that teacher education has a significant role to play in creating teacher leaders, however, is fairly new. York-Barr and Duke (2004) referenced two studies on preservice education for teacher leadership and since their review, teacher leadership at the preservice level has become an emerging field of research. Many studies on preservice teacher leadership suggest ideas and strategies for allowing teacher candidates to demonstrate leadership within their undergraduate work (Mangin & Stoelinga, 2009; Turnbull, 2005). For example, Bond and Sterrett (2014) promote the idea that preservice teachers who serve as officers of student professional organizations such as Kappa Delta Pi are better prepared to be teacher leaders. Holland, Eckert, and Allen (2014) premise their research on the idea that teacher education must help preservice teachers understand school culture and have mentors who are teacher leaders in order to be fully prepared to implement the "fourth wave" of teacher leadership: impacting policy rather than following mandates (p. 436). They argue that current novice teachers see teacher leadership as involvement in school-based decision making, a path to tenure, and administrative responsibilities. Many teachers see teacher leadership as a role that they are given with a certain tasks to accomplish. Anecdotally, as well as through some research, "Lead Teachers" in many schools function as assistant principals with managerial types of responsibilities (Bruce, Jarvis, Flynn, & Brock, 2011). However, leadership and management are vastly different constructs, as Northouse (2016) asserts teachers who are given "leadership" roles that focus on reducing the chaos of the school day or increasing efficiency of the organization are managers, not teacher leaders. Sommerness, York-Barr, and Hur (2008) echo this statement by indicating that teachers share leadership with the administration (i.e., Principal) to "enact the school's vision of advancing teaching, rather than just being communicators or coordinators" (para. 4). So, if teacher leadership requires an "expanded set of capacities and skills, beyond those required for excellence in classroom instruction" (Sommerness, York-Barr, & Hur, 2008, para. 42) can teacher preparation programs really expect their candidates to demonstrate teacher leadership? Some educational researchers (e.g., Quinn, Haggard, & Ford, 2006; Rogers & Scales, 2013) offer a view that preservice teachers have developmental and context constraints in demonstrating teacher leadership, as defined by York-Barr and Duke (2004). The Bank Street College of Education met similar limitations in meeting its goal for their graduates to "be leaders in the creation of a better world for all of our children" (Snyder, 2015, p. 7). While Bank Street preservice teachers took on leadership roles in classrooms and schools and "talked the talk" about advocacy, graduates found it hard to take on these roles (Snyder, 2015). Further, principals reported that Bank Street graduates, while excellent classroom teachers, had trouble "fitting in" to the school culture. Reading between the lines, we imagine that the trouble fitting into the school culture may have been because the culture did not support a vision of teacher leaders that was similar to Bank Street's.

What we have learned from the emerging research on preservice teacher leadership development indicates that helping students understand the culture of schools (Snyder, 2015), offering mentors, intentionally using the language of leadership across courses (Holland, Eckert, & Allen, 2014), and encouraging students to be leaders in organizations (Bond & Sterrett, 2014) may impact their ability to be teacher leaders. In the next section we offer brief summaries of our recent research and findings on teacher leadership at three levels: preservice teachers, novice teachers, and teacher education faculty.

PRESERVICE TEACHERS

The North Carolina leadership standard for teachers served as the basis for the preservice Teacher Leadership Essay state licensure requirement. The leadership standard for North Carolina teachers has five provisions: teachers lead in their classrooms, teachers lead in their schools, teachers lead in their profession, teachers advocate for schools and students, and teachers maintain high ethical standards. Teachers lead in their classrooms by using data to help all students learn and they create a safe environment that promotes learning and collaboration among students. Teachers lead in their schools by participating in learning communities, school improvement plans, and collaborations with colleagues to improve learning in the school. Teachers lead in their profession through their own professional growth by finding development opportunities and participate in professional organizations. Teachers advocate for schools and students by supporting, participating, and initiating in policies and practices that promote student learning. Finally, teachers model the standards in the state's Code of Ethics (North Carolina State Board of Education, 1998).

Three of the five provisions are explicitly related to student learning: Teachers lead in their classrooms, their school, and advocate for schools and students. While our institution's requirement focuses less on student growth, our requirements are for preservice teachers to demonstrate: (1) leadership in the school, (2) professional development, and (3) collaboration with families *through activities that show experience and in-depth understanding of the concept of "Teacher as Leader."* The assignment also gives ideas that "activities must be substantial and meaningful" and can take the form of, but are not limited to, the following:

- *Semester-long participation on a school improvement team*
- *Evidence of planning and collegial work with the cooperating teacher (and/or another teacher in the school) on a project or problem of concern addressed in the school's improvement plan*
- *Involvement and participation in the development of an IEP or an IFSP*
- *Meetings with the parents/guardians at the school, phone calls to the home, etc.*
- *Planning and participation in a school-wide event (i.e., field trip, band performance, assemblies, open house, senior projects, health fair, parent conferences, bicycle safety program, etc.)*

- *Planning and participation in a school system-wide event (i.e., Special Olympics, Odyssey of the Mind, fundraiser, health and wellness initiative, science fair, writing contest, fine and performing arts event, etc.)*

In our analysis of 62 Teacher Leader essays at the preservice level (Rogers & Scales, 2013) we, along with four preservice teacher researchers, independently read 10 essays to determine possible codes. Using a grounded theory approach (Strauss & Corbin, 1998) during the first research meeting, we identified categories from the leadership essays, with subcategories to add detail and depth to the larger categories. Based on evidence within the essays, the research team developed the core categories of *leadership*, *tone*, *resources*, *role*, and *activity* because each essay focused on the activities as ways of being a teacher leader. Subcategories for the leadership category included the level of leadership. Levels of leadership were defined as *witness*, *participation*, and *ownership*. The research team proceeded to code the remaining essays in dyads and shared findings and refinements at subsequent research meetings. We continued this process the following year with 75 additional leadership essays and discovered that our codes held true.

Findings indicated that preservice teachers engaged in activities primarily at the classroom and school-level, and the majority of the activities were of a participatory nature. Indeed, from the two years of data collection and analysis, the 271 reported activities were categorized as afterschool/out-of-school, in-school/classroom, and parent-oriented. Afterschool/out-of-school events were coded as the most frequent type of activities, with 113 (42%) documented activities describing involvement in these activities, such as dances, clubs, fundraisers, field trips, and service learning opportunities. In-school/classroom events were categorized as the second most prevalent type of activities, with 101 (37%) of the activities detailing involvement in meetings/committees and general classroom activities. Parent-oriented events included interactions with parents in an organized way, including parent conferences and PTO nights, with 57 (21%) of the activities describing involvement in these events. The activities rarely went beyond the grade-level and school and, more importantly, rarely were explicitly connected with instructional practices. Following are ways preservice teachers described their activities that were coded as "participation".

To illustrate afterschool/out-of-school events, one preservice teacher wrote, "For this event [school dance], I helped with the planning, I chaperoned, and I was a part of the decorating committee and clean up team."

To illustrate in-school/classroom events, two participants' descriptions stood out. First, by helping lead with the class field trip, this preservice teacher clearly demonstrates participation:

> Little things like this really show me what it means to solve the problems that everyone comes running at you with. You really learn to think on the spot in these situations and

> since I was a "leader" on this field trip, the kids assumed that I was the one with all the answers.

Second, another preservice teacher created an outdoor conservancy education class to teach during the school's Friday enrichment times to middle school students to get them involved with hands-on science around their school. The preservice teacher wrote:

> My cooperating teacher and I agreed that every Friday for the one hour enrichment period, I would teach this outdoor conservancy class. For the most part I sponsored this class in the sense that I paid for the expenses which included, a wood duck box, bluebird box, bird feeders, bird seed, and cracked corn.

To illustrate parent-oriented events, this preservice teacher wrote, "I helped to plan and implement a K-2 Family Reading Night program where students could come with their family to participate in a reading program."

What also seemed to be missing from many essays was a definition of leadership in general and teacher leadership in particular, either from a personal or institutional stand point. Candidates who defined leadership in their essays did so from varying stances: instructional, collaborative, and managerial.

Definitions indicating that leadership was instructional included aspects of professional development, attending conferences, and other activities which helped hone their instruction. One preservice teacher shared that leadership was, "Showing flexibility and engagement in training and planning ahead." This preservice teacher further wrote, "These [curriculum] meetings helped me to realize how vital it truly is for every teacher to be flexible and pursue his/her own professional development opportunities in order to better their own teaching abilities."

Preservice teachers defined leadership as collaborative in the following ways. One preservice teacher defined leadership as working alongside grade-level teachers in the school toward a common goal. They wrote:

> I worked alongside the [school's] third grade team as we compared standards. I typed notes and helped compose a write-up for the team listing current practices, differentiation and new ideas to help implement [the new standards] into the [existing] curriculum.

Managerial definitions of leadership spoke to issues related to organizing events, such as field trips, fundraisers, guest speakers, and parent nights. An illustrative example of this follows:

> I chose and made examples of three crafts to share with the students which included a spider plant with planter decorated for fall, a paper turkey, and a cutout banner of a pumpkin, turkey, or leaf. On November 9th, this idea was shared with the students and I created sign-up sheets in order to gather the materials needed for these crafts. On November 11th, a student and I went to the teacher supply closet to gather materials. That same day,

> I visited local businesses asking for donations, such as, dirt and planters for the spider plant craft.

NOVICE TEACHERS

Next, in our study with novice teachers, recent graduates completed a brief online survey with a follow-up telephone interview option about their leadership activities and perceptions of themselves as teacher leaders at the end of their first year of teaching. The simple descriptive survey contained branched items with sections prompting open-ended responses for elaboration. Fifteen responded, representing 23% of the population surveyed. Three agreed to be interviewed. Qualitative content analysis (Schreier, 2012) was used to determine the content and themes of the surveys and interviews.

Findings indicated that 13 of the 15 first year teachers surveyed remembered their teacher leadership activities completed during student teaching, with nine sharing that the activities were suggestions from their host teacher, 10 indicating that the activities helped them understand what it meant to be a teacher leader, and seven responding that the completed leadership task contributed to their current performance as a teacher leader (Scales & Rogers, 2017). Eleven of 14 respondents indicated their understanding of teacher leadership had changed and provided expanded responses. Responses contained fours themes: Movement within the novice stage, community, change from classroom to community, and subtle leadership. To illustrate this change, one graduate had worked alongside her cooperating teacher to complete a major fundraising event for an international organization during her student teaching, which had multiple steps and included implementing curriculum about the cause, but as a first year teacher her leadership focused on more local community connections. She wrote the following in her response:

> When I look at it now, I think it is very important to be seen in your school community as having part in things. Like we have a garden for the whole school, and 5th grade is in charge of the Berry Garden. I am the leader for 4-H coming into our school, and this is the first time we've had 4-H, so I'll be the head volunteer that they come to for 4-H.

Ten respondents defined teacher leadership from their new mindset as seasoned first year teachers. Four themes emerged: Risks (being open or vulnerable), perceptions from others, advocate, and planner. For example, a respondent indicated that she puts herself "out there—I'm open to being a leader. I shared ideas and resources with my team and my principal."

Perceptions from others also figured greatly in the novice teacher's idea of teacher leadership. One respondent indicated that teacher leaders in her school were "those, they go the extra step. And they're the ones that if we're talking about stuff, they'll take it home and research it to present us with the information." References to their students' perceptions appeared in participants' responses as well. For example, "I now see how much the students look up to you if you are a leader in their school. They want to see that you are involved and you care about them." Another wrote:

> Showing leadership also takes on so many other forms than I once realized. One of my professors once said, "Your students will watch EVERYTHING you do no matter where, or when!" I will never forget that because it is the total truth; you are a leader in and out of your classroom when you are teacher.

Three survey respondents who agreed to the telephone follow-up were interviewed for better understanding. All three indicated their idea of teacher leadership was more complex at the end of their first year of teaching, but their school contexts and how colleagues perceived them as leaders determined their ability to demonstrate leadership. For example, one participant stated, "I was timid in the beginning and got more comfortable over time. I got feedback from my administrators that I needed to share more of my ideas ..." and that her teacher colleagues "... were eager to hear about what I'd learned [from my teacher preparation program] and the technology and (online) resources I had to share."

Another participant shared the following when reflecting on whether she considered herself to be a teacher leader:

> I know there is a lot for me to learn. [The school] paid for me to go to a [literacy] training, and it was really neat. We had to come back and do a presentation for our co-workers on the training. I took lots of notes and lots of pictures. Knowing that you were going to the training to be able to bring it back, you think about everything differently, like: How can I explain this? It helped me to be a part of the school, and show that I'm here and I want to be a part of everything.

TEACHER EDUCATION FACULTY

After analyzing data from preservice teachers and the novice teachers, we used an online survey program to anonymously survey 38 faculty members from our institution and had a 73% response rate. Faculty surveyed represented licensing programs in birth-kindergarten, elementary education, middle grades education, special education, physical education, and secondary content areas. The survey included demographic questions, such as how long have they been working at this particular institution and how long have they been working in teacher education, and contained four qualitative questions on the nature of teacher leadership. The first question asked them about teacher leadership in general, the next two asked about preservice teacher leadership at the beginning and end of the undergraduate experience, and the final question was about what specific activities and skills did they engage in with the preservice teachers to promote teacher leadership.

Conducting a qualitative content analysis (Schreier, 2012) of the faculty surveys, findings were highly variable. For example, while knowledge of content and pedagogy occurred several times as necessary to being a teacher leader, communication and confidence were also important. One faculty summed up the overall results by writing, "Leadership means different things for different contexts, schools and universities. It also means different things for which group leadership is being offered, students or colleagues, a general group or a committee with a mission to accomplish." This wide variety of results fits with research literature on teacher leadership. For instance, York-Barr and Duke's (2004) review of research also defines teacher leadership as "leading among colleagues with a focus on instructional practice, as well as working at the organizational level to align personnel, fiscal, and material resources to improve teaching and learning" (p. 261).

One question asked, "What are your expectations of teacher leadership in preservice teachers at the initial teacher candidate level (beginning of program)?" Responses tended to speak to dispositions and communication skills rather than to teacher leadership. For instance, one faculty member wrote:

> I think we see this [teacher leadership] in our preservice students when we witness: 1) independent and open-minded thinking; 2) whole-hearted class participation; 3) an empathetic attitude toward children, peers, and their university professors; 4) an ability to question the status-quo; 5) respectful, yet skeptical attitude; and, 6) expressing moral autonomy.

Seven faculty members specifically noted communication skills in their responses, such as, "I expect them to be good listeners, express ideas clearly in speaking and writing, collaborate with colleagues," and, "having communication and collaboration skills." Speaking to the developmental nature of teacher leadership, one faculty member wrote, "None," while another commented:

> Preservice teachers initially are so consumed with "checking things off their list" and usually do not understand the importance of teacher leadership or how to be a teacher leader. It takes time for teachers to develop a vision for leadership and preservice teachers at the beginning of programs are often typical college students and are learning to be teachers (which involves surviving the classroom experiences and learning about all of the details behind teaching).

Another question asked, "What are your expectations of teacher leadership in preservice teachers at the student teaching level (end of program)?" During analysis, we noticed that the end speaks to what faculty members consider as lofty goals, such as "begin to be agents of change" and "speak out in various meetings … leadership by example." Some responses were dispositional in nature, such as, "Demonstrated ability to create a positive learning environment for students in which students show academic growth. Reflective. Accepting of feedback and using feedback for growth." Another faculty member wrote:

> The primary goal of [student teaching] is to develop teacher effectiveness at the classroom level, but through collaboration with other teachers on campus and at [the university], I expect that interns BEGIN to understand the larger impact of schooling and BEGIN to think of ways they can be an active participant in those larger conversations.

We found that many of the responses were lofty while also vague. Perhaps this was because of the nature of the survey, but providing operational definitions or clarity through examples would have helped us better understand the responses. An illustrative example follows:

> By this point, teacher candidates should begin understanding more of the global aspects of teaching and have an idea of the importance of leadership. Depending on their experience levels, some become leaders early on in their teaching careers but most leave the program understanding leadership somewhat but not quite being leaders.

To try to connect the dots between the beginning of the program and the end, one survey question asked how faculty members prepare preservice teachers to be teacher leaders through course activities. Most shared the importance of knowledge and the ability to practice course concepts. Practicing course concepts included participation in an IEP, developing interdisciplinary units in teams, analyzing students' time-on-task in the field placement classroom, and completing activities related to school and family involvement. Speaking to the knowledge aspect specifically, one faculty member wrote:

> It is a broad concept without critical points of development outside of later field experiences. Developing knowledge of content and learners throughout the program sets the stage for meaningful participation. Combining that with knowledge of the school setting provides a context for continued refinement. In short, I don't see a specific activity that will develop a leader. It is more organic and borne out of knowledge bases.

One faculty member's response indicated that teacher leadership was being influential, while drawing from the importance of communication and reflecting on their instructional practices. They wrote:

> In a methods course, I have them do a proposal for a conference presentation in which they describe a practice from their own classroom experience, think about how it might be applicable in other contexts, and then develop strategies for communicating the practice to other professional educators in different contexts.

THEMES ACROSS THE LEVELS

In this section three themes that emerged across the findings are discussed. Those themes were: issues of compliance and constraints, creating a functional definition, and the difficulty of measuring the construct of teacher leadership for preservice teachers.

In the list of activities provided by faculty to help students understand leadership, the most common one was the Teacher Leader project, which in the analysis of our program's results indicated was more about compliance with the task than learning about leadership (Rogers & Scales, 2013). Indeed, findings from our follow up study support the compliance idea, as more than one novice teacher indicated that the Teacher Leader essay was "just an assignment," which implied it was not relevant to the real work of teachers. Further, the tasks the preservice teachers completed for this project were predominately based on what the cooperating teachers either wanted them to do or fit within the cooperating teachers' existing projects. Thus, while we, as teacher educators, struggle with preservice teachers viewing the leadership project as a compliance only issue, another layer of that issue is how the cooperating teachers foster or inhibit the notion of teacher leadership, especially what it means and how they model their own teacher leadership for the preservice teachers. Hence, the cooperating teachers could be feeding into the compliance issue while also placing constraints on what is possible for the preservice teachers' understanding and demonstration of leadership. Through two years of analysis of the preservice Teacher Leader essays, we discovered that compliance tasks were measured.

The idea of evaluating beginning, or emergent teacher leadership, leads to the second theme of defining and measuring the construct. Creating a functional, or practical, definition of teacher leadership that spans across teacher development is needed so that we, as teacher educators, can better support preservice teachers in their development while promoting what will be part of their professional lives. Yet defining emergent leadership appears to, at least in our data, focus on participation in certain activities and beginning to think in certain ways. For example, faculty believed emergent leadership should focus on beginning to "think of ways they can be an active participant in those larger conversations" about schooling, to be "involved in activities in their schools," "to begin to be agents of change," "to have an idea of the importance of leadership," and to "lead classes well." Additionally, faculty members indicated preservice teachers learned about leadership from activities provided in their coursework, which included group projects, field experiences, readings, writing and special volunteer opportunities officered by individual faculty.

This directly corresponds with the findings from the preservice teachers' Teacher Leadership essays because most of the preservice teachers defined leadership they engaged in as participating in events and meetings as well as "being in charge" of their classrooms. Further, those opportunities from coursework to learn about and engage in leadership turned into preservice teachers participating in planning field trips, school events (e.g., carnivals, dances), and meetings as evidence of their own emergent leadership.

Similarly, the novice teachers saw their leadership as actively participating as a colleague in grade level meetings, curriculum planning, professional development opportunities [in and beyond the school], in school-wide events, and in the larger community. Many of the novice teachers spoke to their continued professional development to hone their teaching, which included learning from their teacher colleagues about teaching strategies and resources, while being open to share as well. One novice teacher wrote, "It is about participating in everything and not just leading but guiding and being guided." This directly corresponds with findings from the preservice teachers' leadership activities, as participation outnumbered other activities.

Some novice teachers shared about their part in planning and implementing school-wide events, such as reading nights and wellness fairs, or the importance of connecting with the community beyond the school walls, which included child advocacy. For instance, one novice teacher shared that since graduation she became more aware that she needed to speak out in her school and community to advocate for her students to have resources, such as school supplies and shoes.

Given these data, teacher leadership may in fact be a self-fulfilling prophecy. By university faculty members providing preservice teachers with activities that they believe help to shape teacher leadership, the preservice teachers picked up on those activities and beliefs, which ultimately shaped their thinking about teacher leadership in and beyond the teacher preparation program. Hence, faculty members have much influence on shaping teacher leaders, though they may be unaware of their influence.

IMPLICATIONS AND FUTURE STUDY

Comparing faculty and novice teachers' survey results to the kinds of activities described in the Teacher Leader essays provided us with valuable information. While some similarities existed, the wide variation or lack of definitions in the preservice teachers' essays indicate that we are not explicitly addressing a common idea of teacher leadership in our program as a whole or in our individual courses. Additionally, the variety of ideas presented in faculty survey results illustrate this and indicate that we, the program faculty members, do not have a unified concept of teacher leadership, or how teacher leadership fits with individual course objectives. A goal would be, at least, for the program to come to a consensus on a definition of teacher leadership and determine how to best provide teacher leadership activities as part of our coursework.

Further, faculty survey data contained descriptions of dispositional aspects of leadership, which may also have implications for and/or influence on preservice teachers' understandings of and development as teacher leaders. Preservice teachers' dispositions and how they are aligned with or associated with leadership have yet to be explored and warrants closer investigation. The idea that there is a developmental nature to the skills and abilities needed for teacher leadership is also borne out by our findings at each level. The codes and results from preservice data (witness, participant, ownership), the novice teachers indicating their increasing comfort with the idea of teacher leadership, and faculty responses indicating that preservice teachers should "begin" to understand the concept of teacher leadership lend support to the developmental progression within teacher leadership. Just as Levin (2003) found that ideas about pedagogy were still developing years after completing the teacher preparation program, perhaps the same is true for teacher leadership.

CONCLUSIONS AND LIMITATIONS

We acknowledge analyzing a collection of data across three populations (preservice, novice and teacher education faculty) could be seen as limiting the ability to generalize to other institutions, but our purpose is to provide a case of the varying definitions of leadership that emerge from the constituents of one institution. We believe that while this inquiry is assisting in our teacher education program development, it also informs other teacher education programs who are attempting to incorporate leadership preparation and accountability measures. Creating an operational definition of teacher leadership that teacher education faculty and preservice teachers can use to view the work of teachers is an essential task in preparing 21st century teachers. Anders, Hoffman, and Duffy (2000) make a case for investigating how teachers learn and how that learning is enacted in their professional responsibilities. Leadership as a professional responsibility is an emerging requirement for effective teachers along with pedagogical and content knowledge. At this juncture, a dialogue about the vision of leadership that preservice teachers ought to engaged in needs to happen if teacher leadership is to be evaluated in and beyond teacher education programs.

DISCUSSION QUESTIONS

1. How does your institution define teacher leadership?
2. How do preservice teachers at your institution demonstrate teacher leadership?
3. How is preservice teacher leadership evaluated at your institution? Is it an accurate method for assessing teacher leadership?
4. How can assessing teacher leadership at the preservice level be developmentally appropriate?
5. What are some ways you incorporate tenets of teacher leadership in your courses?

REFERENCES

Anders, P. L., Hoffman, J. V., & Duffy, G. G. (2000). Teaching teachers to teach reading: Paradigm shifts, persistent problems, and challenges. In M. Kamil, J. Mosenthal, P. D. Pearson, & R. Barr (Eds.), *Handbook of reading research* (Vol. 3, pp. 719–742). Mahwah, NJ: Erlbaum.

Bond, N., & Sterrett, W. (2014). Developing teacher leaders through honorary professional organizations in education: Focus on the college student officers. *Education, 135*(1), 25–38.

Bruce, C. D., Jarvis, D. H., Flynn, T., & Brock, E. (2011). Lead teachers in collaborative action research: Perceptions of role and responsibility. *Canadian Journal of Action Research, 12*(3), 29–46.

Dewey, J. (1946). *The problems of men*. New York, NY: Philosophical Library.

Holland, J., Eckert, J., & Allen, M. (2014). From preservice to teacher leadership: Meeting the future in educator preparation. *Action in Teacher Education, 36*, 433–445.

Lieberman, A. (2013). Teacher leadership: An introduction. *The New Educator, 9*(3), 169–172.

Lieberman, A., & Miller, L. (2004). *Teacher leadership*. San Francisco, CA: Jossey-Bass.

Levin, B. B. (2003). *Case studies of teacher development: An in-depth look at how thinking about pedagogy develops over time*. Mahwah, NJ: Erlbaum.

Mangin, M., & Stoelinga, S. R. (2009). The future of instructional teacher leader roles. *The Educational Forum, 74*(1), 49–62.

Margolis, J., & Huggins, K. S. (2012). Distributed but undefined: New teacher leader roles to change schools. *Journal of School Leadership, 22*, 953–981.

Northouse, P. (2016). Leadership: Theory and practice. 7th ed. Thousand Oaks, CA: Sage.

North Carolina State Board of Education. (1998). Policy regarding the Code of Ethics for North Carolina Educators. Retrieved from http://www.ncpublicschools.org/docs/effectiveness-model/ncees/standards/code-of-ethics.pdf

North Carolina State Board of Education. (2013). North Carolina Professional Teaching Standards. Retrieved from http://www.ncpublicschools.org/docs/effectiveness-model/ncees/standards/prof-teach-standards.pdf

Quinn, C. L., Haggard, C. S., & Ford, B. A. (2006). Preparing new teachers for leadership roles: A model in four phases. *School Leadership and Management, 26*(1), 55–68.

Rogers, C., & Scales, R. Q. (2013). Pre-service teachers' perceptions of teacher leadership: Is it about compliance or understanding? *Issues in Teacher Education, 22*(2), 17–37.

Sato, M. (2005). Practical leadership: Conceptualizing the everyday leadership work of teachers. *The New Educator, 1*, 55–71.

Scales, R. Q., & Rogers, C. (2017). Novice teacher leadership: Determining the impact of a leadership licensure requirement after one year of teaching. *The Professional Educator, 41*(1).

Schreier, M. (2012). *Qualitative content analysis in practice*. Sage: London.

Snyder, J. (2015). Teacher leadership and teacher preparation: a personal narrative. *The Educational Forum, 79*(1), 5–11.

Sommerness, J., York-Barr, J., & Hur, J. (2008). Teacher leadership. In T. Good (Ed.), *21st century education: A reference handbook*. Thousand Oaks, CA: Sage. Retrieved from http://search.credoreference.com/content/entry/sagetfced/teacher_leadership/0

Strauss, A., & Corbin, J. (1998). *Basics of qualitative research: Techniques and procedures for developing grounded theory* (2nd ed.). Thousand Oaks, CA: Sage.

Turnbull, B. (2005). Facilitating early career leadership through pre-service training. *Teachers and Teaching: Theory and Practice, 11*(5), 457–464.

York-Barr, J., & Duke, K. (2004). What do we know about teacher leadership? Findings from two decades of scholarship. *Review of Educational Research, 74*(3), 255–316.

CHAPTER FOURTEEN

Reconceptualizing Campus Shared Governance AND Leadership IN Higher Education

The Role of Midlevel Administrators

HUGO A. GARCÍA, KIM NEHLS, AND KIMBERLY M. FLORENCE

INTRODUCTION

Postsecondary institutions are complex hierarchical organizations with a shared governance structure as its hallmark. Unlike the other economic sectors of the United States, where there is a strong top-down management system, higher education institutions are comprised of various actors embedded within a loosely-coupled system where shared governance is espoused. Gayle, Tewarie, and White (2003) state that "University governance refers to the structure and process of [collaborative] decision making across issues that are significant for external as well as internal stakeholders within the university" (p. 1).

Much of the literature on leadership and change in higher education focuses on traditional governance roles such as presidents, chancellors, and provosts (Kezar, 2012; Kezar, Carducci, & Contreras-McGavin, 2006). Other research focuses entirely on the role of faculty within the shared governance structure of higher education; indeed, the American Association of University Professors (AAUP) has from its inception in 1915 stressed the importance of faculty participation in the decision making process (Tierney & Lechuga, 2004). With strong foci on positional leaders and tenured faculty, shared governance may present challenges to midlevel staff and administrators. Various higher education associations have stressed the importance of staff involvement in the decision making process and inclusion in shared governance (e.g., Ackerman, 2007).

The purpose of this chapter, then, is to examine how members who have not been traditionally viewed as leaders are able and willing to serve as leaders on campus by participating in shared governance. Empowering midlevel administrators and staff to be leaders may enable and engender input from all levels of the hierarchy. University leadership has come to include individuals who do not necessarily carry leadership titles. When members who have historically been left out of the decision-making process are empowered to join in conversations on campus, it leads to true shared governance. We will first review the literature on midlevel administrators in higher education and the various management theories used in higher education and then present our institutional study on midlevel leaders' impressions of shared governance and leadership.

LITERATURE REVIEW

Midlevel Administrators in Higher Education

Non-instructional professional staff members working as midlevel managers are the largest administrative group within higher education systems (Johnsrud & Rosser, 1999b). Filan and Seagren (2003) report that "midlevel managers outnumber all other types of administrators combined … and are widely regarded as key to the effective functioning of a college or university" (p. 22). Midlevel administrators are "often identified by the administrative units in which they coordinate or direct, and they play a key role within four traditional service areas of higher education: academic support, business/administrative services, external affairs, and student affairs" (Rosser, 2004, p. 319). Depending upon the institution and its staffing, examples of midlevel titles could include director, manager, or assistant dean. They are "holders of non-academic positions below the dean's level" (Johnsrud & Rosser, 1999a, p. 3).

Other key characteristics of midlevel managers are their roles within the hierarchy of the institution. For instance, they often report to a top-level administrator, such as a dean or vice-president, but they also have entry-level staff who report to them. Rosser (2004) indicated, "By virtue of their 'middleness' within academic organizations, midlevel leaders must find balance between superiors' directions and the needs of those who require their support and service" (p. 319). New midlevel staff hires may have advanced from an entry level position or may have made a lateral move from another institution (Mather, Bryan, & Faulkner, 2009).

These staff members typically also have advanced degrees, have been working in the academy at least five years, have attended or been employed by at least two different institutions, and supervise programs as well as staff (Ackerman, 2007; Mather et al., 2009; Renn & Hodges, 2007; Waple, 2006). Overall, the "middle manager plays a vital role in the student affairs function on the campuses of institutions of higher education" (Mills, 2000, p. 135).

Despite the *vital role*, years of experience, and level of responsibility, midlevel managers in higher education are also seen as *the invisible leaders* (Young, 1990) and the *unsung heroes* (Rosser, 2004). They remain largely unseen and usually excluded from the decision-making process. The next section discusses the limited role of midlevel administrators' involvement in shared governance.

Shared Governance for Midlevel Administrators

According to Johnsrud and Rosser (1999a), midlevel managers "have the responsibility of monitoring and regulating policies and procedures, but rarely the authority to change, adjust, or develop regulations" (p. 123). Therefore, midlevel managers may find themselves with significant responsibility, but little power within the scope of the university. Mills (2000) noted the irony of this position in that "they are expected to empower students, but may feel powerless themselves" (p. 135). Other scholars (Mather et al., 2009) suggested that "midlevel administrators serve the formidable role of bridging the gap between university policymakers and front line staff" (p. 244). Precisely because they are situated in the middle of the institution, they are essential to policy implementation, collaboration, and collegiality (Ackerman, 2007).

Policy making and implementation in academia can be convoluted because of the notion of shared governance. Shared governance indicates that decision-making is supposed to be collaborative among faculty, staff, and administrators on college campuses. However, there seems to be misconceptions about shared governance, even if it is encouraged at all levels of faculty and staff. Olson (2009) wrote, "Shared governance is … complex; it is a delicate balance between faculty and staff participation in planning and decision-making processes, on the one hand, and administrative accountability on the other" (p. 1).

Middle managers may find little incentive to participate in shared governance when they are burdened with numerous responsibilities of programming, staffing, budgeting, and working collaboratively within their own units. Johnston (2003) suggested that participation in shared governance at a university level "can quickly become a burden," but also noted that "administrative leaders are most effective when they understand and value academic culture and governance and can apply their understanding within the context of the institution's mission, its organizational needs, and its overall governance structure" (p. 57). Each institution will have its own culture for academic governance and a built-in structure for participation.

Middle managers may seek opportunities to participate because academic policies could have implications for student enrollment, dismissal, and graduation, as well as assessment and program review (Johnston, 2003). All of these areas are important to work within an institution of higher education.

Gap in the Literature

Significant research has been devoted to understanding the leadership skills necessary for senior level positions in colleges and universities. In particular, the president has been the focus of much research on the challenges of managing institutions of higher education (Garza Mitchell & Eddy, 2008; Inman, 2011). However, like Inman (2011), we contend that the prevailing framework of individual agency focused on positional leaders such as presidents is inadequate. Identifying leadership at the midlevels of management in higher education is a necessary step for broadening our understanding of administration and leadership, broadly defined.

Previous research on middle managers in student affairs has focused on the general understanding of the position (Ackerman, 2007; Mills, 2000; Young, 1990), career pathways (Garza Mitchell & Eddy, 2008; Inman, 2011), morale and work satisfaction (Donaldson & Rosser, 2007; Johnsrud & Rosser, 1999a, 1999b); and onboarding and orientation (Mather et al., 2009; Renn & Hodges, 2007). More recent work has focused on midlevel professionals in the community college (e.g., Hornak, Ozaki, & Lunceford, 2016).

THEORIES OF MANAGEMENT

Organizational perspectives in higher education have foundations in political philosophy, sociology, and anthropological theories, which are accompanied by a subset of strengths and weaknesses (Manning, 2013). These strengths and weakness can impact how an institution is perceived by its stakeholders that include administration and staff (Suomi, Kuoppakangas, Hytti, Hampden-Turner, & Kangaslahti, 2013). Therefore, it is important to understand how theory presents itself in management practices in higher education.

Dean and Bowman (1994) discussed the business principles of Total Quality Management (TQM) as critical to serving customer needs. Such principles have since been analyzed in correlation with higher education to explore ways to improve services within a long-established loosely-coupled system (Manatos, Sarrico, & Rosa, 2015). One aspect of quality assurance is establishing a collaborative working environment. Critical to this aspect is the need for creating a community with a centralized purpose (Hamel, 2007). By doing so, managers constructively lead their employees through skills and activities that develop individual employee aptitudes in order to foster team-focused behavior (Pavur, 2012). Buckingham and Coffman (1999) described the role of great managers as follows:

> The manager's role is the role of "catalyst" … speeding up the reaction between the employee's talents and the company's goals, and between the employee's talents and the customer needs. They are expected to be subject matter experts, individual superstars, and sometimes leaders in their own right. (p. 59)

The subsequent section discusses two organizational theories to discern how both perspectives correlate and can, in turn, influence management styles within the organization.

Organizational and Management Theory

There are six prominent theoretical perspectives exhibited in higher education institutional practices; the six predominate theories include: organized anarchy, collegium, political, cultural, feminist, and spiritual (Manning, 2013). The organizational perspective known as organized anarchy is based on the ideology that goals within the institution are constantly shifting (Ruscio, 2016). This shift is primarily due to the systems being loosely coupled: typically, devoid of hierarchical communication and encompassing parts of a system that work independent of one another (Burke, 2014). Purposeful relationships are important to establishing an open knowledge university environment where "managers have been of substantial influence in steering the university knowledge transfer policy and practices" (Sharifi, Liu, & Ismail, 2013, p. 1862). The fact that managers having well-established goals has long been considered an essential aspect to the decision-making process, it is therefore critical to understand how the organizational climate facilitates or disrupts one's ability to lead (Rutherford & Meier, 2014).

The sociological perspective to institutional practice is based on the premise that relationships within the institution are guided by either advantageous positionality, exemplified by the phrase "I'll scratch your back if you scratch mine" or, the belief that everyone is equal and adept with providing valuable contributions to the organization (Manning, 2013). From a systems theory approach to management, goals, membership, and hierarchies are pivotal to operations; collectively each promotes the use of a well-defined purpose with members that have the appropriate skills necessary to accomplish specific activities across varying levels of distributed responsibilities (Kuhl, 2013). Thus, by establishing an environment that honors these elements, middle management can be better supported. According to Boer, Goedegebuure, and Meek (2010) middle managers contribute the following:

> Ideally, they play the role in the formulation of strategic plans by top-level management, they gather and synthesize information, and use resources at their disposal to champion

> innovative ideas and business opportunities linked to overall institutional strategies. (p. 231)

In order to better understand the complexity of middle manager leadership within higher education context and develop new theory, this chapter examines the role that midlevel administrators play in shared governance within complex hierarchical postsecondary institutions. To the best of our knowledge, no previous research has studied the intersection of the midlevel manager and shared governance within a four-year postsecondary context. Thus, the aim of this chapter is to develop new understandings of leadership and shared governance for midlevel administrators. Therefore, the research questions this chapter will seek to answer are:

- How do midlevel staff and administrators participate and define shared governance?
- How do midlevel staff and administrators navigate college environments?

METHODS

Grounded theory was utilized for this qualitative study (Glaser & Strauss, 1967; Strauss & Corbin, 1998). Grounded theory allows researchers to obtain "insight about the phenomenon, not empirical generalization from a sample to a population" (Patton, 2002, p. 40). According to Strauss and Corbin (1998), the researcher arrives at theory through "data, systematically gathered and analyzed" (p. 12). That is, the researcher discovers themes that emerge from the qualitative data (Glaser & Strauss, 1967).

Sampling

For this study, a purposeful sampling procedure was first utilized because the researcher "chooses the sites, persons, and documents that will maximize opportunities for comparative analysis" (Strauss & Corbin, 1998, p. 211). We then proceeded to conduct a snowball sampling technique based on initial participants' responses. By expanding the sample size at different stages in the study, the researchers were able to achieve theoretical saturation (Glaser & Strauss, 1967; Strauss & Corbin, 1998). Strauss and Corbin (1998) have observed that utilizing more than one type of sampling procedure may be called for at different times in a study in order to select participants that contribute to the development of theory. This aligned with what Strauss and Corbin (1998) have suggested during open sampling since "no concepts yet have proven theoretical relevance" (p. 206). As such, no adherence to a predetermined sampling procedure is required. In the study, expanding the sample size, from directors to coordinators provided a broader perspective of staff's experiences and allowed for closer examination of variation and relationships among the concepts (Strauss & Corbin, 1998).

Site

The postsecondary institution selected for this study is a large public research university in the Southwestern United States. It is a minority serving institution and one of the most diverse college campuses in the nation. Institutional Review Board approval was secured to conduct the study.

Participating Midlevel Staff

Nine participants were recruited from various co-curricular offices on campus. Participants had titles such as assistant dean, director/coordinator, or associate director/coordinator. For purposes of confidentiality, participants were given pseudonyms and no specific departments are identified here. Each of the nine participants were interviewed once for approximately 30 minutes to an hour, and interviews were conducted on the university campus.

Data Analysis

All audio-recorded interviews were manually transcribed employing Strauss and Corbin's (1998) three-step approach of (a) generating categories (i.e., open coding); (b) developing and linking categories with subcategories (i.e., axial coding); and (c) integrating and refining (i.e., selective coding) to arrive at the themes. All members of the research team transcribed the data to allow for the opportunity to confirm initial categories identified during the open coding process (Strauss & Corbin, 1998) of the face-to-face interviews and to discern new ones before beginning proceeding to axial and selective coding. Once all interview responses had been transcribed, the data were reviewed multiple times checking for accuracy. Several matrixes were developed to display the data as themes emerged and were coded. Once data and themes were developed, the conceptual model of *Collaboration + Engagement + Inclusion + Involvement = Shared Leadership (CEIISL)* was developed.

LIMITATIONS

There are various limitations to this study. First, the data come from a single institution in an urban setting in the Southwest. Thus, the results may not be applicable to other regions, or suburban or rural institutions. Second, the researchers only examined the experiences of midlevel administrators. Therefore, their experiences may not be representative of other staff members within college campuses. Finally, these experiences are within a large research university, which may not apply to smaller four-year campuses with a teaching focus.

FINDINGS

Research Question 1: How do midlevel staff and administrators participate and define shared governance?

In response to our first research question, three major themes emerged from our data: (a) Limited shared governance participation, (b) Importance of involvement and collaboration across campus and (c) Differences among departments based on funding. Each theme is presented in greater details below.

RQ1 Theme 1: Limited Shared Governance Participation

When asked if they were part of shared governance, several staff indicated they were and gave examples of committees they were invited to participate. Many of the committees, however, revolved around non-academic issues or issues in which campus faculty may not want to be involved. Others indicated that shared governance meant members of the institution are heard even if they do not make the final decisions. For example, Jade states:

> *I've heard of shared governance before. I mean, it's been stated in a lot of higher ed articles, Chronicle of Higher Education. It's definitely a conversation that has been going around. … I would define it as collaboration and sharing knowledge and information.*

Hannah states:

> *I think for me shared governance is being part of the bigger picture of an institution. I think other groups look at it as it's governance just total of an entire institution but I think when its shared that's that key term they're looking at. Being shared everyone has a role within that shared governance.*

RQ1 Theme 2: Importance of Involvement and Collaboration across the University

Various participants in our study indicated it was critical to get involved and work with various groups and decision makers on campus. These collaborations and involvement were strategic in that it allowed them to influence decision-making and provide leadership campus-wide. For instance, Mark indicated that he is aware that decisions are not made arbitrarily by the senior leadership: "*The major decisions of the university are not made blindly from the top but instead those decisions, while still made by the leadership, are heavily informed by the rest of campus.*"

Clara: *To me I think shared governance is really sort of collaboration between faculty and staff, administrators, students. I think it's collaboration in planning and also in making decisions for the university, in a nutshell.*

Frank: *I define shared governance as an opportunity to share ideas on how best we can allocate resources in the best interest of the university. Multiple opinions, multiple thoughts all being able to be shared in a public forum ultimately with the best interest of the university at heart.*

Olive: *I think I know what it's supposed to be, and then kind of what I've experienced it to be. I think it is supposed to be where there is open communication, kind of that visibility on what is happening, major decisions getting input from all areas, for people being able to have a voice and maybe in terms of voting or something along those lines; for data to be easily accessible and more transparency and openness.*

RQ1 Theme 3: Differences among Departments Based on Funding

Unfortunately, some midlevel administrators understood that not all departments are on the same playing field. Jade indicates that individuals can have limited influence based on the department they work in. For instance, when asked to elaborate on "I don't think all departments are on the same footing?" she states:

> *I feel like certain departments are neglected on campus depending on the money that they bring to the institution. My department is grant writing; I call our center a grant writing machine. We bring so much money to the university so therefore, I mean if you look at space, if you look at recognition, my department alone gets a lot of it compared to departments like the women's center or even career services. Because now career services has to share an office with the international office. (Jade)*

Hannah states that voices are muted or amplified based on their position on campus:

> *Some people may end up having a larger role based on their position but I think that everyone should have a voice in that conversation even if the voice isn't necessarily heard but still being part of that experience and being in that room. Hopefully you'll be able to hear all of the voices and even if you don't take in that voice at that exact moment at least they've been a part of that conversation too. (Hannah)*

It is clear to some midlevel administrators, shared governance and leadership is not equally distributed. Although colleges and universities espouse a culture of learning and development of knowledge, these organizations clearly favor departments that bring in external funding, even in a non-academic/instructional unit.

Research Questions 2: How do midlevel staff and administrators navigate college environments?

In response to our second research question, three additional themes emerged from our data: (a) Navigation of the shared governance through their departments, (b) Mentoring from their supervisors and (c) Expressing their voice even when voiceless.

RQ2 Theme 1: Navigation of the Shared Governance through their Departments

Several participants indicated they could be part of the larger shared governance dialog and decision making; however, many indicated they did not want to overextend themselves in campus-wide committees. For example, Mark states he is currently on one committee but that he declined the opportunities to join additional ones. Mark states, "*I get emails to serve on various committees. There seems to be plenty of opportunities, I am intentionally not taking those.*" He states he prefers to focus his leadership energies on departmental issues where there are more shared governance opportunities within his unit:

> *We have the deans, associate deans, all of the advisors, and we even have our executive assistant and office manager, and we are talking about direction for curriculum, or we can be talking about some of the communications projects I'm working and the promotional video I'm working on. Every person here, myself included, has a voice in saying "where are we going as a college and does it make sense?" (Mark)*

Thus, Mark states that everyone in his unit participates in shared governance and has a voice at the table to ensure everyone in his department is represented, which may not be the case on university wide committees. This collegiality by senior, mid-, and entry-level staff has promoted a supportive working environment within all levels of Mark's department. The collegiality seems important in the development of mentorship relationships.

RQ2 Theme 2: Mentoring from Their Supervisors

Several of our participants indicated the importance of being mentored by various individuals on campus. Mentors were members of the campus community that understood the college culture. For instance, Mark states that working for Bill was a great benefit as his former supervisor:

> *I sometimes question how I've ended up with this wonderful situation here at SU. My experiences have been so positive here and … Bill was such a phenomenal mentor to me. He would take me aside and … you know, Bill was working on the major projects at SU and so … he would take me in his office and say "here's what's happening, here's what I'm doing and, here's why. (Mark)*

Therefore, supervisors had opportunities to provide information and pass on knowledge on how to navigate the politics of the organization in order to develop a keen sense of how to participate in shared governance and help lead the organization.

Early career staff and administrators may not believe they are ready to assume leadership positions. However, several participants indicated that midlevel staff helped motivate entry-level staff members to consider mid- and senior-level positions. Jade states that when she was early in her career, a midlevel administrator convinced her that she was ready to make a move within the institution:

> *I knew the program as a counselor but not as a director. So I, and then my staff was like, "Jade, you should really go for it." Especially my assistant director, she's like, "You are so ready to take this position." I'm like, "How? It's a huge job." And she goes, "No. You're ready. You have skills that I haven't seen in anyone else. And people have been holding you back here and its time to move up." So she really for the last two years coached me on this position. (Jade)*

Clearly, Jade believed she was not ready to assume a leadership position within the campus; however, her supervisor was encouraging and convinced Jade that she was truly ready.

Colleges and university campuses, as academic institutions, strive to recruit and retain individuals with advanced levels of education. Many postsecondary institutions require that staff and administrators have a least a master's degree for a midlevel position. Indeed, a master's degree is fast becoming the minimum degree to move up the hierarchical structure of postsecondary institutions. Participants in our study also indicated that supervisors were supportive of them to obtain a master's degree if they did not have one.

> *That's the only reason that I even looked into the master's program, because I kind of got a taste of that world as an undergrad, and it was really in meeting with Amanda and her kind of having those exploration conversations with me, where I was like, "Well, how did you get your job? You're on the college campus, how did this happen?" (Olive)*

Olive states that her interactions with her supervisor encouraging her to get the advanced degrees provides a path to move up the organizational structure as it is cultural capital within these academic campuses. Indeed, because non-academic staff must work and interact with faculty who possess terminal degrees within their field or discipline, midlevel staff earn respect from faculty if they have advanced degrees as well. Therefore, there is a cultural capital incentive to have professional staff with masters and doctoral degrees in all departments.

RQ2 Theme 3: Expressing Their Voice Even When Voiceless

Several participants indicated that many times, there are limited opportunities to make decisions on campus; however, that did not deter them from expressing themselves to ensure they are providing leadership from their midlevel position. For instance, Mark states that senior leadership can provide a sense of shared governance by allowing early and midlevel staff the opportunities to participate in various listening exercises that allow those grassroots staff the ability to provide input. Mark states:

> *I remember years ago when Jim was president and he did these listening exercises ... I attended a few of those. He was actually listening to some of the issues or where are we going ... All of those invitations to get involved, come to this meeting, it appears to be they really kind of opened the idea of shared governance is there. I can't say whether or not it is actually makes a difference. (Mark)*

DISCUSSION AND POLICY IMPLICATIONS

The purpose of this qualitative study was to better understand how midlevel administrators participate in shared governance to ensure they have voice in the higher education enterprise so they may be better positioned to help lead these complex hierarchical organizations. The previous section presented the findings of the study. The purpose of this section is to interpret and synthesize the findings that were presented in the previous section, discuss how they support and challenge the prior literature presented and shed light on new knowledge, and develop theory based on the grounded theory approach utilized in this study.

Upon review of the interviews, several themes emerged that highlighted how midlevel administrators navigate their respective departments as well as how shared governance is demonstrated among campus administrators. One of the themes identified in terms of negotiating the path towards senior and midlevel administration is mentorship. Mentorship was stated to provide some form of guidance and/or encouragement that was significant to the participants' ability to enter and move-up in the realm of higher education administration; furthermore, to understand their individual role within a larger, more complex, university system. A second example of mentorship proved that positional superiority is not always the only type of guidance available. One participant described how encouragement from an individual, who would later become her subordinate, influenced her decision to apply for her current position.

Shared governance was primarily defined by the participants as individuals and departments working in collaboration with one another. However, it was also evident that such collaboration was contingent on the ability to have an opportunity to be involved in decision making. The opportunity to be involved, or invited to join the conversation, in the implementation of change strategies either within the department or across campus was frequently stated as a possibility at the institution. Through committees designed to address various campus initiatives, midlevel administrators were induced either by their superior or a need for campus activism to participate.

However, some discussed how these committees, through opportunities to voice their opinions on specific campus based topics and initiatives, adversely influenced their personal and familial commitments due to the requirement to expend extra time towards work. The inability to establish work life balance for midlevel administrators who might otherwise be more involved in shared governance resulted in the decision to step back from certain opportunities.

Another factor actuating disengagement from shared governance is the unwillingness of those at the top to relinquish power. The need to protect one's positionality out of fear or intimidation can also inhibit shared governance. Additionally, listening is another imperative facet to shared governance. The participants discussed how the ability to be heard led them to feel appreciated and respected for what they brought to their respective departments even if certain changes did not directly influence the campus as a whole. For instance, it is from listening that individuals are able to learn from those most experienced, even if that experience is based on longevity with the institution. There is an invaluable contribution employees provide even if their status within the department or institution is not typically recognized. By speaking up and sharing their opinions midlevel administrators and upper administrators are afforded the opportunity to learn how plans and strategic approaches affect all aspects of an operation.

Finally, the participants discussed how change in higher education is a slow process. Due to the gradual pace of progress, midlevel administrators discussed how it is necessary to recognize that small actions can potentially make a significant difference, if given time. Also, shared governance is about recognizing those

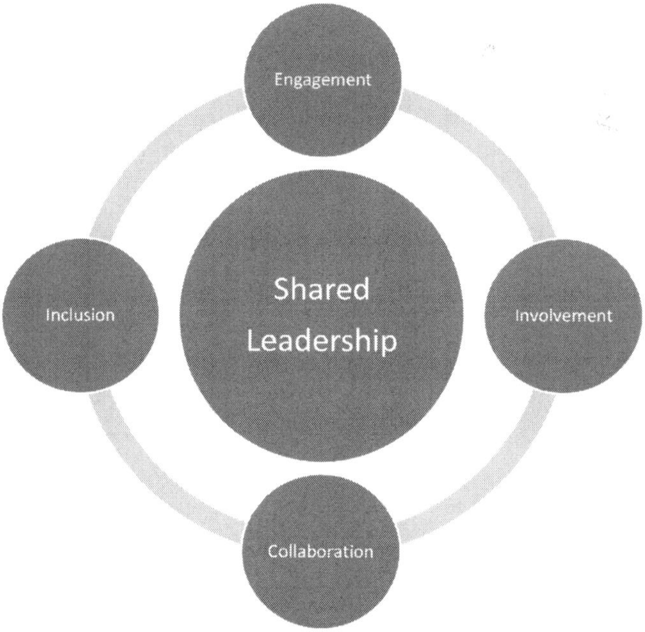

Collaboration + Engagement + Inclusion + Involvement = Shared Leadership (CEIISL)

Fig 14.1. CEIISL Model .

departments and individuals that are critical to the function of an institution. The midlevel administrators interviewed recognized the centrality of the role in the institution but exhibited humility in how that role influenced the campus without the function of teamwork. Each discussed their position as one supported by many others whose work has equally moved the institution forward.

Our conceptual model is derived from participants in our study. Individuals discussed the importance of *collaborations* within and between various departments. These collaborations can be with various other members of the departments across the university. Staff members can provide leadership across the university by removing silos that prevent collaborations in loosely-coupled organizations such as colleges and universities. Our participants indicated that shared governance and leadership are better achieved through purposeful and active collaborations. *Engagement*, which had been described from a student's perspective as "… participation in educationally effective practices, both inside and outside the classroom, which leads to a range of measurable outcomes" (Harper & Quaye, 2009, p. 2) has been shown to be important for college students (Kuh, 2003; Kuh, Kinzie, Buckley, Bridges, & Hayek, 2007; Pascarella & Terenzini, 2005). The same holds for staff engagement. We define *staff engagement* as active and effective participation, within their unit/department and across the university, which leads to shared governance and leadership participation. Thus, staff members should be engaged within their units and across campus on various issues. *Inclusion* is critical to developing engagement and involvement. Inviting staff members to join a university wide committee, as many of our participants indicated they had been, is a step forward in the right direction; however, having only a token staff member only further marginalized staff. For example, if a committee of 20 is comprised of 16 faculty members, 3 students, and 1 staff member, it sends a clear message to the staff just where they stand in the institutional hierarchy. It is important that staff stay involved over time, otherwise midlevel staff become jaded and view their positions within the university as non-influential. Indeed, many staff in our study indicated that they were asked to voice their opinions; however, voicing one's opinion is different from one's voice being heard and influencing the decision making process. Thus, sustained involvement is critical for staff members as they transition from, early-, mid- and senior-level administration. Taken together, *Collaboration + Engagement + Inclusion + Involvement*, these constructs can increase shared leadership that provides the type of shared governance necessary to help steward colleges and universities.

CONCLUSION

Higher education, as an enterprise, needs new leadership perspectives and lenses if it is to be more inclusive. Our literature review and study findings indicate that shared governance has been dominated by select constituency groups (faculty and upper administration) that negate the participation of others (staff). Staff members at all levels within colleges and universities, especially midlevel administrators, are at the grassroots working with students, faculty, alumni, and community members. Unlike faculty, staff members are on campus 12 months out of the year without the benefit and protection of tenure. Therefore, their voices should be included at the shared governance table and dignified with a concentrated ear. A commitment to midlevel administrators' participation in shared governance activities indicates a responsibility to daily operations of an institution and those working hard to manage it and its student body.

DISCUSSION QUESTIONS

1. Why do you think there are more midlevel administrators in higher education than any other level of administrators?
2. Why are midlevel administrators typically called unsung heroes or invisible leaders?
3. What are the benefits of being involved in shared governance on a college campus?
4. What are the drawbacks of being involved in shared governance on a college campus?
5. How would you encourage administrators at any level of higher education administration to get involved in shared governance on your campus?

REFERENCES

Ackerman, R. L. (Ed.). (2007). *The midlevel manager in student affairs: Strategies for success.* Washington, DC: NASPA.

Boer, H. D., Goedegebuure, L., & Meek, V. L. (2010). The changing nature of academic middle management: A framework for analysis. In L. Meek, L. Goedegebuure, R. Santiago, & T. Carvalho (Eds.), *The changing dynamics of higher education middle management* (pp. 31–54). New York, NY: Springer.

Buckingham, M., & Coffman, C. (1999). *First, break all the rules: What the world's greatest managers do differently.* New York, NY: Simon & Schuster.

Burke, W. W. (2014). Changing loosely coupled systems. *The Journal of Applied Behavioral Science, 50*, 423–444. doi: 10.1177/0021886314549923

Dean, J. W., & Bowman, D. E. (1994). Management theory and total quality: Improving research and practice through theory development. *Academy of Management. The Academy of Management Review, 19*(3), 392–418.

Donaldson, J. F., & Rosser, V. J. (2007). Midlevel leaders of continuing higher education: Exploring their satisfaction, morale, and intentions to stay in or leave their positions. *The Journal of Continuing Higher Education, 55*(1), 2–15. doi: 10.1080/07377366.2007.10400104

Filan, G. L., & Seagren, A. T. (2003). Six critical issues for midlevel leadership in postsecondary settings. *New Directions for Higher Education, 124*, 21–31.

Garza Mitchell, R. L., & Eddy, P. L. (2008). In the middle: Career pathways of midlevel community college leaders. *Community College Journal of Research and Practice, 32*(10), 793–811.

Gayle, D. J., Tewarie, B., & White, A. Q. (2003). Governance in the twenty-first-century university: Approaches to effective leadership and strategic management. *ASHE-ERIC Higher Education Report*. San Francisco: Jossey-Bass.

Glaser, B. J., & Strauss, A. L. (1967). *The discovery of grounded theory: Strategies for qualitative research*. New York: Aldine de Gruyter.

Hamel, G. (2007). *The future of Management*. Boston, MA: Harvard Business School.

Harper, S. R., & Quaye, S. J. (2009). Beyond sameness, with engagement and outcomes for all: An introduction. In S. R. Harper & S. J. Quaye (Eds.), *Student engagement in higher education: Theoretical perspectives and practical approaches for diverse populations* (pp. 1–15). New York, NY: Routledge.

Hornak, A. M., Ozaki, C. C., & Lunceford, C. (2016). Socialization for new and mid-level community college student affairs professionals. *Journal of Student Affairs Research and Practice, 53*(2), 118–130. doi: 10.1080/19496591.2016.1143833

Inman, M. (2011). The journey to leadership for academics in higher education. *Educational Management Administration & Leadership, 39*(2), 228–241. doi: 10.1177/1741143210390055

Johnsrud, L. K., & Rosser, V. J. (1999a). College and university midlevel administrators: Explaining and improving their morale. *The Review of Higher Education, 22*(2), 121–141.

Johnsrud, L. K., & Rosser, V. J. (1999b). Predicting and reducing midlevel administrative staff turnover. *CUPA Journal, 49*(1), 1–8.

Johnston, S. W. (2003). Faculty governance and effective academic administrative leadership. *New Directions for Higher Education, 2003*(124), 57–63. doi: 10.1002/he.130

Kezar, A. (2012). Bottom-up/top-down leadership: Contradiction or hidden phenomenon. *Journal of Higher Education. 83*(5), 725–758.

Kezar, A., Carducci, R., & Contreras-McGavin, M. (2006). *Rethinking the "L" word in higher education: The revolution on research in leadership*. San Francisco, CA: Jossey-Bass.

Kuh, G. D. (2003). What we're learning about student engagement from NSSE: Benchmarks for effective educational practices. *Change, 35*(2), 24–32.

Kuh, G. D., Kinzie, J., Buckley, J. A., Bridges, B. K., & Hayek, J. C. (2007). Piecing together the student success puzzle: Research, propositions, and recommendations. *ASHE Higher Education Report, 32*(5). San Francisco, CA: Jossey-Bass.

Kuhl, S. (2013). *Organizations: A systems approach*. Burlington, VA: Gower.

Manatos, M. J., Sarrico, C. S., & Rosa, M. J. (2015). The integration of quality management in higher education institutions: A systematic literature review. *Total Quality Management & Business Excellence*, 1–17. doi: 10.1080/1483363.2015.1050180

Manning, K. (2013). *Organizational theory in higher education*. New York, NY: Routledge.

Mather, P. C., Bryan, S. P., & Faulkner, W. O. (2009). Orienting midlevel student affairs professionals. *College Student Affairs Journal, 27*(2), 242–256.

Mills, D. B. (2000). The role of the middle manager. In Barr, M., Desler, M. & Associates (Eds.), *The handbook of student affairs administration* (pp. 135–154). San Francisco, CA: Jossey Bass.

Olson, G. A. (2009). Exactly what is shared governance. *The Chronicle of Higher Education, 24*. Retrieved from http://chronicle.com/article/Exactly-What-Is-Shared/47065/

Patton, M. Q. (2002). *Qualitative research & evaluation methods.* (3rd ed.) Thousand Oaks, CA: Sage Publications.

Pascarella, E. T., & Terenzini, P. T. (2005). *How college affects students: A third decade of research.* San Francisco, CA: Jossey-Bass.

Pavur, E. J. (2012). Leadership for mangers. *The Psychologist-Manager Journal, 15*, 269–274. doi: 10.1080/10887156.2012.730816

Renn, K. A., & Hodges, J. (2007). The first year on the job: Experiences of new professionals in student affairs. *NASPA Journal, 44*(2), 367–391.

Rosser, V. J. (2004). A national study on midlevel leaders in higher education: The unsung professionals in the academy. *Higher Education, 48*(3), 317–337.

Ruscio, K. (2016). Leadership in organized anarchy. *Public Administration Review, 76*, 219–220. doi: 10.1111/puar.12536

Rutherford, A., & Meier, K. J. (2014). Managerial goals in a performance-driven system: Theory and empirical tests in higher education. *Public Administration, 93*(1), doi: 10.1111/padm.12124

Sharifi, H., Liu, W., & Ismail, H. S. (2013). Higher education system and the 'open' knowledge transfer: a view from perception of senior managers at university knowledge transfer offices. *Studies in Higher Education, 39,* 1860–1884. doi: 10.1080/03075079.2013.818645

Strauss, A., & Corbin, J. (1998). *Basics of qualitative research: Techniques and procedures for developing Grounded Theory.* Thousand Oaks, CA.: Sage Publications Inc.

Suomi, K., Kuoppakangas, P., Hytti, U., Hampden-Turner, C., & Kangaslahti, J. (2013). Focusing on dilemmas challenging reputation management in higher education. *International Journal of Educational Management, 28*(4), 461–478. doi: 10.1108/09513550610669176

Tierney, W. G., & Lechuga, V. M. (2004). *Restructuring shared governance in higher education.* San Francisco, CA: Jossey-Bass.

Waple, J. N. (2006). An assessment of skills and competencies necessary for entry-level student affairs work. *NASPA Journal, 43*(1), 1–18. doi: 10.2202/1949-6605.1568

Young, R. B. (1990). *The invisible leaders: Student affairs mid-managers.* Washington, DC: NASPA.

CHAPTER FIFTEEN

Authentic Leadership at a Hispanic Serving Institution Case Study

HENRIETTA WILLIAMS PICHON

DIVERSITY ISSUES IN HIGHER EDUCATION

The United States higher education community is very heterogeneous. That is, there are multiple public postsecondary education (beyond primary and secondary education or K-12 education) opportunities (e.g., technical college, community/junior college, baccalaureate granting institutions, master's degree granting institutions, seminaries, professional colleges and schools) for students, as well as multiple demographics of students (e.g., first-generation college students, ethnic/racial diversity, socioeconomic status) with various academic needs (e.g., developmental students, high achieving students, students with special needs). These public institutions of higher education are supposed to educate their citizens. So, what happens when the diverse citizens feel as though the public institutions are not meeting their needs?

Thus, it is incumbent upon all affiliated with the institutions (e.g., administration, faculty, staff, students) to fully and intentionally address issues related to diversity. In a Special Report in the *Chronicle of Higher Education* (2016), McMurtrie

Author Note: Several concepts in this case study were presented in a paper, "Leading Diversity Efforts with Authentic Leadership: The University's Social Responsibility" presented at the 13th ADERSE Conference in Lyon, France in June, 2016.

posited that institutions continue to make the same mistakes regarding diversity as they did post 1960s. That is, they continue to be reactionary, only respond to issues once they reach the boiling point, and use ad hoc committees that involve only a few administrators who never really understand what is really going on. Simply stated, not enough people are at the table. McMurtrie advises institutions to do the following: take ownership of the problem and their role in perpetuating it, engage the students, have tough conversations, and hold people accountable. So, what does a genuine commitment to diversity look like? In that same Special Report, a forum included the responses of several scholars as it related to diversity issues in higher education. Shaun Harper noted that "True commitment to diversity permeates every aspect of the campus and is widely collaboratively" (para. 3). He added that it should be integrated into the curriculum and should be appropriately resourced. Sara Goldrick-Rab added that "A genuine commitment to diversity requires institutions to recognize how social class and race/ethnicity structure opportunities to attend and complete college" (para. 9). Commitment to diversity actions include: engaging with the local school districts and community colleges, build relationships with diverse audiences, reject admissions policies that limit access to low-income students, hire diverse personnel, and support students just to name a few. Richard D. Kahlenberg added that institutions must "take steps to make students feel included once they are on campus" (para. 21). In conclusion, senior administrators can no longer engage in rhetoric regarding diversity; they are now forced to take intentional actions. Thus, the remainder of this paper will relay a particular case study related to diversity issues at an institution in the Southwest. The events presented are loosely based on events that occurred at a research institution in the Southwest. Readers will then be asked to examine issues related to authentic leadership and actions.

AUTHENTIC LEADERSHIP

As key stakeholders in higher education tackle issues related to growing diversity, leaders have to be able to demonstrate trustworthiness. Thus, there has become an increased interest in authenticity (e.g., Barnard, 1938; George, Sims, McLean, & Mayer, 2007; Northouse, 2013; Novicevic, Harvey, Buckley, Brown-Radford, & Evans, 2006). *Authentic leadership* is an emergent form of leadership that focuses on the individual's genuineness and conviction to deal with the matter at hand (Northouse, 2013). Northouse posited that authentic leadership focuses on the leaders' intrapersonal skills (e.g., self-knowledge, self-regulation, self-concept, convictions) and interpersonal skills (e.g., relationships, interactions with others)—both can be developed over time. These virtues of authenticity have relied on both philosophical (moral virtue and ethical choices) as well as psychological (trait/state and/or identity; Novicevic et al., 2006) attributes. Five notable traits of an authentic leader are insight, initiative, influence, impact, and integrity (Hyatt, 2010). Terry (1993) defined authentic leadership as knowing and acting on what is really real and true for yourself, the team, and the organization. Inauthentic leadership manifest itself in leadership withdrawal, arrogance, indifference to the needs of the constituencies, allow decisions to hinge on chance, and lack of personal responsibility (Barnard, 1938). This can ultimately lead to a crisis of executive leadership in which the leader becomes paralyzed in the decision making process (Barnard, 1938).

Adding to that, "In such turbulent times, leader authenticity becomes salient because the continuity of organizations as social systems is threatened by multiple discrepancies among leaders responsibilities toward the self, toward the followers, and toward other stakeholders (Badaracco, 1992)." (as cited in Novicevic et al., 2006, p. 65). Walumbwa, Wang, Wang, Schaubroeck, and Avoilio (2010) found that the more authentic a leader is the more likely are the employees to identify with them, feel empowered, do their work, and be good citizens—all willing to work for the good of the organization.

As an authentic leader, George et al. (2007) noted that "we all have the capacity to inspire and empower others. But we must first be willing to devote ourselves to our personal growth and development as leaders" (p. 1). Adding to that, authentic leaders create environments in which individuals believe they can be honest and open about their challenges and concerns, appreciate collaboration across organizational lines, and seek honest and critical feedback (Ramos, 2011). Although not explicitly stated, authentic leadership is aligned with the teaching ethic of social justice. For example, Hytten (2015) offers three habits of teaching for social justice: reflective humility, open mindedness, and sympathetic attentiveness. Reflective humility is required for good character. It is important for individuals to examine their own choices and beliefs as well as examine how they listen to others' perspectives. This leads to intellectual open-mindedness which challenges us to think beyond our own knowledge. Finally, sympathetic attentiveness focuses on caring about others perspectives and experiences. Not only trying to understand the experiences of others but also seeking to understand why they may feel a certain way even when these views differ from ours. George et al. (2007) noted that in order to capture the essence of authenticity, leaders have to examine themselves and really explore the following: people who influenced them early on, what do they value, what motivates them, what kind of team support do they have, is their life integrated, what does authentic mean to them, and so on. Thus, being authentic, one does not show up as different daily or in crisis. An authentic leader "has a steady and confident presence" (George et al., 2007, p. 7). This instills confidence in followers as they know who they are dealing with in all situations.

AUTHENTIC BEHAVIOR

Authentic leadership leads to authentic behaviors in organizations (Harvey, Martinko, & Gardner, 2006). Harvey et al. (2006) argue that authentic leaders can select authentic behaviors even when there are external pressures to be inauthentic. The authors created an Attributional Model of Authentic Leadership in which the authentic behavior is based on the individuals need to understand cause and effect. In essence, "the locus of causality dimension refers to the perceived internal or external nature of the causes of outcomes, whereas the stability dimension refers to the perceived variability of a cause across different situations and time periods" (p. 3). Thus, leaders have to be keenly aware of biases and/or self-interest as they seek to make decisions based on organizational context against their individual factors. In being authentic, George et al. (2007) would argue that the decision making process should be not only balanced but also integrated with the leaders' true self. Harvey et al. (2006) noted that organizations can do several things to increase authentic behavior: decrease ambiguity (define roles and provide clear objectives), increase psychological closeness (leadership performing and understanding task of all employees), attributional retraining (understanding biases in an effort to move toward empowerment), and self-efficacy training (become more efficient). These actions can lead to more authentic behavior.

THE AUTHENTIC ACTION WHEEL

Adding another dimension to authentic leadership and behavior is action. Robert Terry's (1993) Action Wheel was created to answer two questions: What is really, really going on? What are we going to do about it? These two questions should be guided by the authentic self and lead to appropriate actions (Northouse, 2013). Specifically,

> [Terry's] wheel has six components: around the top of the wheel are *Meaning*, *Mission*, and *Power*; clockwise around the bottom are *Structure*, *Resources*, and *Existence*. The center of the wheel is labeled *Fulfillment* and represents the completion of the process. (pp. 255–256)

According to the Action Wheel Leadership Group, the six dimensions represent human actions and can provide appropriate actions by assessing those dimensions using a 60 item Action Wheel Assessment (a sample is available at http://www.actionwheelassessment.com/). Each dimension answers the following questions: *Existence*—"What is the current reality?"; *Resources*—"What do we need?"; *Structure*—"How will we do this?"; *Power*—"Who is driving this?"; *Mission*—"Where are we going?"; And *Meaning*—"Why are we doing this?". By completing the Action Wheel Assessment, leaders will be able to define what is going on, create a common language, focus actions, engage people and systems, and identify challenges, dilemmas, and solutions. Since issues related to diversity in higher education present several different layers and multiple meanings and perspectives, the Action Wheel Assessment could be a great tool to assist leaders in knowing what is really, really going on? And what appropriate actions needs to be taken?

THE CASE STUDY

Background

The University of the Southwest lies in a place of enchantment of which the heavens, the skies, the people, and the earth are all attuned with the universe. With each day, the golden sun gently crosses the sky leaving hypnotic hues of yellow, orange, and red, highlighting the earth's natural beauties of light greens, browns, reds, oranges, pinks and so on. As the sun hits your face, you are constantly reminded of the cycle of life … The ways of enchantment. The state's art, landscape, and culture are dominated by American Indian and Latino/Mexican heritages which provide unique experiences for all who visit and live in the state.

The University of the Southwest is no different. It embraces the states many cultures, customs, and traditions while seeking to be the "university of the people". To date, the University of the Southwest has a total enrollment of approximately 16,000 students and offers 23 doctoral degrees, 56 master's degrees, and 89 undergraduate degrees across five colleges. It has four branch campuses and nine research facilities. It is a Hispanic Serving Institution and is considered a Research I institution. The institution is governed by a state board, which is appointed by the governor. The board delegates authority to the President for the operation of the institution. The institution receives 33% of its revenue from state appropriations, which relies heavily on oil and gas revenues to sustain the budget. The state has performance-based budgeting, which had gone into effect the previous year. Adding to that, the state is anticipating a 3% reduction each year in state appropriations over the next 10 years or unless the state can reconfigure and/or diversify its revenue sources.

The student body is proportionate to that of the region. Approximately 13,000 students are undergraduate and 3,000 are graduate students. Females outnumber the males almost 2:1: 8,500 females and 4,500 males. Majority of the students are traditional-aged college students (24 years old or younger; 10,500) and have an average ACT Composite score of 20.9. With regard to ethnicity and race, the makeup is as follows: 358 (2%) American Indian/Alaskan Native; 220 (1%) Asian; 465 (3%) Black/African American; 32 (0.2%) Native Hawaiian/other Pacific Islander; 7,738 (49%) Hispanic; 1,207 (8%) International; 247 (1.6%) two or more races; 523 (3%) unknown; and 5,039 (32%) White. The six year graduation rate per ethnicity/race was as follows: Black/African American, 32.8%; American Indian, 25.6%; Asian, 48%; Hispanic 41.2%; and White, 50.4%.

The faculty and staff make up is different. There are approximately 1,200 faculty and 2,800 staff. Tenured and/or tenure-track faculty (n = 678) represent the different ranks: 210 (31%) at the assistant level, 244 (36%) at the associate level, and 222 (33%) at the professor level. A majority of faculty are tenured (465; 69%) while the others are tenure-track (213; 31%). The race distribution varies from that of the students in that non-minority faculty make up 74% (n = 499) of the faculty while 26% (n = 179) are minorities. Faculty (tenured and tenured-track) are almost equally divided between males (401; 59%) and females (277; 41%).

For fall 2014, and what appeared to be all of a sudden, a faculty member used the campus listserv to call for a dialogue (A Night of Testimonies) to discuss issues regarding the attrition of minorities and/or women faculty and staff at the institution. All of which appeared to be driven by a mass exodus of faculty and staff of color and women. During that same time, a special issue of a popular magazine related to diversity in higher education, spotlighted the University of the Southwest, calling attention to "ignored diversity issues." The author discussed a culture of insensitivity to diversity issues and cited issues related to request and/or input not being followed up on, loss of funding to support diversity initiatives, and the lack of ethnic studies just to name a few. Another faculty member on the listserv reminded faculty of an earlier study conducted at the institution five years earlier which focused on that same thing. In that report, the authors found that faculty of color and female faculty left for lack of appreciation for their contribution, lack of transparency, unrealistic teaching loads, lack of assistance and mentoring, and limited understanding of diversity. These sentiments were echoed at the A Night of Testimonies in which the Chief Academic/Student Officer (CASO) attended. Faculty, staff, and students alike attended the event and discussed a host of issues: low wages, teaching overloads, unrealistic expectations, lack of transparency in decision making, especially with regard to budget matters, apathetic faculty, lack of ethnic studies programs, minority student retention, underfunded retention initiatives, and blatant racism and sexism.

In response to this session, other conversations were triggered. For example, it was noted that not all persons of color (i.e., Black/African American, American Indian, Asian/Pacific Islanders) voices were heard during the testimonies. Also, some have argued that persons should allow the new administration an opportunity to address the issues because the diversity issues were allowed to grow during times of transitional leadership. Now, the new CASO is being asked to "fix this" or "make it right."

Exploring Several Initiatives

In seeking to address the issues of diversity at the University of the Southwest, the CASO has had a lot to contend with. During times of distrust, broken promises, neglect, and so on, authentic leadership is needed. Authentic leadership is aligned with dealing with diversity issues in higher education in that individuals are more likely to become involved in solution-based processes when they believe in the leader, even when the leader has to make unpopular decisions. There were issues that emerged as the CASO attempted to make things right: Becoming aware of the diversity issues/concerns at the University of the Southwest; Developing a plan to address diversity issues/concerns; and the identification of challenges in implementing your plan.

Becoming Aware of Diversity Issues at the University of the Southwest

The CASO believed that he had a firm understanding of the diversity issues at the University of the Southwest. Having grown up in a diverse setting, he was always keenly aware of diversity and always had diverse friends. Thus, he was always aware that different people had different experiences. For example, if different policies were created, he could always hear the different perspectives of how it impacted persons of color. So, he felt as though he has been keenly aware of other persons' experiences. And he saw institutions as places where everyone should be able to find their place.

When thinking about the diversity issues, he was driven by the mission of the institution. He noted the mission of the University of the Southwest was to meet the educational needs of the state's diverse population. In noting that, he recited the issues with retention rates of the diverse populations, students, faculty, and staff alike. Because of these issues, he knows he had to take action. One of the first things he did was to reach to out to university leaders engaged in addressing diverse issues to hear what were their concerns. From there, he convened a committee of those leaders and others interested in addressing diversity issues.

Although new to the position, the CASO was not new to the institution and was keenly aware of the issues related to diversity. He believed that he began addressing those issues from day one, understanding he was approaching those issues from a point of privilege. So, when the article was published he was not necessarily surprised. He moved to see if there were other issues that he needed to address and incorporate them into his plan.

The Plan

The CASO took a collaborative approach to addressing the diversity issues in which he wanted to include all of the key stakeholders. Understanding his place of privilege and power, as a White male, he chose a collaborative approach. Therefore, he created an advisory group of diverse faculty and staff to advise him on the diversity issues: What do they look like? And what can we do to address them? The committee met periodically throughout the semester and created a list of recommendations that the CASO was able to take to the President for approval. While that committee was working, there appeared to be multiple diversity committees and task forces meeting across campus, yet it was unclear if any cross-talk was occurring between the varying groups. In one meeting, a document may be presented to address diversity issues while at a different meeting, another document may be presented. It is possible that none of those documents represent recommendations shared by the document provided by the CASO. The Faculty Senate had a diversity committee and the Staff Association had a different diversity committee. Then, different colleges had diversity committees.

With regard to data collection, there were several forums held in which faculty and students could voice their concerns. During those sessions, faculty and students voiced concerns about lack of ethnic studies programs, low wages, lack of appreciation for academic and scholarly diversity, and basic climate issues. Additionally, the Faculty Resource Center hosted several sessions on appreciating diversity and understanding the needs of students at the University of the Southwest. During one of the sessions the moderator asked questions of a group of faculty, staff, and students about national diversity issues in higher education and how, or if, those issues were addressed at the University of the Southwest. For example, she asked about heightened harassment of Muslim students in light of the tensions overseas. All of the non-Muslim people indicated that the climate was good and there were no incidents to report. In fact, they believed the institution could be used as a model for tolerance of religious minorities. The Muslim student in the session indicated that the climate was not good. She shared stories of friends being followed as they walked to campus and/or around campus and of being afraid to wear the hijab or other clothing that may identify them as Muslim. She also indicated that several of her friends tried not to go places alone, especially at night, for fear of being harassed or injured, and they believed other students did not want to work with them in groups, disregarded their contribution in class discussions, and were not even being acknowledged by peers—rendering them invisible. Adding to that, they were also concerned about not having their dietary needs met by university dining services. From sessions such as these, we learned that persons were unaware of "others" issues. In another similar session, several faculty voiced concerns about lowering standards. One faculty member indicated that he was fine with embracing diversity but not at the expense of standards. While other faculty mentioned feeling as though they have to do more "hand holding" than they have in the past and feeling like the bad guy when not excusing excessive absences related to family obligations and/or cultural events. It was noted that some personnel were unaware of the Hispanic Serving Institution designation and/or what that meant beyond the numbers and very few understood the cultural significance, especially with regard to the region.

Goals

Several goals recommended by the CASO's committee included: increasing faculty diversity, requiring new faculty/staff orientation so new hires are aware of values, rewarding work with students and addressing diversity issues, as well as enhancing student success of diverse populations through mentoring and advising, academic support services, and financial aid. Lastly, the committee sought to address issues of trust between the administration and the university community. Issues of trust continued to arise as the researcher engaged in casual conversations with faculty and staff across campus. The CASO acknowledged that there were trust issues. He also acknowledged that there was also resistance, noting that some of the resistance could be stemming from the lack of trust. Furthermore, he acknowledged that some of that mistrust was due to changes in leadership or a high turnover in senior administration over the last ten years. There was also acknowledgement that tough personnel decisions were being made that created an environment of mistrust. It was noted that although tough decisions were being made with regard to the budget, the institution remained committed to preserving funds to support diversity.

Longer term goals focused on discussions of whether or not the institution was ready to employ a senior diversity officer. There were continued discussions about the role and scope of such a position. The CASO wanted to ensure that this was the best next thing to do. Others voiced concerned about who's interests would be served by hiring the person: the administration or the university community. One faculty member said that she felt uncomfortable having the CASO make the final decision about the candidate.

Key Challenges

Three issues that arose focused on the following: trust of senior administration, lack of intentionality, and resistance to change. There were significant trust issues discussed by all persons involved. The university community wanted to know: Can we trust that the administration will do the right thing? At this time, the mistrust was not necessarily eased and/or reduced. The students did not trust the faculty and staff and the faculty and staff did not trust the administration. This has led to issues with the lack of intentionality of efforts. That is, although there were a number of initiatives launched to address several of the diversity issues, they were not necessarily marketed that way and so people did not know that they were attempts to address a diversity issue. For example, several of the ethnic programs partnered with several academic departments to bring in speakers, sponsor events, and/or promote student success initiatives. In those cases, the partnerships were sometimes glossed over or not mentioned at all. Although several of these events brought together diverse groups with a common interests and great cross-cultural discussions occurred, no one seemed to know how these events came together or reflected on the experiences.

Adding to that, some faculty and staff were resistant to change. They appeared to be unclear about the challenges of "others" and appeared to not be willing to make changes to address diversity issues. In one of the diversity sessions sponsored by the faculty resource center, several faculty members voiced concerns about working with students. Although the concerns appeared to focus, on the surface, on students issues in general, several other faculty members believed some of the concerns were based on privilege, biases, and prejudices. Because of that lack of awareness, those members were less likely to make changes. In fact, they believed that changing to address academic diversity in the classroom would be dumbing down the course. From those sessions, conversations emerged about how to get people to think differently about the work that they do and how they do it. Questions were raised about how to help students feel included within the academic and social communities on campus and how to get faculty and staff to understand their role in the process.

CONCLUSION

Needless to say, the University of the Southwest continues to struggle with issues of diversity. However, it is important that the faculty, staff, and students look to the institution to engage in authentic behaviors that address the diverse issues head on. That warrants authentic leadership. How then can the CASO create ways to address issues with trust of senior administration, lack of intentionality, and resistance to change? This case study presents several important discussion questions that need to be addressed with regard to the social responsibility of institutions to address diversity issues through authentic leadership. In answering these questions, all institutions will be closer to resolving the issues of diversity and living the social responsibility of the institution.

DISCUSSION QUESTIONS

1. Identify at least five things the CASO can do to address challenges encountered when addressing diversity issues (e.g., trust of senior administration, lack of intentionality, and resistance to change).
2. What are the advantages of using authentic leadership to address challenges encountered when addressing diversity issues (e.g., trust of senior administration, lack of intentionality, and resistance to change)?

3. What are the disadvantages of using authentic leadership to address diversity issues (e.g., trust of senior administration, lack of intentionality, and resistance to change)?
4. How might the CASO incorporate Terry's Action Wheel to address issues of trust between the administration and the university community?
5. What are things the CASO can do to create authentic behavior within the institution, especially as it relates to its social responsibility to meet the needs of its diverse populations?

REFERENCES

The Action Wheel Leadership Group. (n.d.).The action wheel. Retrieved from http://www.actionwheel.com/.

Barnard, C. (1938). *The functions of the executive.* Cambridge, MA: Harvard University Press.

George, B., Sims, P., McLean, A. N., & Mayer, D. (2007). Discovering your authentic leadership. *Harvard Business Review, 85*(2), 1–9.

Harvey, P., Martinko, M. J., & Gardner, W. L. (2006). Promoting authentic behavior in organizations: An attributional perspective. *Journal of Leadership and Organizational Studies, 12*(3), 1–11.

Hyatt, M. (2010). *The five marks of authentic leadership.* Retrieved from http://michaelhyatt.com/the-five-marks-of-authentic-leadership.html

Hytten, K. (2015). Ethics in teaching for democracy and social justice. *Democracy & Education, 23*(2), 1–10.

McMurtrie, B. (May 15, 2016). How do you create a diversity agenda? It takes more than just a plan on paper. *The Chronicle of Higher Education: Special Report, 62*(36). Retrieved from http://www.chronicle.com/article/How-Do-You-Create-a-Diversity/236427

Northouse, P. G. (2013). *Leadership: Theory and practice.* Thousand Oaks, CA: Sage Publications.

Novicevic, M. M., Harvey, M. G., Buckley, M. R., Brown-Radford, J., & Evans, R. (2006). Authentic leadership: A historical perspective. *Journal of Leadership and Organization, 13*(1), 64–76.

Ramos, R. (2011). Being authentic: A different approach to leadership. *Campus Activities Programming, 43* (8), 37–40.

Terry, R. (1993). *Authentic leadership: Courage in action.* San Francisco, CA: Jossey-Bass.

Walumbwa, F. O., Wang, P., Wang, H., Schaubroeck, J., & Avolio, B. J. (2010). Psychological processes linking authentic leadership to follower behaviors. *The Leadership Quarterly, 21*, 901–914.

Afterword

ARNETHA BALL

Finally, a book that brings our conceptions of leadership into the realities of the twenty-first century. This volume serves to remind us that, although we typically think of an educational leader as a man or woman who has a formal leadership role and title, such as the principal, headmaster, dean, president, provost, chancellor, other individuals demonstrate leadership capacity. Just when we need it most, we are reminded by this volume, of what Henry Ford said, "you don't have to hold a position to be a leader" (Moore, 2003, p. 42). Leadership is not even "about a title or a designation. It is about impact, influence and inspiration. Impact involves getting results, influence is about spreading the passion you have for your work, and you have to inspire," as Robin S. Sharma (n.d.) reminds us. John Quincy Adams (n.d.) added an important notation to this chain of thought when he said "If your actions inspire others to dream more, learn more, do more and become more, you are a leader." Most important, at this critical time in our nation's history, it is important to note that "Leadership is not about the next election, it's about the next generation" (Sinek, n.d.).

In other words, this volume is about individuals and groups of individuals who serve in leadership roles within educational institutions, though they do not hold official leadership titles, and it is also about leaders in traditional roles who think and act inventively in fulfilling their responsibilities. This notion of leadership has existed for some time but has received little attention by the research community. The editors of this volume, however, have invited a wide array of authors to offer theoretical perspectives on innovative leadership and to provide unique case studies of instances where people have taken on leadership roles for which they have not been hired or where leaders have creatively redefined their leadership.

This volume presents numerous cases to illustrate how educational institutions are changing. At a time when school demographics are changing rapidly and educational institutions are challenged to meet the needs of diverse students in a growing number of culturally and linguistically complex classrooms, there is a need for innovative approaches to educational leadership and leaders who are willing to creatively redefine their leadership. The authors of this volume offer examples of how individuals may see a void and take it upon themselves to create or redefine leadership roles in an effort to help their programs to survive and thrive despite the complexity of twenty-first century schooling. Some cases tell of teachers serving a leadership role in an elementary school or a group of professors taking on added responsibility in a college or university. In each case, the desire is to advance the institution and to make better the experiences of the students therein. The success of such leadership may require agile programmatic structures and systems to make necessary adjustments to respond to evolving political, economic, and policy influences and to incorporate new insights gained through organizational learning. The emergence of agile structures and systems may also require more democratic program cultures and less hierarchical organizations. When leadership efforts are solely top-down, then innovations may be more limited and they are often conceptualized and implemented in ways that sustain old ways of thinking and accomplishing work. Undoubtedly, conceptions of leadership need to broaden and twenty-first century leaders need to acknowledge the diverse contributions of those organizational leaders who do not hold "official" or "traditional" leadership positions; they need to *support* the work of motivated and knowledgeable others who help to drive and carry out the work of the organization.

This volume is unique and valuable for a number of reasons. First, the editors have gathered a diverse and scholarly group of academics and practitioners to tell this story of innovative leadership. The volume includes the voices of seasoned as well as early career academics, current and former school-level administrators, current and former university administrators, and more. Second, the volume focuses on such leadership at all levels of education: elementary, secondary, and higher education, all in one volume. Third, the authors each provide provocative discussion questions for use by graduate students as well as practitioners in educational institutions. These discussion questions are designed to enable readers to delve deeply into the subject matter. Finally, while the volume explores leadership behavior, it is more than a leadership book in that the authors also explore teachers and other "non-leaders" who are indeed leading.

This book frames all of these unique aspects of the volume within a powerful set of essays that will help researchers, teachers, teacher educators, and leaders of all kinds to take up the critical questions of our times. As they take up questions like "What is leadership and where can we find it?" I am reminded that John Buchan once said that "The task of leadership is not to put greatness into people, but to elicit it, for the greatness is there already" (1950, p. 24). As the volume deals with questions concerning the implications of leadership for students and teachers in relation to diversity issues in the classroom, I am reminded that Reed Markham (n.d.) once said that "successful leaders see the opportunities in every difficulty rather than the difficulty in every opportunity" and that Seth Godin (n.d.) has noted that "leadership is the art of giving people a platform for spreading ideas that work." When the volume deals with questions like "What are the potential outcomes and side-effects of teaching with an awareness of diversity?" I am reminded that Chris Hadfield (2015) has said that "ultimately, leadership is not about glorious crowning acts. It's about keeping your team focused on a goal and motivated to do their best to achieve it, especially when the stakes are high and the consequences really matter. It is about laying the groundwork for others' success, and then standing back and letting them shine" (p. 234). We know that such leadership draws on the contributions and efforts of unacknowledged leaders who work in a wide range of educational contexts to help programs to survive and thrive despite the complexity of twenty-first century schooling. This volume offers examples of how programs are made better by the contributions of a wide variety of educational leaders. Throughout the volume I am reminded that there is "no single formula for success … that some attributes of leadership are universal and are often about finding ways of encouraging people to combine their efforts, their talents, their insights, their enthusiasm and their inspiration to work together" (Queen Elizabeth II, 2010, para. 10) and that sometimes "a leader is best when people barely know he exists, when his work is done, his aim fulfilled, they will say: we did it ourselves" (Lao Tzu, n.d.). Just as I have been inspired by this volume, other readers will find that this volume is a treasure trove of perspectives, answers, and provocations that should stimulate further the essential discussions we must have to create schools that can someday provide all students and teachers with leadership needed to serve a diverse student population. In the past, dialogues on leadership were largely carried on by and about predominantly those we typically think of as leaders—men and women who hold formal leadership roles and titles—or individuals hired specifically to fulfill specific leadership responsibilities. Realizing that individuals do not have to hold a formal position to be a leader, it is time to share the stories and include the voices of leaders from diverse backgrounds and those who lead in unacknowledged circumstances. As we do so, we will find that these voices have much to add that can not only inform, but re-shape current conceptions of leadership practices, research priorities, and policy debates that focus on finding solutions to the challenges that face us as we try to improve schooling for all populations in twenty-first century educational institutions and beyond.

REFERENCES

Adams, J. Q. (n.d.). Retrieved from https://www.brainyquote.com/quotes/authors/j/john_quincy_adams.html.

Buchan, J. (1950). Montrose and leadership. In *Lectures on leadership: Delivered before the University of St. Andrews (under the Walker Trust) 1930–49*. London: Oxford University Press.

Moore, J. D. (2003). *Quotations for martial artists: Hundreds of inspirational quotes to motivate and enlighten the modern warrior.* Lincoln, NE: Writers Club Press.

Godin, S. (n.d.). Retrieved from http://www.goodreads.com/quotes/560088-leadership-is-the-art-of-giving-people-a-platform-for.

Hadfield, C. (2015). *An astronaut's guide to life on earth: What going to space taught me about ingenuity, determination, and being prepared for anything*. New York, NY: Back Bay Books.

Markham, R. (n.d.). Retrieved from http://www.goodreads.com/quotes/377618-successful-leaders-see-the-opportunities-in-every-difficulty-rather-than.

Queen Elizabeth. (2010). Address to the United Nations General Assembly. Retrieved from http://www.americanrhetoric.com/speeches/queenelizabethunitednations.htm.

Sharma, R. S. (n.d.). Retrieved from https://www.brainyquote.com/quotes/authors/r/robin_s_sharma.html.

Sinek, S. (n.d.). Retrieved from https://www.brainyquote.com/quotes/quotes/s/simonsinek568178.html.

Tzu, L. (n.d.). Retrieved from https://www.brainyquote.com/quotes/quotes/l/laotzu121709.html.

Authors' Biographies

Arnetha Ball is a Professor in the Graduate School of Education at Stanford University in the Curriculum Studies, Teacher Education, and the Race, Inequality and Language Programs. Her most recent research investigates successful paradigms, principles and practices in preparing teachers for diversity across national boundaries in countries that serve large numbers of historically marginalized students—including the US, South Africa, Australia, and New Zealand.

Rosa M. Banda is Assistant Professor of Educational Leadership at Texas A&M University-Corpus Christi. Formerly, Dr. Banda was a Research Associate to the Samuel DeWitt Proctor Chair in Education at Rutgers University. Dr. Banda's primary research interests include: Latinas in engineering, faculty diversity, leadership, and qualitative research.

Ira Bogotch is a professor of educational leadership and research methodology at Florida Atlantic University and adjunct professor at Griffith University Institute for Educational Research. His interest in social justice as an educational construct leads to exploring critical theories and methodologies for studying educational leadership nationally and internationally. He is currently co-editing an International Handbook of Educational Leadership.

Patricia Bricker is an associate professor of science education and associate director of the School of Teaching and Learning at Western Carolina University. Her research interests include inquiry-based science education, integrated curriculum, experiential education, and teacher professional development.

Isiah Brown is a Visiting Assistant Professor of Management at SUNY Oswego in the School of Business. His primary areas of interest include managing diversity, leadership, culturally responsive pedagogy and accreditation and assessment.

Gary M. Crow is Professor in the Department of Educational Leadership and Policy Studies and Executive Associate Dean of the School of Education at Indiana University (USA). His Ph.D. is from the University of Chicago. Crow is a past president of the University Council for Educational Administration and founding editor of the Journal of Cases in Educational Leadership. He is also a recipient of the Roald Campbell Lifetime Achievement Award presented by the University Council for Educational Administration.

Robert Crow is an assistant professor of educational research at Western Carolina University. Previously, he worked in faculty professional development. He received his PhD in Educational Psychology & Research from the University of South Carolina, in his home state. He currently lives in the scenic Appalachian Mountains in Weaverville, NC.

Rebecca Ensley is a school principal and doctoral candidate in the Educational Leadership program at Western Carolina University. She has worked in public education for 15 years. Mrs. Ensley began as a special education teacher and then transitioned to school-level leadership. She also has experience as a district level leader.

Levon Esters is an Associate Professor in the Department of Youth Development and Agriculture Education at Purdue University. He holds degrees from Florida A&M University and North Carolina A&T University.

Kimberly M. Florence, Ph.D. received her doctorate in Higher Education from the University of Nevada, Las Vegas. Her research interests include college preparedness, academic transitions, student success, retention and persistence, and first-generation students. In 2016, she received training to become an educational college consultant and became an Associate Member of the Independent Educational Consultants Association (IECA). Afterward, Dr. Florence started her own business titled College Literacy, LLC aimed at providing college knowledge and academic assistance to students and families in Clark County, Southern Nevada.

Alonzo M. Flowers III is Assistant Professor in the School of Education at Drexel University. Dr. Flowers specializes in educational issues including academic identity development of African American and Latino males in STEM education. He also focuses on diversity, leadership, teaching & learning, and college student development.

Hugo A. García is an assistant professor at Texas Tech University. His research interests pertain to access and equity in higher education, retention of underrepresented students at two- and four-year postsecondary institutions, international higher education, diversity in higher education, and P-20 education pipeline. Specifically, his work focuses on conducting research on community colleges and their impact on underrepresented students' academic success, student transition to community colleges and four-year institutions, institutional responses to globalization and the internationalization of higher education, and educational outcomes for students of color throughout the educational pipeline.

Marybeth Gasman is a Professor in the Higher Education Division at the University of Pennsylvania and also serves as the Director of the Penn Center for Minority Serving Institutions.

Adriel Hilton is director of the Extended Campus, Myrtle Beach Metropolitan at Webster University. As the chief administrative officer for the extended campus, he is charged with implementing programs and policies that achieve the overall goals and objectives of the University. Most recently, Dr. Hilton has held positions at Grambling State University where he was chief of staff and executive assistant to the President and at Western Carolina University where he was an assistant professor and director of the Higher Education Student Affairs program.

Sonya Douglass Horsford is an Associate Professor of Education Leadership at Teachers College, Columbia University. Her research interests include the political and policy contexts of education leadership with a focus on racial inequality, resegregation, and reform in the post-Civil Rights Era. Her work has been funded by The Spencer Foundation and published in numerous journals and edited volumes to include Educational Administration Quarterly, Teachers College Record, The Urban Review, and the Handbook on Critical Race Theory in Education. She is editor of three books and author of Learning in a Burning House: Educational Inequality, Ideology, and (Dis)Integration (Teachers College Press, 2011), which received a 2013 AESA Critics' Choice Award. Prior to joining Teachers College, Horsford served as an Associate Professor of Education at George Mason University and Assistant Professor of Educational Leadership at University of Nevada, Las Vegas.

Joann Horton is chief operating officer and consultant with Pacific Crest, a foremost educational consultancy known for transformation of teaching and learning in higher education for thirty years. Dr. Horton has extensive senior executive level experience including the presidency, facilitating transformational change in higher education and state government. She has a degree in higher education administration. In addition to leadership, her interests include mentoring, coaching, learning and strategic planning.

Melvin (Jai) Jackson is an Assistant Professor at Zayed University. A native of North Carolina, he earned both his Bachelor and Master degrees from Appalachian State University. Dr. Jackson has served in several capacities in higher education including: Academic Advisor, Student Affairs Administrator, and Director of Orientation.

Kofi Lomotey is the Bardo Distinguished Professor of Educational Leadership at Western Carolina University. He received his PhD from Stanford University and has previously taught at SUNY-Buffalo and LSU. He has served as chancellor at Southern University-Baton Rouge, President at Fort Valley State University, Provost at Medgar Evers College-CUNY, and Provost at Fisk University. His research and publications focus on urban education, black students in higher education, African-centered schools and black principals. His research has been published in such journals as *Educational Administration Quarterly*, *Urban Education*, *The Journal of Negro Education*, *Education & Urban Society* and *Educational Policy*. He has authored, edited and co-edited more than a dozen books on race in higher education, urban education and the education of black people.

Kendra Lowery is an assistant professor in the Department of Educational Leadership at Ball State University. She received her PhD from the Department of Educational Leadership and Policy Analysis at the University of Wisconsin–Madison. She previously taught at University of Arkansas at Little Rock and prior to that, was a teacher and administrator in traditional public P-12 schools. Lowery's research interests include: school desegregation and urban education; leadership practices of black and Latino administrators; leadership for social justice; and organizational inclusion and diversity.

Kim Nehls has served as the Executive Director of the Association for the Study of Higher Education (ASHE) since 2008. Additionally, Kim teaches classes for both the educational psychology and higher education programs at UNLV. Kim earned a PhD in higher education administration and a master's degree in communication from UNLV as well as bachelor's degrees in political science and speech communication from University of Illinois. She is also back in school for her MBA from Duke University. Her research interests include philanthropy, leadership, and student engagement.

Henrietta Williams Pichon is an assistant professor in the Educational Leadership and Administration Department in the College of Education at New

Mexico State University. Her research interest focus on access and persistence of historically underrepresented groups in higher education, college teaching, and multicultural leadership. To her credit, she has several publications in peer reviewed journals and book chapters. Adding to that, she has presented at international, national, regional, and state conferences. She earned her doctorate from the University of New Orleans and a master's and bachelor's degree from Louisiana Tech University.

Carrie Rogers is an associate professor at Western Carolina University in the School of Teaching and Learning. She earned her doctorate after being a classroom teacher in Minneapolis for several years. Her research interests are practical leadership and teacher agency. Her areas of expertise are action research and teacher leadership, in particular connecting the two while assisting teachers as they conduct research within their own classrooms to improve curriculum delivery and student learning.

Mistilina Sato holds the Campbell Endowed Chair for Innovation in Teacher Development at the University of Minnesota. Her research focuses on teaching across the career continuum including teacher preparation, performance assessment of teachers, teacher evaluation, teacher leadership, and National Board Certification. Sato holds a PhD from Stanford University.

Roya Q. Scales is an associate professor of literacy education and Program Coordinator for Elementary Education and Middle Grades Education at Western Carolina University in Cullowhee, NC. She taught kindergarten through second grade in NC public schools for 11 years prior to moving to the university level. Roya's research interests include literacy teacher preparation, teachers' visions, how they are enacted in their teaching, teaching adaptations, and teacher development.

John J. Sherlock is an associate professor at Western Carolina University in the College of Education & Allied Professions. He serves as director of the master's degree program in Human Resources. John is an active scholar in the field of human resources and leadership, with forty (40) published articles and over seventy-five (75) live presentations. Prior to full-time academia, John worked in the wireless communications industry for 20 years in various management/leadership capacities, overseeing functions including business development, operations, and human resources.

Linda C. Tillman is Professor Emerita of Educational Leadership, School of Education, University of North Carolina at Chapel Hill where she taught courses in school leadership, central office leadership, and research design. A former public school educator with teaching and administrative experience,

Dr. Tillman is a nationally recognized scholar and leader in higher education. Her research and scholarship is focused in three primary areas: school leadership, the education of all children and particularly African Americans in K-12 education, and culturally appropriate research approaches. Her work has been featured in top tier educational leadership and education policy publications including *Educational Administration Quarterly*, *Journal of School Leadership*, *Educational Researcher*, *Review of Research in Education*, and *Review of Educational Research*. Most recently she served as editor in chief of the *SAGE Handbook of African American Education*, co-editor of the *Handbook of research on educational leadership for diversity and equity* (with J. J. Scheurich) and co-editor of *Identities and the educational leadership of Black women in the USA* (with S. D. Horsford).

Kathleen Topolka-Jorissen is a retired associate professor of educational leadership in the College of Education and Allied Professions at Western Carolina University where she served as director of the Executive Ed.D. in Educational Leadership. Prior to working in higher education, she was a public school and district level leader in suburban and rural districts in Minnesota, where she facilitated school improvement and professional development. Her research has focused on policy and practice related to leader effectiveness and capacity building.

Kelly N. Tracy is an associate professor of literacy at Western Carolina University. Her research interests primarily focus on writing pedagogy and writing professional development.

Michelle Vaughan is an assistant professor at Florida Atlantic University. She teaches courses in curriculum design, action research, and school reform. Her scholarship explores teacher growth and change through action research, online learning, and the integration of technology into practice. She works with local school districts to train teachers in curriculum design, action research, and inclusion strategies.

Amanda Washington is a Ph.D. candidate in higher education at the University of Pennsylvania. She also serves as a research associate at the Penn Center for Minority Serving Institutions. She graduated from Spelman College.

Jessica R. Weiler is an assistant professor of educational leadership in the College of Education and Allied Professions at Western Carolina University where she serves as director of the Executive Ed.D. in Educational Leadership. Dr. Weiler also works with schools and school leaders across the western North Carolina region, helping them to develop, grow, and sustain effective learning communities. Before Western Carolina, she served as a speech and language pathologist, clinical and adjunct instructor at UW-Milwaukee in the Department of Communication Disorders, and as a high school assistant principal in Western North Carolina. Her research has focused on the leadership of learning communities.

Daria J. Willis is the Provost and Senior Vice President of Educational Services/ Academic Affairs at Onondaga Community College in Syracuse, New York.

Questions about the Purpose(s) of Colleges and Universities

Norm Denzin,
Shirley R. Steinberg
General Editors

What are the purposes of higher education? When undergraduates "declare their majors," they agree to enter into a world defined by the parameters of a particular academic discourse—a discipline. But who decides those parameters? How do they come about? What are the discussions and proposed outcomes of disciplined inquiry? What should an undergraduate know to be considered educated in a discipline? How does the disciplinary knowledge base inform its pedagogy? Why are there different disciplines? When has a discipline "run its course"? Where do new disciplines come from? Where do old ones go? How does a discipline produce its knowledge? What are the meanings and purposes of disciplinary research and teaching? What are the key questions of disciplined inquiry? What questions are taboo within a discipline? What can the disciplines learn from one another? What might they not want to learn and why?

Once we begin asking these kinds of questions, positionality becomes a key issue. One reason why there aren't many books on the meaning and purpose of higher education is that once such questions are opened for discussion, one's subjectivity becomes an issue with respect to the presumed objective stances of Western higher education. Academics don't have positions because positions are "biased," "subjective," "slanted," and therefore somehow invalid. So the first thing to do is to provide a sense—however broad and general—of what kinds of positionalities will inform the books and chapters on the above questions. Certainly the questions themselves, and any others we might ask, are already suggesting a particular "bent," but as the series takes shape, the authors we engage will no doubt have positions on these questions.

From the stance of interdisciplinary, multidisciplinary, or transdisciplinary practitioners, will the chapters and books we solicit solidify disciplinary discourses, or liquefy them? Depending on who is asked, interdisciplinary inquiry is either a polite collaboration among scholars firmly situated in their own particular discourses, or it is a blurring of the restrictive parameters that define the very notion of disciplinary discourse. So will the series have a stance on the meaning and purpose of interdisciplinary inquiry and teaching? This can possibly be finessed by attracting thinkers from disciplines that are already multidisciplinary, for example, the various kinds of "studies" programs (women's, Islamic, American, cultural, etc.), or the hybrid disciplines like ethnomusicology (musicology, folklore, anthropology). But by including people from these fields (areas? disciplines?) in our series, we are already taking a stand on disciplined inquiry. A question on the comprehensive exam for the Columbia University Ethnomusicology Program was to defend ethnomusicology as a "field" or a "discipline." One's answer determined one's future, at least to the extent that the gatekeepers had a say in such matters. So, in the end, what we are proposing will no doubt involve political struggles.

For additional information about this series or for the submission of manuscripts, please contact Shirley R. Steinberg, msgramsci@gmail.com. To order other books in this series, please contact our Customer Service Department at: (800) 770-LANG (within the U.S.), (212) 647-7706 (outside the U.S.), (212) 647-7707 FAX, or browse online by series at: www.peterlang.com.